REVIEWS

"In *From Contempt to Dignity* Dr.Rustomjee uses her wide clinical experience as an individual and group psychotherapist to elucidate many of the principles of psychoanalysis While there are many references to the core psychoanalytic literature the clinical vignettes demonstrate Dr. Rustomjee s cultivation of an open mind (Keats negative capability) and an ability to learn from and with the patient or group.

There is a lifetime of learning distilled in these pages."
— Oliver Larkin M.B B.S DPM FRANZCP

"From a long and rich professional journey Sabar presents a wide and deep range of experiences — personal and clinical. Her reflections, case studies, quotations and lessons from art and literature flow as in a wonderfully productive conversation.The book focuses on the origin and consequences of the most destructive element in human relationships - contempt. Contempt, controlling and triumphing are manic defences against anxiety. Sabar shows how these can be addressed in therapy and turned towards self-regard and dignity. A receptive, non-judgmental and containing therapist is essential. Her commentaries on many issues linked to contempt are illuminating. Her deep compassion has led her to understand and assuage her patients' suffering through her practice of group psychotherapy and group psychoanalysis. This book is her testimony to her exceptional journey in her field and in her life."
— Dr. Alan A. Large, F.R.A.C.P., F.R.A.N.Z.P., D.P.M., M.R.C.P.(U.K.) Consultant Psychiatrist (Retired)

i

"Here is a book that shows us how a group analytic psychotherapist practices across a wide spectrum of people seeking help. The poignant case descriptions take us to the moments of understanding that underlie success. In disclosing her reflections during group work, Dr Rustomjee reveals the art of her practice, such a difficult thing to teach and rarely revealed publically. The material drawn from the training programs that she initiated reveals the underlying rigour required of such practice. Patience with the almost free associative style of the book will reward the reader."
— Graeme Smith, Emeritus Professor of Psychiatry, Monash University Australia

"In this fascinating book Dr Rustomjee gives generously of her professional and personal experience. The theoretical passages are illustrated with numerous examples from literature, philosophy and art. One could say that the book is a reflection of her philosophy of life, both as a physician and human being in which core values of respect and equality have a central position. I highly recommend this book to anyone who wishes to learn from someone with clinical wisdom, a high level of scholarship and a belief in the human dignity."
— Christer Sandahl, Professor of Social and Behavioural Sciences, Karolinska Institutet, Stockholm, Sweden and Past president of the International Association for Group Psychotherapy and Group Processes (IAGP).

"Dr Rustomjee's book is about much more than psychoanalysis. It is a book about the life and work of a highly experienced and talented psychoanalytic psychotherapist, psychiatrist, teacher and supervisor.

She generously shares the wisdom gleaned from a career working in a broad spectrum of therapeutic contexts.

Her capacity to integrate her deep understanding of the writings of great theoreticians and therapists, and the work of poets and artists, is reflected in her discussion of contempt and in her many case examples.

Features of her approach to working with patients, both individually and in groups, include a focus on sensitive listening, showing sustained curiosity to understand, and an openness to adapt her therapeutic style to the particular needs of each patient or group. This has enabled her to achieve impressive outcomes which may elude less skilful practitioners.

There is much in this book to interest and engage not just those with an interest in analytic psychotherapy, but also anyone with curiosity about how a young person may overcome challenges to build an admirably successful career in psychiatry as well as a fulfilling life generally."

—Roger D Glass MBBS, DPM, FRANZCP, CSCATChild Psych Consultant Child, Family & General Psychiatrist.

"A rare combination of sensitivity and sensibility runs throughout the reading of this book. Poetry, art, open sharing of personal history and a very extensive professional experience adorn it.

Dr. Rustomjee has created an interesting piece that fuses feelings and knowledge making the reader be loyally curious to the end. Remarkable is her open generosity in recognizing and appreciating those from whom she has learned.

An outstanding book highly recommended to boths professionals and public in general."

—Dr. Roberto Deinocencio, Psycotherapist. Psychodramatist
    Santander, Spain

"Born in Sri Lanka of Parsee Zoroastrian heritage, Sabar's formative years were in India and deeply influenced by the death of her GP-father when she was six. She identified with his career, trained in medicine in Mumbai, and paediatrics in the UK. Having married a surgeon, they migrated to Australia when civil war broke out between the Sinhalese and Tamils. Her culturally enriched background enhanced her psychoanalytic training, shared here as the narrative of her life, interspersed with the theory that guided her, stories of patients that intrigued her, and with her commentary about how dignity is achieved through her extraordinary and wholesome life. She offers a great history of group psychotherapy!"
— David W Kissane, AC MD, Professor of Psychiatry, Monash & Cornell Universities

FROM CONTEMPT TO DIGNITY

DR SABAR RUSTOMJEE

Sid Harta Publishers
ABN: 34632585203
17 Coleman Parade
GLEN WAVERLEY VIC 3150

First published in Australia 2019
This edition published 2020
Copyright © Sabar Rustomjee 2020

Cover design, typesetting: WorkingType (www.work ngtype.com.au)

Front Cover image
Ginevra de' Benci (1474) by Leonardo da Vinci
Ginevra de' Benci with an element of self-contempt, withheld identity
with half closed eye-gazing over her shoulder

Rustomjee, Sabar
From Contempt to Dignity
ISBN: 978-1-925707-00-7
pp466

Image information

Page 127   Narcissus and Echo ---- en.wikipidea.org/wiki/Echo_and_Narcissus

Page 172   The Ambassadors (1953) by Hans Holbein the younger ----- The National Gallery London Souvenier, St. Vincent House, London Wc2H

Page 174   Lower portion of previous picture - National Gallery, London

Page 175   Ginevra de' Benci (1474) by Leonardo da Vinci --- National Gallery of Art, Washington, DC USA

Page 177   Cecilia Gallerani: The Lady with an Ermine (1489) --- Location— Czartoryski Museum, Wavel Castle.

Information from Wikipedia text under cc-BY-SA-Licence

Page 178   Mona Lisa (1503-1506) BY Leorardo da Vinci - Location Muse'e du Louvre, Paris.

Data from Wikipedia text under cc-BY-SA Licence

Page 179   Edvard Munch (!893) From Edvard Munch- 1993 – Benedikt Taschen Verlog GmbH

Page 180   Puberty - (1894)   (c) Benedikt Taschen Verlag GmbH

Page 181   The Scream (1894) Located at the National Gallery, Oslo, Norway.

CONTENTS

Appreciation from the Giver and the Receiver.
Correspondence from Emeritus Professor Graeme C Smith.

Dear Sabar

Many thanks for the copy of your book, *From Contempt to Dignity*.

Thanks also for your acknowledgment of me.

Congratulations on its publication.

So, few psychiatrists bother to record their life's work and the concepts that have really mattered to them.

This means that few remain well known, as you will be.

The book epitomizes your ability to get to the heart of issues.

It helps the reader to understand what you were trying to do with your patients and why they and your students got so much from you.

As Head of Psychological Medicine at Monash University, I had much cause to be grateful to you for your commitment to teaching at undergraduate and postgraduate levels.

You served as a wonderful role model in that respect.

I have also greatly appreciated your friendship and support over the years.

Warm regards,

Graeme Smith.

Dr Sabar Rustomjee, AM
Member of the Order of Australia (General Division)
M.B., B.S. (Bombay), F.R.A.N.Z.C.P., D.P.M. (Melb)

President International Assoc. of Group Psychotherapy (IAGP)
(2000-2003)

Past Adjunct Senior Lecturer Monash University, Melbourne

Clinical Member Group Analytic Society London

Clinical Member American Group Psychotherapy Assoc.

Past Course Co-ordinator of Group Analytic Studies Monash
University

Member Australian Assoc. of Group Psychotherapy

Fellowship Award — IAGP (2018)

I have given papers in Melbourne, Sydney, London, Tokyo, Greece, Trivandrum and Spain.

I worked in Sri Lanka in the casualty wards and inpatient wards.

I also worked in the Royal Liverpool Children's Hospital, U.K., in the medical and surgical units, as well as in Emergency.

Since emigrating to Australia, I have worked as a Psychiatrist at the Monash Medical Centre in many units for the past forty years, prior to retirement.

Piloo and his dog Duke
I dedicate this book to my beloved husband, Piloo,
who has been a most loving and containing partner
with whom I have had the good fortune of sharing my life.

FOREWORD

This leads towards the development of fundamental principles in all forms of exchanges between individuals, groups, professionals, families, as well as during educational and organizational work. In all forms of interpersonal and professional discourse. It also provides the basis of courageously overcoming inhibitions, resistances and anxieties resulting in eventually restoring freedom of thought, speech and human dignity.

Adjusting between cultures, acknowledging similarities and differences of race, colour, caste, economical and religious beliefs are other factors, which are also an important component of everyday life today.

Every human being is vulnerable without exception. Let us look briefly at examples of two great men, Nelson Mandela from South Africa and Mahatma Gandhi from India. Mandela, one of the greatest political leaders of our time, describes in his book — *Long Walk to Freedom* (1995, p12) how at a very early age, he played with a group of friends, trying to climb up and down 'an unruly donkey'. Suddenly the donkey bent its head and unseated him into a thorn bush. The thorns pricked and scratched his face all over. Mandela stated "*I had lost face amongst my friends. I learnt that to humiliate another person, is to make him suffer an unnecessarily cruel fate. Even as a boy, I defeated my opponents without dishonouring them.*"

Mahatma Gandhi's life also has many similarities. Both have inspired me greatly towards my journey through life. The similarities in their ethical values in life, gave most persons hope for the future persistence of Truth and Loyalties in their own countries.

On 10th May, 1994, *Mandela* installed South Africa's first democratic, non-racial government. Similarly, *Mahatma Gandhi planned the Independence of India, without forcing violence and bloodshed. India became an Independent country in 1945.*

Life of John Keats, the Poet

> *"Beauty is truth, truth beauty — that is all*
> *Ye know on earth, and all ye need to know."*
> John Keats, (1820) Ode on a Grecian Urn

John Keats leads us, his readers, to explore his own unique wisdom, expressed through his romantic poetry. Keats and other renowned persons in the fields of art, literature, music, religion and politics have enriched our awareness that there is more that unites us than that which divides us.

It was fifty years ago, in 1963, that Martin Luther King Jr. gave his famous '**I have a dream**' speech which moves people to tears, and inspired the world to work towards seeing the day when *no child* would be *"judged by the colour of their skin, but by the conduct of their character"*. This paved the way for the American Civil Rights Act of 1964.

Yet, there remains a lot of work to be done.

In the field of psychoanalysis, especially Group Analysis, John Keats has been likened to a natural conductor of an orchestra, who, together with select musicians, brings out hitherto concealed, repressed, denied or disavowed emotions in a safe and receptive atmosphere of truth and beauty. Keats was capable of remaining creative and full of inspiration until the very end when he, like most of his family, died of tuberculosis. He carried feelings of jealousy, envy and harsh criticisms about his work by successfully "holding and containing" his disappointments, with the help of his true friends who sincerely loved him.

In one of his letters to his own brothers at Christmas 1818 (Keats 2009), he describes a disagreement he had with a friend while walking home from a pantomime, in which it struck him as to what qualities went to form a "man of achievement", especially in literature. It was then he conceived his concept of "**Negative Capability**".

> *"A Man capable of being in Uncertainties and having the capacity of Enduring Ambiguity, Doubt and Mystery without Irritably Reaching after Fact and Reason."*
>
> John Keats, defining negative capability

Psychoanalysts, especially those from Australia, have revered these lines of Keats. The lines highlight the importance of working closely with ambivalence in one's work. Just as every coin has two opposite sides to it, so have our conscious and unconscious thoughts.

"Negative Capability" is an important skill in every psychoanalytic discourse. It encourages reflection and prevents the therapist from using her own interpretation hastily, which comes naturally from the unconscious of the analyst (and not of the patient).

I consider Keats similar to SH Foulkes, who was the founder of modern group analysis. My respect for John Keats is bound to the fact that I have never read him ever to denigrate anyone by the use of Contempt. This aspect of his personality reveals his deserved dignity. In addition, I have never observed Keats resorting to any Manic Defence to protect his own ego. He courageously faced the most envious of his critics.

He limited his writing to his relationship with his fiancée, Fanny Browne, only due to his fast advancing tuberculosis. He was determined to keep on writing his brilliant poetry as long as he lived.

In Keats, we can also see examples of "repeating and remembering". Kierkegaard once stated that "people don't want to remember; they only want to repeat". (Our modern-day poet, Felix de Mendelssohn, has been a source of inspiration for me. He was particularly fond of this sentiment.) In Keats' poetry we see this desire, amidst his ambiguity. The eponymous woman in "La Belle Dame Sans Merci" is both a figure of myth and a representation on Fanny Browne; in some variations, the kissing of the brow can be interpreted as kissing "four wild eyes", one pair of which must belong to his fiancée. He is warned in his dreams of "La Belle Dame", yet he keeps "repeating and remembering" by returning to the cold hillside, clinging to the hope of enjoying this desire once more.

GUILT, SHAME and CONTEMPT are important features in the aetiology of THE CRIMINAL MIND.

These will be considered separately in this book. Sigmund Freud has discussed the above, including the life of Fyodor Dostoevsky. Wilfred Bion's book has included Grotskien's work on Raskolnikov in his editorial. The title of Bion's book includes the feelings "How dare I Disturb the Universe?". To explore the Criminal Mind appears to be a multifocal enterprise.

Shame

"Shame lurks unseen", is described by many authors including Nelson Mandela and Paul Mollon. This book will investigate shame and how it relates to contempt, and guilt resorting to humiliation. I have mentioned Nelson Mandela successfully overcoming the humiliation earlier in this Foreword.

Use of Philosophy in Group Therapy

My principle experience for treating shame in individuals has arisen in group therapy sessions. The benefits of such a practise are covered in this book, as well as in the works about large groups covered by Irwin Yalom, when describing Schopenhauer.

Contempt

Regarding contempt, Mahatma Gandhi said, "It has always been a mystery to me how men can feel themselves honoured by the humiliation of their fellow beings".

This book describes the vicissitudes of contempt through numerous examples. Contempt is projected, with resulting injury to the victim, through both unintentional humiliation, as well as planned, humiliating, contemptible actions. The one who projects contempt onto others rarely intends to consciously reveal his or her true motive in doing so. Moreover, there may have been long standing, disowned self-contempt which had already started in early childhood. It may well be openly a result of unbearable jealousy towards another or supressed, contemptuous rage belonging to various castes, races, religions and countries. Current or recent traumatic events may bring up repressed feelings in persons harbouring self-contempt from a young age.

Contempt, Control and Triumph are three Manic Defences, initially described by Melanie Klein (1945):

Loss of face of the victim is the greatest humiliation a contemptuous person can possibly inflict onto another.

Any one of these defences, or all of them, can work at a partially unconscious level, in an attempt to deny past and present painful losses and traumas.

Shame can also be a point of origin. If shame is isolated and treated in its early stages, there will be no self-contempt. The relationship between shame and self-contempt is revisited in Part 5 of this book by considering the criminal mind.

Part 1 of this book considers the untimely death of the author's father when she was aged six, totally unaware of the consequences of such an event. Edvard Munch expresses it very vividly in his picture *The Dead Mother and Child*. When I first came across this painting, I realised how familiar the scene was for me. Everyone was consoling my bereaved family and probably considered that children as young as myself would have minimal feelings, able to get over this trauma far quicker than an adult would. Highly experienced psychoanalysts like Sigmund Freud, Joan Symington and Esther Bick, as well as Alice Miller, vividly describe the difficulties and realise the vulnerabilities of very young children who need trust and constancy in their environment and feel bereft when they are left for long periods of time by themselves. The psychological considerations of infants and children are covered in greater detail in Part 2 of this book.

Issues with compliance, grandiosity and narcissism are offshoots of these considerations and are covered in detail, mostly with Part 7 of this book.

Need for differentiating similarities and differences

In a light hearted conversation between Alice and the Hatter, at the tea party in *Alice's Adventures in Wonderland*, the Hatter corrects Alice by saying, "You can see everything you eat, but you cannot eat everything you see".

Those people who are unaware of the addictions and jail sentences following murders lead a very unhappy life, as is described in Part 5 of the book. In relation 'culture of containment' is a core concept of discussions in Part 8.

The political thinking of Nelson Mandela and Mahatma Gandhi is also described in this book in detail within various sections.

Sigmund Freud describes the psychoanalytic fact in his essay "Beyond the Pleasure Principle" (1920), during which a manic phase in adolescence or adulthood can lead to alcoholism and taking non-prescribed addictive medication (E Hopper, 1995). Violence is described by James Gilligan (2000) as our "deadliest enemy".

This book describes the art and science leading to the eradication of contempt. M Gandhi and N Mandela describe how they were able to encourage a life of non-violence.

Gandhi describes how civil disobedience is different from contempt. This is demonstrated in his famous Salt March.

> It is only by facing a problem and seeing what it really is about, that we can live a Life of Freedom without carrying burdens of Contempt belonging to others.

Guilt

Guilt is the key work of this book. Where shame comes from external factors, it is my opinion that guilt manifests within. Criminality stems from guilt, as considered by Friedrich Nietzsche and Sigmund Freud in their respective attention to the idea of the 'Pale Criminal'.

The nature of shame and guilt will be considered in Part 5, with criminal cases such as that of Robert Stroud, aka "The Birdman of Alcatraz".

Where guilt develops from infantile neurosis, therapy is required to solve the resultant issues.

This book also addresses the uniquely Japanese concept of

amae in Part 2. This cultural factor can be commonly mistaken for and related to a sense of guilt and apologetic gestures, but Takeo Doi offers a nuanced take on this concept in his text *The Anatomy of Dependence.*

This book will also seek to investigate these various principles as seen in other cultures, particularly in Part 6. — Transcultural Psychotherapy -

Sabar Rustomjee

P7 "Traversing one's Human Vulnerability so as to arrive at a Safe Space in Life" (2013)

This paper is dedicated to Hidefumi Kotani from Tokyo, during the time of the Hiroshima bombing, when he was merely a youth. He has been an active leader and participant in all recent traumas in Japan. He followed the famous lines presented by John Keats, the English romantic poet.

"The capacity for Enduring Ambiguity, Doubt and Mystery without Irritable Reaching after Fact and Reason"

John Keats lived a short life of 26 years. Many family members had died prematurely of tuberculosis, as he did too. Psychoanalysts, especially those from Australia, have revered these lines of Keats greatly. The lines highlight the importance of working closely with ambivalence in one's work. Just as every coin has two opposite sides to it, so have our conscious and unconscious thoughts. Dr George Christie and Dr Ann Morgan used Keats' frame of analysis named *Negative Capability* to help infertile couples. As co-therapists they encouraged infertile couples in groups as well as individually to be aware and open to verbalise their unconscious negative feelings about becoming parents themselves. These couples then worked seriously towards overcoming their hitherto unconscious resistances. Christie and Morgan's (2000) published papers show their excellent results, especially in those who had not benefitted even by IVF.

These examples also openly revealed the importance of recognising both transference and countertransference interactions and the enriching effects of observing successful results which reinforced further morale and faith in their already existing desires to become good-enough parents.

One of Keats most popular odes is *'Ode to a Nightingale'*. He writes:

> *'tis not through envy of thy happy lot,*
> *but being too happy in thine happiness'.*

The song encourages Keats to give up his own sense of self and embrace the actual feelings that were evoked within him by the nightingale.

In his work on 'Ode on a Grecian Urn' its most profound lines are:

> *'Beauty is truth, truth beauty — that is all*
> *Ye know on earth, and all ye need to know'.*

The Urn depicts timeless beauty.

This theme is brought up in the book in many chapters of clients of all ages.

A Clinical example

A 3 year old autistic child, whom I treated: When his birthday cake was brought out, he got into a total tantrum with tears streaming down his face. He was settled down and then said in his own words "Where is the house of the cake? It has no home now!!" The child was absolutely correct, there was no box in which the cake had 'been born' a short time ago. Where and how had it suddenly disappeared? In Dr Kotani's words the child could not see or feel a safe space for the cake to live in anymore.

In the concept of Margaret Mahler (1975) the cake of the autistic child was without even a soft shell, like that of a fully formed egg to hold itself together without contents overflowing.

Wilfred Bion's *holding and containing* by the teachers was insufficient to help the child. The child could only perceive himself in bits and pieces. Naturally this little boy was totally overwhelmed.

CONTEMPT

One of the most important points that all grown-ups, as well as children and teachers, need to be aware of is to realise that society itself is totally unaware of the long-term consequences of hurtful contemptuous behaviour and patterns starting from pre-school or school life. Contempt was considered by Hanna Segal and Melanie Klein as a Manic Defence. Some books consider it to be similar to humour or for it to be simply a way of life, hence unknowingly confused children and adults. As years go by there can be a misuse of alcohol, bullying verbally, physically, stealing, corruption, drug addictions and even jail sentences.

An Example: HUMAN BONDAGE BY SOMERSET MAUGHAM

The feeling of being in bits and pieces is well described in the life of Philip Carey, the main character in Somerset Maugham's book '*Of Human Bondage*'. Both his parents had died and he was under the care of an Uncle, a Priest, and his Aunt, in the role of his guardians. Friends were never invited to play with him and he was sent to boarding school where he became even more unhappy. His whole life is described in one of the later chapters that follow in this book.

He became involved in an unhappy bondage with a female, 'Miriam', who kept on behaving in a contemptuous manner towards him. Eventually he realised what was happening and when finally, he admitted that she was a heart-breaking female and he needed to make his distance from her. He failed once more. Miriam gave birth to a child belonging to another male and hoped this would work, she continued to see other men sexually and tore up a beautiful painting done by Carey some years ago. He then finally encouraged her to leave living with him. She eventually suicided.

It was after her death that he was able to return to a healthier relationship with a suitable lady whom he later married.

Need for Differentiating Similarities and Differences.

We read these in Alice in Wonderland. In a light hearted conversation between Alice in Wonderland and the Hatter at the tea party, the Hatter corrects Alice by saying 'You can see everything you eat, but you cannot eat everything you see'.

Those people who are unaware of the addictions and jail sentences following murders lead a very unhappy life as is described in Part 5 of the book.

Hidefumi Kotani always demonstrated his 'courageous, fearless, honest and open nature', which is similar to the timeless poem by Leigh Hunt which starts with "Abou Ben Adhem, may his tribe increase".

The political thinking of Nelson Mandela and Mahatma Gandhi is also described in this book in detail.

Sigmund Freud describes the psychoanalytic fact in 'Beyond the Pleasure Principle' (1920) during which a manic phase in adolescence or adulthood can lead to drinking excessive alcohol and taking unprescribed addictive medication (E Hopper, 1995).

Violence is described by James Gilligan (2000) as our 'deadliest enemy'.

This book describes the art and science leading to the eradication of contempt. M Gandhi and N Mandela describe how they were able to encourage a life of non-violence.

Mandela's words were 'FREE AT LAST'. He strongly believed that lack of human dignity was a direct result of white supremacy.

Gandhi describes how civil disobedience is different from contempt. This is demonstrated in his famous Salt March.

'It is only by facing a problem and seeing what it really is about, that we can live a Life of Freedom without carrying burdens of Contempt belonging to others.

COMMENTS
FROM THE EDITORS

Beau Hillier — Version 20 Editor

From Contempt to Dignity has a scope that belies its most basic mission statement. As a work of psychoanalysis, it transitions between the viewpoint of the author and supporting groundwork of eminent persons in the field, interspersing them with cultural analysis. As a more philosophical rumination on the human mind in various emotional states, it aims at an insight through a journey in art, religion and literature, using these as a collective window into what constitutes our driving passions and motivations. A deeply personal work, Dr Sabar Rustomjee shares her life and the way her circumstances throughout the decades have shaped her approach to her work.

Dr Rustomjee's experiences are primarily, but not solely, focussed on both Group Therapy and Individual Psychoanalysis. Her extensive experience in the field is apparent. Working with her on this Edition was daunting at first, because of is aforementioned scope, but fascinating. This text takes rudimentary terms like shame, dignity, contempt and arrogance, and addresses them with nuance and deep consideration. In all measures this is a unique text, a long time in the making, and a fitting coalescence of Dr Rustomjee's contribution to literature in general.

TONY TRUMBLE — Editor prior to Version 20

Dr Sabar Rustomjee is a respected psychoanalytic psychoanalyst who has specialised in individual and group psychotherapy.

She started her professional life in 1952 in India and migrated to Australia in 1960.

Her book *From Contempt to Dignity* is an encapsulation of her life's work, her professional passions and her hopes for bringing greater insight and understanding to the study and treatment of those suffering the belligerence and indifference of others.

Her book has been written in a style that will be of interest to the mental health professional, as well as the general reader. Sabar has drawn widely on the influences in her personal and professional life that provide sources of human contempt. Sabar skilfully manages to explore this theme through literature, art, analysis and professional case studies. She brings her compassions for the suffering and isolation felt by so many into focus. She hopes this will provoke greater discussion and attention to the many issues she raises.

While Sabar's approach is academic, her style will engage and introduce new readers to the lives and works of some of the seminal practitioners of both individual and group psychoanalysis. This includes Sigmund Freud, Wilfred Bion, Melanie Klein, S.H. Foulkes, Pat de Maré, Rocco Pisani, Jacques Lacan, Walter Stone and many others. I'm sure you will find the results readable and compelling.

My role has been to work with Sabar over the course of her writing by lending her encouragement and providing feedback on the direction the work was taking. The result is not meant to be a complete record of her life in psychotherapy. Nevertheless, it is a valuable reflection of one who has offered so much to group and individual analysis in Australia and around the world. Amongst other achievements namely Consultation-Liaison work, her kindness and compassion for the suffering of others and the wish to bring new perspectives, is evident in '*From Contempt to Dignity*'.

It has been a fascinating and rewarding time collaborating with the author of this book.

ALEX READMAN

Assisting Editor prior to Version 20 Understanding the intricacies of psychoanalysis through the eyes of the author has been a rewarding and academic experience. I have found great revelation in scribing the ideas and wisdom into 'From Contempt to Dignity' from the well-educated mind of Dr Rustomjee. Throughout the book there is presence of the power to understand one's own life through the vision of the author's own experience. It has been a pleasure to work on this project.

PROLOGUE

Our vulnerabilities in life and the courage to face contempt

All human beings are born free and equal in dignity and rights.
Universal Declaration of Human Rights, *1948 Article 1.*

Following the above can lead towards the development of fundamental principles in all forms of exchanges between individuals, groups, professionals, families, as well as during educational and organisational work. It is the basis of courageously overcoming inhibitions, resistances and anxieties. This restores freedom of thought, speech and human dignity. Acknowledging similarities and differences of race, colour, caste, economy, intellectual and religious beliefs is an important component of everyday life. Every human being is vulnerable without exception. Nelson Mandela, one of the greatest political leaders of our time, describes in his book, *'Long Walk to Freedom'* (1995), how at a very early age he played with a group of friends, trying to climb up and down 'an unruly donkey'. Suddenly the donkey bent his head and unseated him into a thornbush. The thorns pricked and scratched his face all over. "I had lost face among my friends. I learnt that to humiliate another person, is to make him suffer an unnecessarily cruel fate. Even as a boy, I defeated my opponents without dishonouring them."

Loss of face in public is a manifestation of self-contempt. This book has provided examples of those who have been able to overcome obstacles in their lives by valuing truth, honour and compassion, leading to regaining self-dignity which may have been lost in the early years of their lives. Talented poets like John

Keats, William Wordsworth and artists including Michelangelo, Edvard Munch, Leonardo da Vinci, as well as numerous literary geniuses of different persuasions. These artists are able to demonstrate contempt either through art, music and/or literature. They are also able to normalise an individual who is already traumatised by contempt. There are many examples given in this book which demonstrates contempt, which can either be seen by all or hidden secretly.

Contempt as a manic defence described by Melanie Klein

Melanie Klein (Control, Contempt and Triumph)

Melanie Klein was born in 1882 and was the first psychoanalyst to bring into light the importance of contempt which was projected into carers/parents, those who were unable to defend themselves. For these people it becomes a temporary solution to overcoming their own depression and dissatisfactions in life. Psychoanalytically this is defined as Manic Defences. The three manic defences Klein describes are:

Control

Contempt

Triumph

This can lead to carers concealing their own pain and self-contempt, rather than working to overcome their self-inflicted defensive mechanisms.

I have read books written by numerous authors in the field of psychoanalysis and psychotherapy, both group and individual, but found that it was mainly the psychoanalyst Melanie Klein (1952, 1975a & 1975b) who had originally explored the topic of Contempt in great depth. She was a pioneer who focussed on the origins of contempt, starting from infancy. Klein, along with Hanna Segal (1975), who had been analysed by Klein, also describes in detail the use of Manic Defences in life.

Alice Miller, Psychoanalyst, describes the Vicious Circle of Contempt

Alice Miller, a psychoanalyst, silently suffered the pain of "incest" without complaint. This was a result of being totally controlled by her mother. She describes this very clearly in many brilliant books. Two of these are '*For Your Own Good: The Roots of Violence in Child-Rearing*' (1990) and '*The Drama of Being a Child*' (1993).

Parents and carers using contempt as a manic defence do great harm to their children, as described vividly by Alice Miller in her published works. She describes a variation of events ranging from severe, as in the case of Hitler to a chapter on '*Vicious Circle of Contempt*' (pp. 85-141), which parents consider a big joke. They do not allow their child to enjoy a lollipop while they are all walking on the beach. The poor child is initially devastated, enraged and humiliated. They then allow the child to lick their lollipops to quieten the child. Even incidents like this, which appear to be inconsequential, can carry a weight in the memories of a young toddler. It is very puzzling for an adult to realise later in life as to why their child is not obeying their wishes and remaining under their control.

Alice Miller writes in her preface, 'This discovery convinced me that if, we either are, or are not, willing to open our eyes to the suffering of the child who lies within us, then as adults we could turn the same newborn into monsters or let them grow up into feeling responsible human beings'. She concludes that *'a child responds to, and learns both tenderness and cruelty from the very beginning'*. If a mother respects both herself and her child from the very first day, she will never need to teach him respect for others and the child will lead its own life based on its true self. On the other hand, if one's true self has not been able to engage in open and truthful communication, then it needs to live a life based on its own protection. 'One who lives in a glasshouse cannot conceal anything without giving oneself away, except by hiding it under the ground. And then you cannot see it yourself either' (Miller, 1993, p. 36). This then becomes self-alienation.

Self-contempt: The roots of violence as depicted by Alice Miller

Self-Contempt often results 'from projective identification' of others — especially one's carers.

It is not an easy task for any person to overcome their own Self Contempt. It is also not a familiar feeling to live with, during our entire lives. From birth, the newborns attribute their own physical discomfort, tummy pains of whatever reason, to parents, carers and others in their vicinity.

Parents, who cannot tolerate their baby's cries and wriggles, even when their jump-suits are being put on, can cause intense feelings of helplessness. This turns into rage and at times even loss of control.

How and when does self-contempt start?

History has revealed destructive brutality arising during wars, which were ignited mainly through Contempt, Control and Triumph. Alice Miller (1933) describes details of Hitler's childhood, ranging from hidden to manifest horror and its consequences.

It has been demonstrated that 'Personal Analysis' is an integral part of psychoanalytic training. During this period, there is time and space for reflection and exploration of both the here and now as well as one's infancy and early childhood.

Alice Miller (1933: New Preface viii) wrote, 'I was amazed to discover that I had been an abused child. From the beginning of my life, I had no choice, but to comply totally with the needs and feelings of my mother, and to ignore my own'. Miller's aim has been to search within a psychoanalytic framework, how a parent/client can regain his or her authentic sense of being truly alive, without living in human bondage to anyone. She believes that feelings of unresolved contempt towards a certain person or persons can be an important indication of the linking having been unknowingly displaced from a previous person onto another. This is termed Transference which will be discussed in detail later. The discourse and response of the recipient is termed Countertransference.

Children learn both tenderness and cruelty from a very early age.

A child responds to and learns both tenderness and cruelty from the beginning. 'One living in a glasshouse cannot conceal anything except by hiding it underground and then you cannot see it yourself either' (Miller, 1993, p. 36). This then becomes self-alienation. Anne Shutzenberger also contributed significantly to the above.

Major disasters following ignored contempt

We have all come across people, ranging from adults to children, who have silently suffered the pain of incest without complaint. This is a result of being totally controlled by both of their parents. The father has often threatened the child with murder should the child speak about the intrusive act of incest, when the child becomes a victim of the father. Similarly, mothers have encouraged the same silence so as to keep up the appearance of being a very stable, wise, charitable and admirable member of society. However, the truth comes out at some time in the child's life.

During manic phases in adolescence or adult life, this can lead to drinking alcohol in excess regularly or taking unprescribed addictive medication. Whenever reality is limited during a manic phase of life, it does not necessarily result in death. (This is because an amount of reality is still functional.) Freud has mentioned this important fact in his description of '*Beyond the Pleasure Principle*' (Freud, 1920b).

Hence, it is vital to understand the complexity between *self-contempt vs aggression* towards others, leading to murder. As mentioned by Melanie Klein, there are only three manic defences, namely control, contempt and triumph. Violence is not included by Melanie Klein.

Difference between contempt, humiliation, shame and violence

James Gilligan describes violence as 'our deadliest enemy' (Gilligan, 2000). Violence resulting in death can be described as being part of one's *death drive*. These destructive consequences to mankind also present as loss of dignity, scorn, disdain, indifference, alienation, in addition perversions and ruthless aggression. It is vital to understand the complexity of origins and the extreme motivation needed to bring about violence.

You the reader, may well ask the author "Why have you written this book regarding contempt?" and "Why now?" The answer for myself is similar to that given by Somerset Maugham when he wrote *'Of Human Bondage'* (1915). Issues such as contempt, shame and unhealthy parasitic bondage are exceedingly difficult to reveal to those near and dear to us. One may have years of experience in the field in psychoanalysis and psychotherapy, but to actually write the truth about subjects which the author feels is very personal to oneself and has played a central role in one's life, is truly difficult.

Manic defences are helpful only when used within constructive boundaries. Psychic reality of the recipient needs to be intact. Here is an actual example: On winning an important match, a certain player drank alcohol to an extreme amount and presumably went to bed. He was found dead in the morning! As no other cause was detected 'Accidental death' was the Coroner's verdict. There was no evidence of control, contempt or triumph. His capacity to think clearly was impaired by being under the excessive influence of alcohol.

Manic Defence mechanisms of the Ego can protect the self-worth of the person who has a tendency to undermine him or herself.

Contempt towards others, as part of a manic defence, is used destructively when encouraging projection of one's own pre-existing self-contempt. This, when projected onto a vulnerable part of the other, can lead to Triumph temporarily overcoming Self-contempt, which may give the subject only a limited period of elation. It may then be followed by Demoralisation as soon as the elated person feels dethroned by another competitor. For those who are psychologically minded, they may join a psychotherapy-oriented program working to overcoming their self-contempt.

Why explore the subject of contempt?

I had published an article on *'The Solitude and Agony of Unbearable Shame'* in 2009. Until then, obviously I too felt uncomfortable about fully exploring consequences of Shame. It seemed too private a subject to publicise. So, why do I focus on contempt now? I attended an excellent presentation on contempt by Dr Michael Honnery from Sydney, at a conference in Melbourne, which led to my avid reading of Somerset Maugham's *'Of Human Bondage'* (1915). Maugham also had difficulty in publishing it at first. He was thirty-seven years old then. He had initially given it a different title, namely *'From Beauty to Ashes'*". He then changed his mind. The book's original publication under the present title was in 1915. He enforces the authenticity of incidents concerning contempt by explaining that his book, *'Of Human Bondage'*, is not an autobiography, but 'an autobiographical novel'. The emotions were felt by Maugham, but he states that some of the incidents described were not from his own life. They were from the lives of persons with whom he was intimate. Maugham was surprised and elated that for eighty-five years this book has attracted the attention of numerous writers. The success of the book has continued, increasing as years went by! It highlights the extent of contempt which a crippled orphan had to endure, before he was able to overcome his difficulties.

The Romantic English Poet John Keats (1795–1821)

The romantic young English poet John Keats has enriched us greatly when we read his works. These are filled with a wide variety of subjects ranging from Truth and Beauty, from *'A Grecian Urn'*, an *'Ode to a Nightingale'*, and *'La Belle Dame sans Merci'* who is very beautiful and loving. She is described as a 'faery's' child, who kisses him, puts him to sleep and then leaves him. He is now 'alone and palely loitering'. This had been done by her to many other kings and princes.

Keats, like most of his family, had tuberculosis from an early age and dies young. Nevertheless, despite all the sadness in his life of knowing he would die at a young age, he greatly enjoyed his love with Fanny Browne, to whom he gave an engagement ring. He could not go further with their relationship as he wanted to spend the last few months of his life in the warmer climate of Italy while he completed as much as possible of his poetry.

My respect for 'John Keats the Man' is bound to the fact that I have never read him ever to denigrate anyone by the use of Contempt. This aspect of his personality reveals his well-deserved dignity. In addition, I have never observed Keats resorting to Manic Defence either, so as to protect his own ego. He courageously faced the most envious of his critics. He limited his writing to his relationship with his fiancée Fanny Browne, only due to his fast advancing tuberculosis. He was determined to keep on writing his brilliant poetry as long as he lived.

He highlighted the importance of ambivalence in 'Negative Capability', He described this as *'the capacity to endure ambiguity, doubt, and mystery without reaching out irritably for fact and reason'.*

Dr Sabar Rustomjee

ACKNOWLEDGEMENTS

The path each of us has traversed through life provides us with our strengths and weaknesses. Throughout my academic journey I thank all my loyal, loving and caring friends and colleagues who have been by my side during good times and difficult ones. The late Dr George Christie, the late Dr OHD Blomfield, Jocelyn Dunphy Blomfield, Emeritus Professor Graeme Smith, Prof Russell Grigg and Dr Tom Murray are the main persons from Victoria to whom I will always remain indebted. They were very caring and containing in their own ways. I have spent a major part of my professional life learning many aspects of my work from them. Their warmth, wisdom, truthfulness and clarity of thought were precious attributes during the first few years of my training to become a consulting psychiatrist, then engaging in paediatrics and finally resulting in psychoanalytic psychotherapy.

I am most grateful to Beau Hillier for his concentrated effort and energy in his editing of the content of this book. Also, to Michael Richards for his insightful contributions and Joy Richards for typing and proofreading.

The International Association of Group Psychotherapy (IAGP) has proven to be an additional milestone in my life. It gave me the opportunity of widening my horizons greatly. I was elected President of IAGP for a period of three years in the year 2000 and attended seven international congresses, including four Pacific Rim congresses and regional congresses in three cities. I have co-chaired Pacific Rim Congresses in Melbourne with Susan Daniel a psychodramatist.

I will remain grateful to Jay Fiddler, Walter Stone, Earl Hopper, Malcolm Pines, Rocco Pisani, Esther Stone, the late

George Christie, Ann Morgan, Anne Schutzenberger, Christer Sandahl, Paul Foulkes, Roberto de Innocencio, the late Felix de Mendelssohn, Howie Kibel, Richard Billow, Hidefumi Kotani, Oliver Larkin, Morry Rottem, Jocelyn Allen, Robi Friedman, Margarita Kritikou, Catherina Mela, Nikolaos Stathopoulos, Haim Weinberg, Leila Navarro, Martha Gilmore, Ben Roth, Peter Ellingsen, Dr. Christine Hill and the late Dr Fern Cramer-Azima.

I then started working in the International Christian University in Tokyo, Japan. Certain members of the IAGP were also committed to this work. I would like to thank the late Dr Felix de Mendelssohn, who sadly passed away in 2016.

I then founded the Melbourne Branch of International Organisation of Group Analytic Psychotherapy (IOGAP) in Australia in 2012. I thank all those who assisted me in compiling this book, namely Emeritus Prof. Graeme C Smith, Earl Hopper, Tony Trumble, Assist. Prof. Russell Grigg, Prof. David Kissane, Assist. Prof. David Clarke, Herbert Hahn, Oliver Larkin, Vanessa Murray, Lynn Davis and Anne Jeffs.

Russell Grigg from Deakin University, Melbourne, has been one of the main Coordinators of Training from 2013 to 2015. Herbert Hahn helped greatly in 2012.

I thank all of you, my trainees and patients for enriching my life and sharing with myself numerous precious times together. I wish all of you the very best in your health and happiness. You will all remain in my memory forever.

With my gratitude always,

Dr Sabar Rustomjee

INTRODUCTION:

S.H. Foulkes: His Life and Journey
by Dr Paul Foulkes – Psychoanalytic
Psychotherapist and Consultant Psychiatrist

This book starts with an introduction to the life of S.H. Foulkes, a great world renowned psychoanalyst and especially the founder of group analysis. Dr S.H. Foulkes' grandson has become a very well-appreciated psychoanalytic psychotherapist in Australia. Paul now gives us his memory of his grandfather.

"S.H. Foulkes: His Life and Journey" by Dr Paul Foulkes – Analytic Psychotherapist and Consultant Psychiatrist

S.H. Foulkes

My grandfather, S.H. Foulkes, variously called Siegmund Heinrich, Heinz and Michael, became the founder of group analysis and a pioneer in group psychotherapy. He lived in the middle half of the 20th century; one of the most volatile, violent and yet creative periods of history. He was a doctor, psychiatrist and psychoanalyst and moved from a highly individualist way of thinking to seeing people embedded communally through communication. This was a dramatic and profound shift within himself, but it also inspired others to make that journey. Today, it is commonly recognised that we, as human beings, have a deep need to belong to grouping. But this was not always so. This talk examines the life of one man who journeyed far in the search for truth about the human condition. This presentation leads us to understand more of the reasons why he chose to embark on this voyage.

S.H. is how he always chose to be known professionally. He was the youngest child by far in his family. He had three older brothers, one sister and was an unplanned pregnancy. He was born in Karlsruhe, Germany, of a Jewish family who lived in Germany for centuries — since the Middle Ages. As was common for Jews living in Germany, his family idealised Germanness, desired 'symbiosis with Germany' (Elon: 2003) and identified themselves as Germans. For the most part, this view was not reciprocated. So S.H.'s father fell in love with Wagner, who so hated Jews, that he named all his sons after Wagnerian characters.

S.H.'s parents, Gustav and Sarah, had much in common both being born into wealthy merchant families; timber and wine respectively, and both losing fathers in their childhood. Mother was a beautiful woman to be admired and desired rather than to forge a connection. She seemed more distant and occupied with the other children. He was not the favourite! On the other hand, Father who enrolled in the family business as a teenager, looked after by older brothers, to become more interested in leisure pursuits of riding and music, was seen as a figure with which to have a closer relationship. There were other members of the family group, his mother's maternal uncles, who were described as having a formative influence on this development; Uncle Richard, the architect, Gottfried the soccer champion who scored ten goals in an Olympic match for Germany, and his uncles the physician and surgeon. So S.H. was a lonely child, sitting for long periods contemplating what it was that he knew concluding it could only be thought itself.

Emulating his family, he studied architecture and then the study of the body, medicine. However, even at that early stage the desire to learn more of the mind interested him and psychology was a serious option. Strikingly, his first love, though forbidden by his family, was that of the theatre. He wanted to be a director and had he followed this wish; it would have been his first group.

It was during his initial years in medicine at Heidelberg, that he first became avidly interested in Freud and psychoanalysis, described by S.H. as 'the greatest influence on my professional life... from then on I knew exactly what it was that I wanted to be, namely a psychoanalyst'. This is reflected in his final medical examination when, examining a patient with diabetes, was asked by the patient if it could be due to disappointment. S.H. agreed, whereupon the rest of the time was spent on listening to the patient's retelling of her loss. The medical side was quietly forgotten. Notably S.H.'s interest after graduation for many years was psychosomatic medicine. The above story reveals his great capacity as a listener, a quality that was most remembered by his patients in a group.

The first signs of group thinking were formed by his postgraduate work with the great neurologist, Kurt Goldstein, who believed that nerves function not in isolation, but always as part of a communicating network. S.H. started to feel 'a liberation from the limitations of received knowledge... [to throw] light on one's unacknowledged hidden prejudices' (Fuchs: 1936). The whole became greater than its parts. This ability to form his own views was perhaps helped by Goldstein serving as a supportive father figure.

During this time, S.H. married a woman from a wealthy family of jewellers enabling him to continue his medical studies, despite the economic woes of the time. Notably, she also came from a family with a far more strongly Jewish orientation. This fight within himself, as to which cultural group to identify with, was enacted out by the fights between himself and his father-in-law as to whether to circumcise the first child, a son. Should he be declared a German or a Jew? S.H. lost, but this was the start of many conflicts between this doctor with a Wagnerian name and his Jewish wife.

At this stage there was little conflict about his professional orientation, his seeking of a career and identification. Psychoanalysis was his chosen goal, and after advice from Karl Landauer, applied to train in Vienna, moving there with his wife and two children. Although he wished to apply to Freud directly, he was persuaded to write to Helene Deutsch, and in turn, she became his training analyst for two years. Interestingly, she also analysed his wife Erna. S.H. lost out on his mother's attention and had to share his analyst too. He didn't like this, but accepted it rather compliantly. Taking into account the 'notion of a whole', S.H. was concerned with not forgetting the brain, the corporeal aspect of mind. He studied psychiatry concurrently with his psychoanalytic training, chiefly being interested with spending long hours trying to understand the delusions of the psychotic.

Our dreams are not always fulfilled and our images of how we want our lives to be can sometimes be shattered. Sometimes this can enable us to put the pieces together in a better way to find a different direction in life. Sometimes we are just left with a jagged collection of pieces. Over a period of two years from 1931 to 1933, S.H. suffered the destruction of his culture, the loss of his country and homeland, the death of his father and the dissolution of his family of origin. This was to usher in a new phase of his life with dramatic and far reaching consequences.

Gustav, S.H.'s father, died in 1931, suddenly of a stroke. Although S.H. was much older than Gustav was when his father, Bernhard, died (i.e. in teenage years), it still left a major impact. This was chiefly displayed in his distancing from loved ones, especially his wife. We see the same cutting off in both his wife Erna and granddaughter who, following her father's death, had a breakdown on their marriages. We can only speculate on the underlying mechanisms of the impact of this paternal death, so we have to rely upon interpretation without the benefit of response from S.H., our subject.

My impression was that S.H. had deeply loved his mother and always wished to push out his siblings and father. This would imply a degree of guilt regarding his father's death. When he changed his name some three years later, the stated reason was the sexual connotation of his surname, "Fuchs". S.H. had a life-long interest in language; his first paper being on the 'significance of a name'. Cutting off from sexuality and intimacy with others, was perhaps his response to Gustav's death, a sense of punishment for Oedipal guilt.

Now I must turn to the social, the cultural loss that would have a decisive impact upon S.H., namely the cutting off of Jews from the German corpus. It's hard for us now living in a multi-cultural land to truly have an understanding of the utter rejection, the disowning that can only occur to a minority within a nation. The Germans had gone through massive deprivation following the First World War and Depression, but like Saturn, had chosen to devour their own children. In order to devour, to cannibalise, you must first dehumanise and Jews in aspects of society began to lose their jobs and their identity as citizens. S.H. was Director of the Frankfurt Psychoanalytic Institute and, as such, did not rely upon outside patronage of the State. Book burnings were common in cities including Frankfurt. Arnold Zweig, the author, writes of one such event:

"They were cheering, laughing, joking… simple people, obtuse, passive — they were marked by animal-like, smug stupidity. They would have stared as happily into the flames if live humans were burning… I was the only one among thousands who did not sing or raise his arm when the swastika flags passed by… That same night [I] made up my mind… not to remain. We had to leave for better or worse."

In 1933, on the night prior to the date when Jews had to surrender their passports, S.H. and his wife and three small children fled to Switzerland, never to return as a family. The Fuchs family was dissipated to the four corners of the world; two brothers were to be sent to concentration camps, although one managed to escape. His sister was consigned to the flames. S.H. was very sadly only to see his beautiful mother, Sarah, for one day in London, before she died penniless in Canada in 1941.

The sense of belonging, both in his identity as a German and also in his family, was considered by S.H. to be the primary impetus for human beings, to have been annihilated. Although he quickly decided (after one day) to settle in London at the invitation of Ernest Jones, the loss of Germany caused him great angst. He suffered a series of asthma attacks in the early stages of resettlement. In retaliation for the sense of being a 'foreign body', as he described himself repeatedly, he rejected his Wagnerian German names. Instead, he chose the most English of names, Michael, and a very English spelling of his surname, to Foulkes.

Professionally, he fell on his feet however. He was able to gain British medical qualifications after studying at Westminster and was invited to join the British Psychoanalytical Society, after a short time, in 1937. This was described as his second home and, in fact, he felt more welcomed there than by the Berlin Society when he was in Germany. In fact, this acceptance involved in mainstream psychoanalysis continued for many years. He was a teacher, training analyst and Council member and always saw some patients individually in psychoanalysis to the end of his working life. Sometimes the second home becomes the first home when pain needs to be avoided. S.H. spent long hours, including weekends, at work and study.

Worse was to follow. Erna, soon after her father's death, had an affair with another German Jewish refugee, later to become her husband. The marriage broke up, but Erna continued to blame S.H. for her chronic depression for many years afterwards. The three children were split up with the youngest child, Vera, remaining with her mother and the older children, Thomas and Lisa staying in England with S.H.

As Europe slowly slid into madness and destruction, S.H.'s continuing anxiety was how his daughter, Vera, and her mother fared. They ran from country to country like mice evading the Nazi cat. Luckily, they obtained visas for Mexico where they were to see out their lives. "What future was to emerge from all this uncertainty and loss?" S.H. thought as he looked out at the world. Freud, in fact, in their only meeting warned him, "What terrible things await you to be seen?", when S.H. was only thirty eight years old.

However, this was not to be. S.H. did not cave into despair or resort to revenge, but turned to construction, creatively seeking new solutions. Getting out of London during the period of the Blitz, he set up practice as a psychotherapist in Exeter, linked to a child guidance centre and psychiatrist. Seeing patients one to three times per week, he put into practice ideas he had had for years and had only lain dormant, like seeds in the desert awaiting rain. He fantasised about putting his patients, who lay on the couch, together in a room talking to each other, wondering how they would interact. One day in 1940, he put this into practice. Excitedly, he rushed back to his new wife, Kim, who he had married eighteen months beforehand, to tell her of this event. "A momentous event has happened today, but no-one has realised it yet", he declared.

Over the next two years, fifty patients were to be treated, some in a co-therapy situation with Eve Lewis, a psychologist. The results were remarkably good and this was written in his first paper on Group Analysis in 1942, although War service delayed its impact until publication in 1944. His experiences in Exeter enabled S.H. to develop his ideas using the groups as his laboratory and was to set the scene for the next act.

Northfield Park was an Army psychiatric hospital near Birmingham and hosted a military neurosis centre where Bion spent a period developing his concepts of group process. S.H. took over and started running his groups using patients from the wards. As he became emboldened this expanded and he (with others) transformed the whole hospital into the world's first therapeutic community, groups being used at all levels of the hospital. The world was in chaos and Jewry was being obliterated, but in a small hospital a very lively and creative community flourished with the ideas generated to have a major impact upon post-War psychiatry and psychotherapy. The major portion of his ideas of the social construction of individuals, the matrix, and the practice of group analysis have their genesis in these formative times. His first book, *'Introduction to Group Analytic Psychotherapy'*, written in a scant three weeks, was an outpouring of his ideas created in this period. This set out the experience of the second Northfield Experiment.

As the war ended, his ideas brought fruit. S.H. and interested colleagues formed the forerunner of the Group Analytic Society in London which was formally founded in 1952. The concept of group processes spread widely around the world with group analysis as a means of treatment, finding great success. Later, a journal was to be founded and an Institute to help train future generations of therapists. S.H. was recognised in mainstream psychiatry to some extent. He was a consultant at St Bartholomew's Hospital in the dermatology unit and at the Maudsley.

He always identified himself as a psychoanalyst and continued to be very involved in the affairs of the Psychoanalytic Society. However, there was also always a degree of mutual suspicion with each side blaming the other for holding back and withdrawing. He was not welcomed at the Tavistock, being a rather denigrated figure. Perhaps the presence of strong women, such as Melanie Klein, rather than a male figure, such as Freud, put S.H. off somewhat. Grosskurth called him one of the ineffective 'continental males', but who castrated him? Certainly, the analyst would have viewed his move away from the intra-psychic to the systemic with a mixture of disdain and uncertainly. What was this man doing? Might his actions have been seen as a cry for help by Mrs Klein, who might have believed he needed more analysis, as was oft believed in those times?

A few more storms were to pass his way in his personal life. Erna, his ex-wife died in 1950 of lung cancer, once again producing a psychosomatic response in S.H. who promptly fell ill. Kim, his then wife, died also of cancer in 1950. A long period of mourning was not really for him when faced with a massive loss and he rather quickly married his much younger cousin, Elizabeth. She, however, proved a tower of strength for him providing a degree of care and interest in his work that sustained him for the rest of his days — she even became a group analyst herself.

S.H.'s devotion to groups continued until the end. In a staging worth of Gorky, whom he admired intensely, he died suddenly of a heart attack in the middle of a group, aged seventy seven. Interestingly enough, this was the penultimate session of a group that consisted of the future generations of group analysts. Dennis Brown, one of the participants, relates that he was angry at S.H. for ending the group, as were a number of others. He saw S.H. clutch his chest out of the corner of his eye and fall lifeless to the ground. A few hours later Dennis was to suffer a detached retina in the exact same quadrant that viewed the death scene; a bodily punishment indeed for a destructive thought, but one that resonated with S.H.'s psychosomatic tendencies.

S.H. left such a tremendous creative legacy to the society he founded and to those interested in his work. But, perhaps the manner of his death might have passed on a rather darker cloud to those who were to continue his work.

So, what are we to make of this man, who journeyed so far and in such new directions? Who belonged to an intellectual culture rooted in the notion of the individual and yet became so embroiled in the social construction of the psyche? He identified strongly with Germany yet tried to be so very English, but ended up with his children being scattered across the world. What made him set out on such a voyage, with such determination, to never look back?

Intellectually, we know that Foulkes paid a debt to Kurt Goldstein (individuals like nodes in a neuronal network), Gestalt psychology (figure ground configuration) and the Frankfurt School of Sociologists, especially Norbert Elias. But these were just the building blocks, not the will nor the external forces behind the construction.

Foulkes gives us the clues himself in his writings. He states again and again that the primary impetus of humans is to experience belonging (Dalal) and that the systems in which humans

are embedded are vital to understanding the individual and his
motivations.

Man "is basically and centrally determined by the world…
[and] community of which he forms a part" and "the individual is preconditioned to the core by his community… and his
personality and character are imprinted initially by the group
in which he is raised". Inner processes are seen as internalized
group dynamics.

If we are to take Foulkes at his word, then we must believe
that the culture of German Jewry, and its destruction, must have
played a vital part in his journey. His family of origin was so oriented to the wish to belong to the German corpus that S.H. and
his brothers were named after characters created by one of the
most notorious anti-Semites in pre-war Germany. This family
grouping transmitted these values to their children, only for the
culture to reject them forcibly. It is said that only the Jews truly
loved the Germans, the rest of the world feared them. Yet S.H.
had an unusual response to being rejected. Most German Jews
who fled mourned their lost motherland, still admiring German
values to the end. Some replaced Germanness with Jewishness.
But he did neither. He became English. He married a British
woman. His son married into an ancient titled English family.
Others invariably described SH as having made a good adjust-
ment to his new home, but this is more likely to mean that he
did not fall sick or talk interminably of Germany. I suggest that
Foulkes was not able to mourn adequately for his losses and that
creating groups and, naturally, a society to study them, was his
way of dealing with death and emptiness. It was not just his culture, but his family of origin and his wife and children, who also
felt lost. We have some evidence of his difficulties with mourning, from his rather quick remarriages after the ending of his first
two unions.

Foulkes's concepts of the essential connectedness of human beings, of the ideal of the group matrix as a container symbolically linked to the generative mother, of resonance that creates identifications, speak of a world where people are not alone. The pain of separation, the pangs of grief, are not feelings that come immediately to mind when reading his works. What better way to deal with the massive losses in his life and in a post-war world then to project his need for belonging and communication into the patients in his group? Personally, he was able to get a sense of belonging by drawing together a group of like-minded professionals, a collection of lively and intensely creative people who were to later form the nucleus of the Group Analytic Society. And he was their leader. No wonder that Foulkes thought of groups in terms of a primordial craving for a father figure (Dalal), a rather Freudian concept indeed.

Foulkes's journey was not just from one country and culture to another, nor just from individual to group analysis. He was able to move from a position of being the excluded one, viewed from a position of contempt by Nazi Germany, to one of acceptance and admiration for his great creativity. The shame that he must have felt, which must have resonated with the aloneness experienced in childhood, became transformed into a generative idea — the realisation of the intrinsic interconnectedness of human beings. More than just an intellectual concept, Foulkes broke from the analytic tradition of the individual and internal world, to forge a new path of group thinking and using other people as a means of resolving emotional difficulties. The practice of Group Analysis began. It is a wonderful illustration of the transformative power that can be harnessed from external difficulties and losses, provided that contempt doesn't become the dominant driving force.

Although losses and difficulties in mourning provide such a stimulus for creativity, other issues were a consequence, and have been cited in some of the chief criticisms of Foulkes' work.

He retained a rather over-idealised view that groups in general and group analysis, in particular, "therapeutic group analysis is the foundation upon which a new science of psychotherapy can rest. By and large, the group situation would appear to be the most powerful therapeutic agency known to us" (Foulkes 1964). It is not uncommon to declare such claims for a new treatment, but the harsh reality of our limitations tends to aid the work of de-idealisation and mourning of our lost omnipotence. This does not seem to have occurred for Foulkes who is still idealised by the Society he helped found.

Surrounded by some of the most destructive and aggressive events in history, S.H. held up a terribly optimistic view of human behaviour in groups. He believed that destructiveness was to be centred in the individual, to be there corrected by the socializing forces of the group, seen as essentially constructive and normative. And what of the destructive group? It is not to be mentioned rather surprisingly. In such dark times, in war-torn England, in the Holocaust, such optimism is a sign of hope in humanity, but little work of reality correction seems to have been done thereafter.

S.H. himself struggled with the issue of aggression. Personally, he had a very calming demeanour, 'the master of the unfinished sentence', who, like his way of conducting a group, had a very 'indirect', 'permissive' (E. Foulkes) manner of speech. He valued unobtrusiveness and explicitness and yet instilled a 'curiosity and spirit of inquiry' (Skinner, 1982) in those who heard him. A colleague at the Society said to me of him "When Foulkes listened to you, you felt as though you had never been listened to before". He was rarely heard to raise his voice or to act in an aggressive manner, rather he was seen to be unfailingly polite. An eruption, when he chased his son around the dining table with a pen knife, seems to be the exception that proves the rule.

Denial of destructiveness is suggested in a famous anecdote.

Foulkes went shopping for some curtains for his consulting rooms. After making his choice he and his wife were alarmed upon their arrival some time later. The recurring pattern on the curtains was scenes from a battle, where a variety of means of death and mutilation of the most violent nature was depicted. S.H. had no conscious awareness of what he had chosen.

There were no signs of his being overtly destructive, but his attempt to suppress his more intense emotions could lead to a withdrawal from people close to him. Colleagues said of him that he was distant and not particularly effusive (Hopper). His emotional and physical distance from his first wife, especially after the death of her father and the lack of emotional closeness with his children, in particular, are examples of this. His wedding present was a fox stole, given to his daughter-in-law. Of course, one can only speculate upon the unconscious meaning of dying in a group of future group leaders, and what kind of 'present' was being given. It is said that he was more ambivalent to 'sons' and 'brothers' in his profession, potential rivals, than younger ones, 'grandsons' (Hopper).

Yet, on balance, Foulkes impresses as a highly original and creative man, who forged a new way of conceiving the nature of human beings and who was able to use this conception in the development of a new treatment for human problems. That he did this as a stranger in a strange land, in the shadow of war time and his own sense of personal losses. Perhaps his failings, as regards mourning and aggression, only make him more human, more a person with whom we can identify.

As S.H. always believed and practised:

"In the end it is the individual that matters most."

INTRODUCTION:

From Contempt to Dignity
by Sabar Rustomjee

This book describes the vicissitudes of contempt through numerous examples. Contempt is projected, with resulting injury to the victim, through both unintentional humiliation, as well as planned, humiliating, contemptible actions. The one who projects contempt onto others rarely intends to consciously reveal his or her true motive in doing so. Moreover, there may have been long standing, disowned self-contempt which had already started in early childhood. It may well be openly a result of unbearable jealousy towards another or supressed, contemptuous rage belonging to various castes, races, religions and countries. Current or recent traumatic events may bring up repressed feelings in persons harbouring self-contempt from a young age.

Contempt, Control and Triumph are three Manic Defences initially described by Melanie Klein (1945).

> Loss of face of the victim is the greatest humiliation a contemptuous person can possibly inflict onto another.

The book starts with the untimely death of the author's father when she was aged six years and totally unaware of the consequences of such an event. Edvard Munch expresses it very vividly in his picture 'The dead mother and child'. When I first came across this painting, I realised how familiar the scene was for me. Everyone was consoling my bereaved family and probably considered that children as young as myself would have minimal feelings and would get over this trauma far quicker than an adult. Highly experienced psychoanalysts like Sigmund Freud, Joan Symington and Esther Bick, as well as Alice Miller, vividly describe the difficulties and realise the vulnerabilities, of very young children who need trust and constancy in their environment and feel bereft when they are left for long periods of time by themselves.

Problems with separation individuation

This realisation led me to start understanding children's difficulties when their mothers quietly slipped off to work while the child was asleep and returned hours later. This theme appears in various forms in the child's later years. Then, a period occurs which is very well put into place, by Freud. The child practices mastery by playing with a cotton reel, throwing it over the bed actively and then happily reels the thread back. The child now feels in control of the cotton reel, and says forte–dah (in German) if that is the language used in that house. The child now is confident, knowing he/she can take an active role playing with the cotton reel and not remain passive all day. It allows the child the individuality to enjoy an active playing role. Later in life, the child will want parents to buy a Barbie doll or Batman outfit, depending on the child's wish. However, buying material articles does not solve separation anxiety. Young boys are known to remove the Batman outfit and hide themselves behind their mother's apron. (The Batman outfit was too premature for the child to enjoy.)

As an example, take Maria, a new member starting group therapy at the local Community Centre. Initially, Maria appeared pressured, repeatedly criticising her preschool daughter. The bulk of group members also appeared to feel uneasy about the future of the little girl. They felt reluctant to say the obvious, namely that the child, Julia, felt 'like a fish out of water', staying at home most of the time. The group suggested that it seemed to be a good idea for me to see Maria's little daughter Julia, even once, so as to assess her briefly and then suggest a well-supervised children's play group, similar to the one associated with the local library next door. This programme had times set aside for children to sing and dance. As Maria — the mother — could not afford to send Julia to a full-time nursery for children her age, this suggestion seemed appropriate.

The next week, at the allocated time for Maria and Julia to see me, they arrived promptly at the Community Health Centre. I had kept paints and a drawing board for Julie, along with some toys. I suggested Maria remain in another room nearby, reading some magazines. This was done to give Julie special time for herself.

As soon as the mother left, Julia saw the painting materials which I had left for her to use. She immediately went for the colour black. She drew a tree with black leaves, a bare house and a Christmas tree just outside the house. The tree was totally black, and had no presents or coloured decorations. I asked Julia to describe her painting. She flew into a temper and said, "Can't you see? There is no-one in the house". I pointed to the Christmas tree and she said again, more angrily, "Can't you see? — It is bare! There are no presents for anyone". She told me her parents had divorced and she would only see her mother late in the evening after she returned from work. Her babysitter would be "around somewhere". Julia continued, "Sometimes after she gives me some breakfast, I do not even know where she is". The story was crystal clear. She had no-one who had realised the importance of containing her fears and hugging her when she felt annihilated. There was no responsible person to take her for a walk. She had lost her omnipotence and felt she was 'a nobody' — just existing in 'bits and pieces'. Obviously, she knew what she was lacking when she compared herself to other children in her age group. She knew her mum earned the money, but it was never enough compared to what other children had. They could go everywhere they wished. She saw her own drawing again and said softly to herself, "This is how I feel every day". She was always very truthful.

Over the next couple of weeks, the group members tried to do their best to help Maria. Julia was now able to start pre-school in the new term. A number of parents were unaware that children who are separated from their own parents for long periods during their infancy or early childhood experience hindered their healthy growth (Bowlby, 1973).

Little Julia re-enacted a similar sad scene a few weeks later at her first playschool. She was outside, playing alone during lunch time, when it began to rain heavily. She saw an old Greek lady dressed in black getting totally drenched and yet hobbling slowly, due to her old age. Julia could hold herself no longer. She screamed at the woman, "Run, you bloody bitch, run!" Needless to say, the teacher on duty heard her and wanted to expel her from the school! This led to my approaching the teachers with her mother and explaining the sensitivity and hidden goodwill of the child who felt helpless once more. She knew the Greek lady needed to be dry, but could not express in words exactly what could be done. The incident ended well, especially as the teachers realised that the limitations of little Julia were a result of the teacher's own limited ability to ask those around her for help. For example, the teacher could have run and given the old lady an umbrella! The little girl's own goodwill to keep the old lady dry gave her feelings of remaining helpless. Sadly, others who witnessed the scene did nothing to help either, which made Julia more furious. She could not accept the passivity of the old lady and of others doing nothing to stop the old lady from getting totally drenched.

The book goes on to describing Manic Defence Mechanisms, compiled by Melanie Klein and Hanna Segal (Segal, 1975). In addition, Alice Miller's two great books '*For your own Good: The Roots of Violence in Child Rearing*' and '*The Drama of being a Child*'. Often the child bears a lot more pain than the parents do.

Narcissism is often compared with contempt. Bateman (2002) describes the 'thin-skinned' person and the 'strong-skinned' one. The latter requires less protection from exposure to trauma. The nymph, Echo, could not speak on behalf of Narcissus, as all she could do is echo his words. Narcissus dies admiring his own image in the water while getting closer and closer to his own beautiful image.

This reveals the importance of progression towards 'Separation and Individuation' as described by Margaret Mahler (see Part II, Chapter One).

The Early Origins of Humiliation and its Consequences

The book goes on to examine the early origins of murderers and those who massacre innocent citizens. These murderers invariably have a history of being *humiliated* in unbearable ways during their early life. The examples given are the *Birdman of Alcatraz*, *Martin Bryant* from Tasmania, *Raskolnikov*, the main character of Fyoder Dostoyevsky's brilliant book *Crime and Punishment*, *Anders Behring Breivik* from Oslo, Norway, and others. These murderers have been humiliated and disgraced during their lives, to the extent of feeling self-contempt arising from poor behaviour of their siblings, peers and community.

Self-contempt and lack of courage lead to problems attaining healthy self-identity. Persons with Obsessive-Compulsive Disorders present with an air of perfectionism. They see others as inferior. This is often seen in couples who have not been able to compromise on their differences. *Anna Karenina* is described as a very thin-skinned narcissist in Leo Tolstoy's novel. She is described by Neville Symington as needing proof that she was loved at all times. This is even after a broken marriage and agreeing to leave her son whom she loved dearly, but agreed to keep her only son in the care of his father. This seemed the way to enjoy loving the young handsome man she had chosen for herself.

Contempt with social isolation

Early life traumas starting from congenital deformities are also discussed, such as the clubfoot of Dr Philip Carey, a brilliant medical doctor, as described in Somerset Maugham's biographical novel 'Of Human Bondage'. The young orphan boy's club foot caused him intense contempt from the start of boarding school and later as a medical student. Carey then suffered major projected contempt from the barmaid Mildred whom he loved dearly till the day she died. He fell in love with her, and was unable to end the destructive relationship, forgiving her until he finally realised she worked as a prostitute and had destroyed his most precious hand paintings in a fit of anger. Only following her death, Philip was able to seriously consider surgery in order to normalise his foot. Following this, he was able to seriously choose an appropriate partner to love and share married life.

Although individual and combined group psychotherapy methods have proven to give a good result, it is sad that a large percentage of individual psychoanalysts do not add weekly or bi-weekly group sessions in their regular work. These include Small, Median, Large, time-limited, slow Open Analytic Groups and Supportive Expressive Groups. It is sad that a large percentage of individual psychoanalysts do not add weekly or biweekly group sessions in their regular work.

Different types of groups are suited for working with different categories of patients. There are varieties of groups in children's hospitals, including mother/infant groups, preschool children groups, parent groups and others. Expert supervision is an important component.

Tom Main's *'The Ailment'* described a unique project of inpatients with serious disorders, which could not be treated appropriately in other settings. This is considered a very important experience, the details of which are discussed later. It can be discussed in three categories, namely:

a) The staff, relating to the patient as if they belong to the category of 'The Special Patient', and so deserve special treatment!

b) Nurses accepting the plea of 'The Sentimental Appeal' for extra help asked from certain patients who appeared more vulnerable than others.

c) Bringing about a feeling of 'Omnipotent Arousal' in the nursing staff looking after the patients. The nurses felt elated by accepting the praises with which they were showered. There was, of course, accompanying fear in the nurses, that they may disappoint the 'Special Patient' and Senior Staff. This brought about immense strain on the nurses, leading to resignation.

Transference and Counter-transference issues are examined through the works of Donald Winnicott, Malcolm Pines, Earl Hopper, Jacques Lacan, Farhad Dalal, Morris Nitsun, Bennett Roth, Richard Billow, Nancy McDougall and others.

Another important issue discussed in the book is Jacques Lacan's subject of Desire. This includes an examination of Leonardo da Vinci's world-famous paintings, Mona Lisa, Ginevra de' Benci's withheld identity, soft, beautiful complexion and downcast eyes, as well as Cecilia Gallerani hugging an Ermine. Leonardo's exceptional, multi-dimensional, work *'The Virgin of the Rocks'* shows another of Leonardo's ideals of beauty. Leonardo's understanding of how the body influences the mind and his theories of character and expression have affected other great thinkers (Syson, 2011).

Transcultural psychotherapy is important in the multicultural world in which we all live. It is imperative to be knowledgeable and clear about transcultural orientations.

A very important chapter is one about Noncompliance. This can apply to a variety of instructions given to patients who are told quite categorically and at times have even been made to sign that they understand the complications. Different illnesses need different restrictions. A number of case histories have been written where, despite the above, there is total non-compliance with resulting disappointments in the outcome. However, the most important issue is that *not all non-compliant patients have a tendency to die prematurely*. I have worked in Consultation Liaison Units for nearly forty-five years. It is such a pleasure to see the most unexpected non-compliant patient attain total normality following what was probably a successful renal transplant. A few months ago, I got the shock of my life when suddenly a familiar voice said to me, "Hi, Doc!" I turned around in surprise to find the most non-compliant patient I had ever seen, smiling from ear to ear and showing off his strong muscular arms while saying, "I am working as a fencer now". I believe with similar patients that enjoying one's own individuality is a very important component to attain recovery.

The following picture reveals a young girl painted by Diego Velázquez (1659), who without asking for permission pushes aside a thick curtain and enters a tapestry room. As she was doing this with great care, no-one appeared to be disturbed. She left the tapestry room in an excellent mood as she was overawed to see the magnificent work that was being done by those she knew well. This room was ordinarily forbidden for children. However, her carefulness and maturity led the workers in this large room not to be worried about her, but to respect her individuality.

Had she been scared and demoralised by peeping into the room, the team leaders would have asked her to leave. They would have taken it as granted that non-compliance is a pathway to failure.

The Tapestry Weavers (1659) — Diego Velázquez

In present day consultation medicine, we often see seriously ill patients who become highly dependent on those around. They demonstrate feelings of demoralisation and depression, as described by Professors Kissane, D. (2003), Clarke, D. (2005) and others. It results in believing that those who are not easily demoralised or depressed, due to minor trauma, responds with optimism, self-assurance and encouragement. They then start to think positively about their own future.

This year I suddenly needed an acute abdominal emergency operation. The majority of the senior consultants were most encouraging. I now feel that my quick recovery within three weeks was a result of the expertise of these experienced professionals. This has also helped me considerably in completing this book. I thank them and their staff most sincerely.

Similarities and differences between Contempt, Controll ,Arrogance ,Triumph

Contempt as a Manic Defences

1. Features of	Symptoms	
⊥ CONTEMPT	⊥ Self Contempt hidden— ⊥ Contempt to Others is openly expressed	⊥ Result ⊥ Causes considerable Emotional trauma ⊥ Can lead to death ⊥ by Suicide ⊥ Serious psychiatric and ⊥ Medical Illnesses
Occurs openly without Shame 'ѵ	➤ To discredit the victim, ➤ to condemn painfully and scornfully	➤ Result ⊥ Extreme Hostility ⊥ Death wishes 1. Devaluation of Self ⊥ and loved ones of victim ⊥ Competetive and envious of Others.

| Lack of Empathy for others

 Lack of Empathy

 Indifference

 Eg rather than receive an invitation | ➤ Demoralization

 ➤ Lack of Faith and

 ➤ Lack of Hope from others | ⊥ Avoids Psychic Reality

 ⊥ Self contempt projected onto rest of family.

 ⊥ Can lead to psychiatric illness in those living |

		Partner treated as object, bolstering Narcissists self esteem. Cool indifference
Non compliance	Included in DSM 1V includes Self-centeredness, pervasive Grandiosity, self-importance, Self-accomplishments	

SHAME	**SYMPTOMS**	**Result**
LURKS UNSEEN Helen Block Lewis 1971 discovered high no of unexplored Shame markers	Demoralised Clarke and Kissane	**Does not commensurate with** **Analytic work done** **Can turn analysis to acting out.**
Witkin et al 1954 discussed Shame more openly with better results	Patients too ashamed to expose their own shame	

Important Reference **W Bion *Second Thoughts* (1990)Chapter 7 pp86-92, Karnac.England.**	"When life instincts predominate PRIDE becomes Self Respect." "When Death Instincts predominate, Pride becomes Arrogance"	"Arrogance of Oedipus in vowing to lay bare the truth, at no matter the cost" "Sphinx destroys herself when the riddle is answers"

OMNIPOTENCE

Omnipotence	Symptom	Result
a) Infantile		
b) in Adults	Poor Reality Testing-eg wearing socks in the hospital.	May need amputation below ankle.
		Kidney Failure needing 3 times a week hemo-dialysis.
	Developed ulcers on feet because was a diabetic.	Narcissistic Personality
	Would drink more than prescribed water, although kidneys could not excrete urine-	Can have lethal results
		Lack of empathy
		Intense envy
		Expect to be recognized as fragile
		Responds to shame with shame-rage cycle
		Friendship formed only if there are benefits for them.

Features of Arrogance

ARROGANCE	SYMPTOMS	RESULT
Where there is mainly evidence of Life Drive, there is pride.	*People dislike an Arrogant Person as they cannot identify themselves with such a person.*	Only a person who lives with Self Contempt is likely to marry an arrogant man +
Where there is mainly evidence of Death Drive, there are Asks for **Impossible Demands**	*Haughty and Condescending* *"Illusion of Omnipotence"* *"I am not Bookett, I am Mrs Bouquet!" in TV series Keeping up appearances.* *No apology given by Mrs B.*	Endless disagreements+ Success does not last long + Projective Identification.++ Real problems remain unresolved ++++++++
Wants to Keep Up Appearances. (Quality of life is hollow inside)	*Lives with a False Self on the outside.* *Great Painter E.Munch painted a philanthropist " Rathenhau" as being arrogant.* *Reply by R" That's what you get when you go to a great artist like Munch "(disappointed)*	Marriages may last, if a)either husband or wife keep arguing with each other, just to prove a point that only one person is correct. Marriage problems remain unresolved. OR b) One partner remains subservient
Denial that a son or daughter is not able to budget for his own needs or luxuries.	*Controls son by sending him constant money.* *Son not taught to be accountable.*	Son never sees parents for sharing love Relationship with father is poor .Identifies with weak father by being gutless.
Unhealthy friendships.	Choices of friendship, based on ability to control them.	Self- Defeating Behavior

	medication, combined with **Expressive Supportive therapy**	
	Example: Loss of Psychic Reality as in **Freud's case of Female Homosexual**	**Result can be LETHAL.** **And LOOKS of Contempt can KILL.**

INTRODUCTION (B):

A Vulnerable Journey from Contempt to Dignity

This journey is achieved by crossing the bridges starting from between the "Survival of Primitive Omnipotence "described by Joan Symington (1980) and Esther Bick (1987). This entails Holding and Containing their baby, by accepting their own and their baby's ambivalent feelings as being a part of the process of giving a Psychological Birth to one's own child.

Next comes Stage of Manic Defences, demonstrating Control, Contempt and Triumph, described by Melanie Klein (1935) in "A Contribution to the psychogenesis of manic-depressive states."(IJP, 16:145-74). No one needs to go "Beyond the Pleasure Principle" as described by Sigmund Freud. We need to remain safely within boundaries which prevent us from getting into any danger.

Separation and Individuation stages as described by Margaret Mahler occur during this period. The child should not remain symbiotically attached to the mother, and neither should the mother encourage pushing the child away. The child needs to show to himself/herself that it is possible to develop the Capacity to be Alone in the presence of the mother (Winnicott, D. W.). This phase is the start of an independent life for every child.

Mourning of a loving relative,

The story of Cinderella shows how she needed to mourn her dead mother, to feel free to lead a wonderful life with her Prince!

Her step mother and step sisters gave her a rough time. They were jealous of Cinderella's beauty and her warm, forgiving nature. They tried to treat her with scorn, disdain and envy, but she did not accept their contemptuous attacks. She rose about it. Even after marrying her prince she never took revenge on them, and treated them only with respect. This is the most important part of all our lives, namely to accept the Reality of the Losses in our Lives.

As long as we have not nurtured a life of Self Contempt, we can overcome the Contempt of others, and stop their cruelty from destroying us as well as innocent others. The final goal needs to be Self-acceptance and Creativity. We will then not be affected by *Nameless Dread* (Stephens, K., 1941 & Bion, W., yyyy). As long as we do not consider that we are so-called Superior beings, similar to what Razkolnikov (the hero of Crime and Punishment by Dostoevsky), we do not need to prove anything to anyone.

As a medical doctor initially I chose to work in neonatal paediatrics in Liverpool, UK, while my husband was on scholarship. We then returned to Colombo where I worked once more in neonatal paediatrics in a maternity hospital.

In the next few years there were severe political unrest with riots in the late 1960s. Medical doctors needed to go to the hospital morgue regularly. The most painful encounter, I was to witness is a very well groomed child with long shiny light blue satin ribbon tied in her hair probably less than half an hour ago. A bomb had exploded near her and suddenly ended her life. There was no justification for such an atrocity. Violence became more rampant daily. We decided to migrate to Australia.

And so we called Australia Home.

Although we had relatives in the UK we preferred Australia. At that time racism was high in the early 1960s in the UK. I asked the secretary of the consultant whom I was working with for an appointment. She turned that pages and replied emotionlessly "He is busy till February next year." I thanked her and left quietly. I knew my English consultant would have answered my query the same day but thought it was more respectful to aske his secretary first. Subsequently I got the reply from him the same day directly. Even at hospital parties both new Zealanders and Indian doctors were treated rudely and asked when are you going to go back to your own country? There was tremendous economic poverty in rural villages in Sri Lanka at the time.

In this book I have explored the topic of contempt starting with self contempt and going onto malignant bonding. Somerset Maugham's book *Of Human Bondage* (1915) gives the best background of a crippled medical student who was treated most contemptuously because of his deformity. I would recommend this book for everyone who is interested in understanding contempt. And the humiliation it delivers to the person whom it is projected. Contempt can be overcome by courage using Oratory Skills, Jokes and Cartoons.

Section two in the book gives numerous examples of curative factors in small groups and the advantages of being a member of an analytic group. Groups for terminal cases of metastatic breast cancer and unexpected deaths are part of these groups. It gives lot of support to group members who are suffering similarly.

This section also describes narcissistic grandiose arrogant and omnipotent members in small groups. Theoretical issues arising during transference and countertransference need to be understood if the groups are based on analytic framework. Heinz Kohut's version of transference is idealising and mirroring transference. Marrone describes the both negative and positive transferences are equally important to psychoanalysis. It is very important for analyst to know if they are annoyed or contemptuous towards those in treatment even if it is for a brief period of time. Members get very humiliated and lose faith in their therapist if they observe signs of contempt. Everyone has their own technique. Margaret Little a well known analyst has written a book of her own personal analyses by three different analysts each of which was very different.

Section three is on Lacan's views on Gaze and Perception. When done by world famous painters like Leonardo da Vinci, Edvard Munch and Hans Holbein and others show their emotions very clearly. Munch's famous painting of the *Scream* described by him both verbally and in his painting. Similarly *Mona Lisa* is the most popular painting where visitors move all around the painting to see her from all angles and enjoy her beauty. It reminds me of the su   which is always fixed but the earth revolves around it.

The section four is on forensic psychotherapy on murders and mass murderers, also, those with remorse and without remorse.

Section five describes transcultural psychotherapy which describes differences in cultures as well as feeling s of unbearable shame and guilt. Indigenous Australian culture with Freud's version of totem and taboo is also important in understanding the Australian aboriginals.

Section six includes dealing with autistic spectrum disorder grandiosity and dangerous non compliance. Consultation Liaison Psychiatry reveals the importance of non compliance and its relationship to the life drive and the death drive. The latter is part of conservation withdrawal. (Ironside, W.,

PART I

THE HIDDEN TRUTH WITHIN THE DEPTHS OF THE UNCONSCIOUS

CHAPTER 1:

My early life enduring ambiguity and méconnaisance

I am starting with the words of John Keats
La Belle Dame Sans Merci **by John Keats (18200**

Oh what can ail thee, knight-at-arms,
Alone and palely loitering?
The sedge has withered from the lake,
And no birds sing.

O what can ail thee, knight-at-arms,
So haggard and so woe-begone,
The squirrels granary is full,
And the harvest's done.

I see a lily on they brow,
With anguish moist and fever-dew
And on they cheeks a fading rose,
Fast withereth too.

I met a lady in the meads,
Full beautiful a faery's child,
Her hair was long, her foot was light,
And her eyes were wild.

I made a garland for her head,
And bracelets too, and fragrant zone,
She looked at me as she did love,
And made sweet moan.

I set her on my pacing steed,
And nothing else saw all day long,
For sidelong would she bend and sing,
A faery's song.

She found me roots of relish sweet,
And honey wild, and manna-dew,
And sure in language strange she said –
"I love thee true".

She too me to her elfin grot,
And there she wept and sighed full sore,
And there I shut her wild, wild eyes
With kisses four.

And there she lulled me asleep,
And there I dreamed — ah woe betide-
The latest dream I ever dreamt
On the cold hillside.

I saw pale kings and princes too,
Pale warriors, death-pale were they all;
They cried — "La Belle Dame sans Merci
Hath thee I thrall!"

I saw their starved lips in the gloam,
With horrid warning gaped wide,
And I awoke and found me here
On the cold hill's side.

And this is why I sojourn here,
Along and palely loitering,
Though the sedge is withered from the lake,
And no birds sing.

My Childhood

Personally, overwhelming and challenging experiences started in my own very early life in Sri Lanka, coping with unexpected sudden grief as a child, with my father dying unexpectedly when I was aged six. It started with a short journey in a large ship, followed by a smoke-filled dusty train journey into a very different country, India. I felt bewildered and lost. All I remember was my father, Maneksha, a medical practitioner, giving my fourteen year old sister Manijeh and myself, an inoculation of smallpox vaccine on the ship. It was on the inner part of our calves and served as a lifelong protection. He carefully chose the site so that the scars were not visible or disfiguring for a female. I felt proud that although my father, himself very ill, always had his wife Mehra and us, his children in his mind.

As Sri Lanka at that time had no chemotherapy or radiation treatment for him, I overheard that India, being more advanced, was the only hope for recovery. I had heard about death, but knew nothing more as to what would happen next. Fortunately, my maternal grandmother, who loved me dearly, came with us to live in Mumbai, India. She was a very courageous and practical person, but not one with whom I could share any deep and meaningful conversations. She was more my protector than a friend. Then tragedy struck our family.

Two days after reaching Mumbai, my father died suddenly one evening. We were staying in a huge hotel by the sea at that time. As the sun was setting, everything seemed dark. The scene before my eyes even now is very much like the painting of Edvard Munch when his mother died. Edvard's mother lying lifeless on the bed, with adults huddling on one side, and with his six year old sister, Sophie, on the opposite side, closing her ears so as to 'block out the painful screams of death' (Munch, 1897-1899), '*The Dead Mother and Child*'. All I remember was that about half an hour ago, my father advised my mother that as there would be visitors in our hotel room that day, she needed to buy bread, butter, biscuits, tea and milk and keep it ready for them! Being a loving and obedient wife, she arranged it all.

The Dead Mother and Child, 1897, Edvard Munch

The funeral was a nightmare. As both my parents had been born in India, there was a large crowd of their friends and relatives who surrounded my mother all the time during the four days of the funeral. Thankfully, she felt held and contained and able to express her sorrow. Our Sri Lankan relatives could not come for the funeral at short notice, so all who came were totally unknown to my sister and myself. We just sat absolutely stunned, side by side. We were almost lifelessly watching and feeling totally bewildered. We saw and heard four Zoroastrian priests in their sonorous voices praying to God in unison. That became gradually very comforting as lots of fresh flower petals were constantly sprinkled on my father. Then, freshly cut up fruit and sweetened food 'malido' which had been blessed during prayers, was distributed to everyone to be eaten. All this was done in a holy atmosphere with calm and precision, in the ancient Avesta language, translated into English by my uncle Framroz.

Uprooting oneself and the difficulties of migration to an unknown country

The reality of what life was going to be like, without my own father, mother and grandmother all living in a large house in Sri Lanka, with servants and luxuries could not be imagined. I was now living in a foreign land, with not even one friend, no common language and no familiar surroundings. Life felt cold and very bleak. My mother, grandmother, sister and myself lived for the first two months in the country with my maternal Indian uncle, aunt and their nine children whom I had never met before! My own belongings had mostly been given away or auctioned before my very eyes! Most of our daily wear clothes were locked up in trunks had yet not arrived by sea. I did not own a single toy or even a children's book. Most of all, I greatly missed my own cupboard full of very expensive English dolls which had been locked safely away for me, till I was "old-enough" to play with them. That day never arrived. I felt cheated. This has remained as an internalised loss within me. I presume my sister Manijeh felt the same. We never discussed our grief, even with cousins our age, as we had never met them before.

The only toys I could now see were cheap ones in local shops which were most unattractive. I was well aware that we could not now afford anything even a fraction as beautiful as before, on my father's limited pension, which arrived monthly from Sri Lanka. My love for my mother stopped me asking her for any toys at all. As an analytic psychotherapist, I now realise my ambivalence of mixed up love and anger towards her and my maternal uncle, for auctioning and giving away, the few belongings which had been promised to me all my life. Later in life I realised that these were not toys but were expensive ornaments. My grief subsided after knowing the explanation.

It was the first experience I had in my life, that it was not only people I loved, like my father, whom I missed, but that material things also had a transient life of their own. In retrospect, it is clear, I must have been equipped with enough love in my heart from both my parents, so as to be able to overcome all these obstacles.

I do not remember feeling particularly strong, but neither did I ever feel weak. Reality seemed easier to bear in India. Most of all, I never felt sorry for myself. I hardly ever felt sick either.

I had the capacity for reflection, e.g. "Since everything is transient, how can anyone suddenly develop trust, and if so, in whom, in what and for how long?" I became thoughtful and somehow knew that I needed to face my new life as it was then and make important decisions mostly by myself. My mother, now a widow, was going through her own grief. She only wore white sarees, white blouses and even white shoes for the rest of her life. The colour black depressed her; hence her choice was white. My sister was eight years older than myself and lived her own life. My mother valued education above everything else and would often say "A lot of material things can be stolen, or lost, but no-one can steal your brain away from you. So, make good use of it".

There was one memorable family group, which my uncle arranged for all of us to attend. My mother pleaded that being only six years old, I be exempted. My uncle insisted for myself to be included as he felt I was old enough to understand that my mother felt dissatisfied with him. My sister and myself had heard all this before, so were not moved by it. We did not take sides and neither did his children. My uncle said he had been wrongly accused for charging my mother his expenses for coming to Sri Lanka and settling all loose ends financially, so we could all move to Mumbai. My mother, on the other hand as a widow, had been shocked that her own brother had actually charged her! This had apparently been decided between them before he came to Sri Lanka. Nevertheless, there remained a coldness between them. As far as I was concerned, I felt recognised by my uncle in insisting on my presence at the meeting of about twenty adults. This was my very first Family/Median Group. After a few civilised exchanges the meeting was ended. Shortly afterwards my uncle moved to Pakistan, with some of his children, while others remained with their maternal grandmother in Mumbai at a location much closer to us.

A few weeks later, we said goodbye to our uncle and aunt who lived in the country and rented a flat in a very busy and lively part of Mumbai. All the remaining cash available for us was enough to buy four beds and four electric light bulbs. We bought the rest of our furniture gradually, whenever we could afford it. This suburb had the reputation of having one of the best girls' schools in Mumbai, which was walking distance from our flat.

Despite going to one of the best schools in Mumbai, I would feel a heaviness in my heart leaving behind all the security of having a well acclaimed father and being respected by the city of Balapitiya and my relatives in the capital Colombo. What I was now suffering was that I did not feel I had a clear sense of identity any longer.

At the age of six I started at Queen Mary's private girls' school, in Mumbai. The headmistress before accepting me asked me to read a simple sentence. It was a children's storybook. It had a word, 'grandmother' which I couldn't pronounce. So, she felt I was more suited to start in the form below which was the beginners' class. That made me feel defeated, as I could read the rest of the book quite eloquently. Also, I hadn't yet started knowing the other children in my class. I wasn't used to sleeping all afternoon which is what the rest of the class was expected to do. Having been used to a much more independent life at home in Sri Lanka I felt rather miserable. Looking back now it was part of self-contempt which is commonly present with children who have lost one or both parents.

All victims of contempt carry their unwanted burden for varying periods of time and in different ways. It is similar to demoralisation. It is not connected with shame as no shameful behaviour belonging to myself had been made. I now realise that I was going through early stages of mourning for my father. As time went on, I gradually got to know certain friends at school.

I now gradually started to develop my own identity. I clearly remember that maybe on my first or second day at my first school, a very kind English teacher put out a lot of cut outs for calendars and gave all of us a choice of whichever one we fancied to paint and assemble. I knew which one I wanted from the start. It was a pretty calendar with lovely flowers and a beautiful little house. It had the words, 'To my Darling Daddy with Love'. printed on it. (Maybe the teacher did not remember it or my mother had not told her or both had repressed it for whatever reason that I had just lost my father less than a month ago.) I rushed and grabbed that calendar and hugged it. I felt very happy as I proudly painted it with beautiful colours and then joyfully skipped home to show it to my mother. She hesitated for a split second, when it suddenly dawned on me, that maybe that calendar was inappropriate for me. My mother quickly realised what I was feeling and said gently and lovingly, "Don't worry darling, your Dad will be very pleased with your calendar. It is so beautiful". The memory of this reassurance, with my mother being perfectly in tune with my initial feelings of worry, has always been invaluable. Her loving and empathic feelings were also internalised and have served as a strong foundation stone for my later life. I felt calm and peaceful. I realise I had not hurt anyone or even had a fleeting desire to do so.

To my darling daddy Manekshaw Rustomjee, with love

This portrait of my father has hung in our lounge room for most of my life in India. It has also made the journey to our home in Australia where our family can admire him always.

Gradually, all of us adjusted to life in Mumbai. Our cousins who lived close by with their maternal grandmother visited us weekly. My sister and myself could play games together with our cousins now. 'Carrum' was a popular game with a wooden board and round wooden pieces. Each new piece needed to be struck from the boundaries by the striker piece so as to get other small pieces into four pockets. The rules were somewhat like a miniature billiard game. One of my cousins always brought fruits and music records for our grandmother while we enjoyed playing Carrum. My mother's grief had also lifted significantly.

However, only once over a period of twenty years of our migration, we were all invited for a family holiday at a friend's seaside holiday home. The next holiday was when I was a medical student in my late teenage years. This was exactly the same for many other friends of ours in Mumbai. No-one considered it peculiar. It is very different in Melbourne where a greater percentage of migrants go regularly for holidays or to visit the relatives they left behind in their country of origin. We were too financially disadvantaged to afford that.

We made life-long friends from school in Mumbai, who have remained true and sincere to this very day. Of course, I felt jealous when I saw some homes of wealthy friends with their expensive toys, their families, the food they ate and the chauffeur driven cars they travelled in, as well as the pile of magazines they could afford to buy regularly. Thankfully it was a reality, that there were fewer children from wealthy families in our school compared to the majority of lower middle-class students. What we all had in common was our school education, the colour of our skin and the high educational standard of the school. Our school was founded by Zoroastrians who are well known to be philanthropists and well respected. We all sang Christian hymns each morning at assembly, regardless of our religion. There were no separate religious classes for anyone. Indians in those days coped with differences in custom, race and religion, very much better than many countries do today. Nevertheless, economic difficulties affected me, greatly. It felt a sense of deprivation, to be relatively poor, but I did my best to conceal it. Compared to today's Western society, there were only two school friends in our class who could afford to have a yearly birthday party, inviting all classmates. I was well aware that my mother could not afford to have parties, buy me storybooks and many other things. Thankfully, very few families owned cars, fridges or telephones. If there was an urgent need, I would walk to the pharmacy down the road and make a phone call. So, being one of the majorities of lower economically classed students in our school helped me to feel normalised, much more than if we had lived among the wealthy in Colombo, Sri Lanka. There, the class system and the religion to which one belonged made a huge difference as to whether you were or were not accepted in certain circles. Most private schools also only accepted certain children of that particular race and religion or those who donated very generous admission fees. Thankfully, memories of Sri Lanka were now starting to fade, as I became friendlier with like-minded friends in Mumbai. I had also picked up at least three Indian languages, which helped me to converse with most Indians.

Restoring Self Dignity

My mother having been born and brought up in Mumbai did not think twice about bartering with tradesmen and even tram drivers when we went shopping. She would ask them to have pity on us children saying that my sister and myself were "fatherless children".

She would also routinely plead with tram conductors to allow us standing space in a fully crowded tram, when it was raining or at night time. Since then, I promised myself that I would never ever plead or beg for anything. I would study hard, and get scholarships. I never pampered or self-indulged myself either. At our home, we could never afford to buy imported cheese or ham for school lunches or to dress in clothes bought from expensive shops. Nevertheless, it did improve our self-image and dignity to dress always in clean clothes which our mother washed and ironed daily.

The average Indian went to tailors they could afford and pay them to sew their blouses. Sarees did not need tailoring. My sister and myself instead decided to sew all our own dresses. We bought materials we liked, became good dressmakers and dressed attractively with pride. My sister's schoolmates were clearly wealthier. One became an air hostess who gave me her beautiful expensive hand-me-down dresses bought by her from overseas. This friend and myself were luckily the same in size too. I did not live the life of a 'false self' as described by D.W. Winnicott (1960). Step by step, my sister and I overcame our obstacles without resorting to denial.

The only social exposure was with a like-minded elderly man who worked at the Pension office where we would go weekly to collect our pensions from Sri Lanka. A friendship grew between his family and ours. One highlight of my life was that his family had a selection of antique books regarding the lives of kings and queens who lived in the United Kingdom. They were very generous in lending them to me one by one to read and enjoy.

Life as an Indian may not be what most Westerners imagine

It was never a priority in our home for us to look for jobs after school, cook meals or even wash dishes! Our mother made it very clear that she expected us, in her words "to have a noble profession", by studying hard. I believe my mother was contemptuous of certain other mothers, as she thought it a great pity for their children to cook and clean, at the expense of studying.

Mother's own main passion was her love of embroidery. She spent months producing beautiful work with silky embroidery in bright colours. Sometimes she accepted orders from bridesmaids and was offered money for her work. She made it clear she did not work for money, but for the love of the work. The routine for teenagers after a light snack at home was to go out with their school friends together most evenings or with family or friends by train to the sandy beaches around Mumbai, sit on the sand, have an ice cream or two and return home for a delicious meal cooked at home by our elders.

After some rest, I would start doing homework for at least three hours, starting at 9.00 pm, almost daily. My sister would go out with groups of much older male and female friends to rather high-grade clubs such as Cricket clubs, Yacht clubs, Clubs near racecourses etc. These clubs attracted members, whose fathers and their children had been dedicated members for generations. Each club had more than one dining room, a swimming pool and a library. She would return home while I was still burning the midnight oil.

I went through my mourning for my father by looking daily at a life-sized hand painted portrait of him done in Sri Lanka. When alone I would talk to the portrait, recalling events of the day or week. My attachment to my father remained alive and strong.

Regular visits to our religious temples were also a regular feature of our lives. Watching cinemas was a rare treat. My first and only priority in life was to pass my Secondary School Certificate with high marks, so as to enter a well reputed college namely, The Elphinstone College, where I could learn advanced Physics and Chemistry. Having studied at a girl's school, I had missed out on these subjects which were only taught at boy's schools. So, I needed to study most nights, with very little sleep, so as to gain entrance to a certain Medical College I fancied. It was the Grant Medical College (GMC) in Mumbai. After so many years of dedicated studying, GMC had a reputation of being both a prestigious college, as well as a 'fun-loving college', students could miss a few lectures, and take time off and go to the movies. The missed work could be made up by borrowing notes from senior students. I really believed God helped me all my life. When the marks were announced it was absolutely unbelievable to realise, I not only got admitted to GMC, but had the highest marks in Chemistry in the State of Maharashtra, compared to all female Zoroastrian students. This enabled me to receive the N.M. Wadia Zoroastrian scholarship. I could now buy all brand-new books that I needed every year, as long as I returned them all, at the end of passing out as a Medical Doctor. It was the dream of a lifetime come true! I can hardly believe it even today! There were about 250 vacancies in Medicine in Mumbai every year with over 10,000 applicants from other states at that time in 1954. The rest of the students either went abroad to study if their parents could afford it, changed careers or went to other universities in nearby states where the standard for entrance into Medicine was lower.

I gradually grew to love India and can honestly now say that I would not swap my own life which I had in Mumbai, with that of anyone else I really knew in any part of the world. I still enjoy India and am very patriotic to it. We were very proud of Mahatma Gandhi as a leader of non-violence, wisdom and independence without relying on any foreign country. I feel I learned reality-based values of conducting oneself. I enjoyed sports, and became a university hockey player and a 100 metre sprinter. Anyone who was part of a University sports team got one and a half per cent added for each sport to their final marks to enter medicine, law etc. For the first time in my life, I now became popular with a network of friends. We still had no car, no phone, no money for taxis or even small luxuries, like a slice of cheese, and travelled by tram or train. My mother still had to pay my tram fares, as medical interns did not earn enough. In today's currency it would be much less than two Australian dollars a week!

After graduating as a Medical Doctor, I finally felt an equal to everyone, leading an emotionally cohesive group life with like-minded friends, tolerant of differences as to whether or not one belonged to the same culture, intellectual capability, race or religion. My internalised self-dignity and self-worth were restored. I no longer felt like a '*fatherless child*' who had lived in near economic poverty and been treated at times with contempt. However, I knew I was loved dearly by my mother and my close friends. Migration to Mumbai and saving money for our education was certainly one of the best decisions made by my mother. The cost of remaining and living in Colombo, the capital of Sri Lanka, was very high. Even recently most private schools only admitted children of their own religion, unless a charitable grant was given to the school by the parents.

Trans-generational transmission of courage

I now realise that my own courage probably was transmitted to my sister and myself, from my maternal grandmother, as well as my father. Prior to the birth of her children, my grandmother had lived fearlessly on her own in comfortable government quarters in Central India. My maternal grandfather was an engineer who built railways for the Indian Government and would often be home only on weekends. Although it is uncommon for an Indian female to live without her own family nearby, my grandmother obviously enjoyed most of her life. My maternal grandfather was also very highly respected in his work.

There were similarities with my own father's bachelor days in Sri Lanka. My father too lived alone, as he was a solo medical practitioner and was transferred by the government to work in different towns when needed. District Medical Officers were always given very luxurious homes with servants to clean the house and garden. My father was the only obstetrician in the district. He delivered both my sister and myself. My father worked most of his life in townships with a large criminal population in South Sri Lanka and did major and minor operations on patients who had suffered 'grievous wounds', as it was then termed. However, soon after my parent's marriage, my mother invited my grandmother to live with us. It may have been very scary for her to live under these frightening conditions on her own, where bloodshed was rampant. My father worked in the hospital all day. Nurses from the hospital were also sent to assist my father when needed in the evenings. A small operating room had been built at the rear of our home and was kept for emergency patients at night, if that was adequate. All I can remember is feeling curious, rather than scared. As a child of three or four years, I remember wearing my father's hat and walking up and down the garden saying, "I am a doctor". I felt very dignified, identifying myself with my father. School teachers also came home to teach my sister Manijeh. Being the daughter of the sole doctor in the town, she was also respected. However, having only one car, my sister had to go to a nearby school daily, standing upright in a bullock-cart, and accompanied by a female government worker. This was a common means of transport in small villages in that era.

Initially I felt all alone at home, after my father went to work and my sister went to school. My mother was also very busy either enjoying her great talent in embroidery with silk which was specially imported from China. To amuse myself I would pull at the tassels on our cotton curtains. The servants would either throw away the torn balls of cotton or I would secretly play games with them.

My sister was also fearless in many ways. She became one of India's first female glider pilots! She was also an excellent dentist. She married a Chemical Engineer, Sarosh, who was a very religious, kind and generous husband. Manijeh too was very generous with her time, listening for hours to the problems of the staff of a Yacht Club and Hotel in Mumbai in which she and her husband Sarosh, did honorary work. Many of my male cousins and a female cousin living in the UK have a similar disposition. Possibly living with my courageous maternal grandmother for over fifteen years has influenced both of us and our cousins in India not to become overwhelmed with every single obstacle we encountered in life.

My focus on contempt

So, why do I focus on Contempt now? It was after reading Somerset Maugham's book '*Of Human Bondage*' with his description of a contemptuous and narcissistic barmaid who had a lack of feeling for an innocent and crippled medical student who loved her dearly and kept on trying to please her until her death. It reminded me of certain persons, including family, whom I have come across.

Wilfred Bion in his writing in Second Thoughts (1987) states that contempt projected onto the victim is premeditated. Verbal abuse and actions result in devastation. When anyone's painstaking lifelong work and self-dignity are ruthlessly denigrated, the projection of contempt needs to be accepted as an Act of Violence. The perpetrator may have previously been a victim. This circulated the pain of contempt to wider a circle of unsuspecting children and adults starting from childhood. It involves open projection of scorn, disgrace and condemnation from another.

Shame on the contrary arises from within, but it tends to be repressed and then projected onto another. "Where life instincts predominate, pride become self-respect. Where death instincts predominate, pride becomes arrogance".

Contempt is the most destructive affect anyone can convey to another knowingly or unknowingly. Boundaries for contempt have never been clarified so far. We see ongoing daily evidence of cyber bullying, political contempt from any one ruling party to the opposition, difficulty in accepting differences in cultures, racial discrimination, prejudice against mental illnesses, physical illnesses (e.g. AIDS, epilepsy, congenital deformities (similar to Philip Carey's congenital club foot), physical disabilities) and other illnesses.

Hiding the deformed right foot.

Injustice in violence

The Third of May 1808, Francesco Goya.

Francesco Goya portrays a very severe injustice that he saw from outside his window. He was so upset that he was unable to paint it till some years later in 1814. A group of peasants were exploring what effects there were on Napoleon's army entering their land. He saw the scene below where innocent peasants were held at gunpoint by Napoleon's army. The figure in yellow, with a light shining on his face, shows his feelings of grave injustice. He was furious that unarmed peasants were being killed without any reason. The other peasants accompanying him lacked his courage and very few were able to look straight at Napoleon's gunmen. This picture is typical of sheer contempt to innocent unarmed peasants.

See p358 for further discussion of this painting.

CHAPTER 2:

A Hope for Equality fo Take Place in the World

There is hope for equality to take place in the world when contempt, humiliation and destructivity are abolished and creativity takes its place.

> "This above all: to thine own self be true,
> and it must follow, as the night the day
> Thou canst then, be false to no man."
> ### Shakespeare, Hamlet Act 1; Scene 3

My first ambition in life was to work as a competent paediatrician. Every paediatrician loves children. It is not possible to do so, unless one has been loved for oneself.

I knew I was loved dearly by those who had demonstrated their feelings clearly in their own way. My father had written Shakespeare's lines in my first autograph book and on the first page. This was given to me just before we left Sri Lanka to go to Mumbai, India, for his chemotherapy. I was only a child and could read children's story books, but understood that these lines from Shakespeare were written by my father were precious as they were written especially for me, with all his heart.

Exposure to violence starting from infancy

My childhood experience was that we were highly respected in Sri Lanka (formerly known as Ceylon), mainly because my father had accepted the Ceylon Government's offer for him to work in the most murderous rural environment, which all other medical practitioners had refused to do so. The environment was full of impulsive, aggressive folk, who would react violently, even if a coconut from their tree fell with the strong winds into the next door neighbour's property and was not returned immediately! An argument would start resulting in slashing each other with long knives penetrating major areas of the body! The patients would be transported to the district hospital where my father would sew the serious ghastly wounds. Minor injuries which did not need hospitalisation would be sutured by him in a separate, special operating room at the back of our home with the help of an assistant. If the door was slightly ajar, I would have a quick look. Possibly I felt scared, but had total faith in father's skill. I cannot remember any of us being truly worried. We never discussed our father's work issues once he returned home. My maternal grandmother lived with us and was always a pillar of strength.

The wider perspective: rural economics and death

An unbearable situation in the rural villages was extreme poverty. I lived and worked as a doctor of medicine in Sri Lanka for the first three years after marriage, when I was in my early twenties. It was then that I witnessed horrendous sights. One day, I saw a woman dressed in an old, torn and dirty cotton saree who had walked many miles carrying a little baby. She ran towards me, whilst hugging and kissing her baby. She put her baby in my arms saying "My baby won't eat. I gave an egg today morning, but it dribbled out again". All I could do was to hug her. How does anyone say to this mother, "Your baby is no longer alive"? I felt totally helpless, but more and more determined to become a doctor and help other people. My father had worked till his retirement and had died when I was only a little child. All I could do now was to share her sorrow. We both knew what sudden death of a close family member feels like. Our servants took over helping her with the practical details like a shower, fresh clothes and bed to sleep on for a couple of hours with her deceased baby. When she was ready, she was taken back to her home for funeral ceremonies.

There are two sides to every story. It is possible that in my anger towards the villagers for not helping the Sri Lankan mother with the dead baby, it may be that the mother was pretending even to herself that her baby was alive and just not eating. Similarly, the villagers may have been duped into thinking that this lady was not in any emergency and hence refrained from offering assistance. This is another example of Silence being the Real Crime (Segal, 1987).

It is only by facing a problem and seeing what it really is about, that we can live a Life of Freedom without carrying burdens of Contempt belonging to others.

In comparison Mahatma Gandhi states "I hate the ruthless exploitation of India, even as I hate from the bottom of my heart the hideous system of untouchability for which billions of Hindus have made themselves responsible. But, I seek to reform them in all the loving ways that are open to me" (Gandhi, 1983, p. 52).

History

Ceylon had lost its independence first to the Spanish, then the Portuguese and finally to the English. Sri Lanka eventually got its independence from the English in 1948. By then, riots and massacres had started between the Sinhalese and Tamils. It left its mark on all of us in Sri Lanka. This massacre was purely racist. The Tamils had migrated from South India, were very hardworking and wanted to own part of Sri Lanka as their own territory. This was unacceptable to the Singhalese who were ruling Sri Lanka.

During my work at the Colombo General Hospital, it was part of our curriculum to attend the city morgue. My most painful memory was during the Singhalese-Tamil riots. I saw the body of a very well-groomed young girl probably aged ten, with long, freshly ironed blue satin ribbons in her hair. It appeared that she had left home hardly half an hour ago. A bomb had exploded near her school and ended her whole life in less than a minute! She had done nothing wrong. She was spotlessly clean and obviously well dressed with tender loving care. She may have been dropped by car to her school. No one would have imagined that fifteen or so minutes later, she would be in the city morgue!

The post office nearby was also bombed. We received news in Melbourne from our own youngest daughter, that she had just posted a letter to us and reached her medical college, minutes before the post office was totally flattened by bombs. She was not physically hurt, but there were threats that her medical college was also going to be bombed shortly. Naturally, I flew from Australia, and stayed with my daughter for a period of time helping her to recover from the shock.

Gandhi's policy of non-violence won independence for India. Sadly, after he was killed, the world has not continued in his footsteps. Most politicians' largest aim today is to please the party who voted for them. Gandhi was one of the great orators. He fought valiantly for equality in taxation laws for the British and the Indians residing in India.

Gandhi's outstanding leadership

In 1930 Mahatma was fully equipped in himself. He was the undisputed leader of the Congress Party. He had spent two years in jail, one year planning how to start rebuilding an Independent India being away from British Rule. This freedom would rebuild India.

The English collected 800 million pounds sterling, yearly from taxing the Indians, while the English contributed only twenty-five million yearly! These outlandish differences in taxation, broke Gandhi's heart. Revenues were mainly obtained from the sweat of the poor Indians.

Gandhi wrote to the Viceroy Lord Irwin, "Dear Friend… I hold the British Rule to be a curse. Yet I do not intend to harm a single Englishman or to any legitimate interest he may have in India. My ambition is to convert the British people through non-violence… I want to serve them, even as I want to serve my own". Gandhi received an emotionless reply from the secretary.

On March 11th Gandhi gave what he thought was his last speech on the banks of the Sabarmati River. "We have used all our resources in the pursuit of an exclusive Non-Violent struggle. Let no-one commit a wrong in anger."

There was an Indian army, clad only with a Khaki cap, but not showing any rank. Gandhi was the leader. Jawaharlal Nehru was placed in Ahmedabad, to continue to lead the Indians, if Gandhi was hurt or disabled.

Satyagrahis were also available. They were well trained in controlling, propagandising and using Gandhi's rules of prayers, giving lodging, spinning one's own clothes and writing a diary.

The press surrounded them from all parts of the world. They walked together twelve miles daily for twenty-four days. 50,000 Indians were jailed before Nehru even looked around him. Native policemen, hit open skulls and injured male testicles! Women were not allowed by Gandhi to join the Salt March.

Churchill scoffed at Gandhi, but the English Viceroy complimented Gandhi.

In May 1930, Rabindranath Tagore wrote in the *Manchester Guardian* that, "Europe had lost its prestige in Asia". He prophesised that this will lead to mutual recognition, of what a handful of brave men can do for the world.

Civil Disobedience is different from Contempt

Gandhi's letter shows his leadership for an independent India, rather than an abusive or scornful India.

Satyagraha indicates a policy of political resistance, especially that, which was advocated by Mahatma Gandhi by organising the Salt March in order to equalise the British and Indian taxation system of acquiring natural salt from the Indian Ocean.

Nelson Mandela's fight for freedom

Mandela was born in 1918 in Transkei. He attended a Methodist school. Later, he became a lawyer graduating from the Witwatersrand University. He was in the armed wing of the political party of the African National Congress (ANC) and then became a political activist with the banned political party.

In 1964 he was imprisoned for life for plotting for an anti-apartheid and anti-racist cause. He was released in 1990. In 1994 he won the South African election and became President of the ANC.

"FREE AT LAST" were the first words he spoke. He strongly believed that the lack of human dignity and growing up with feelings of inferiority for being black, experienced by Africans, was the direct result of white supremacy.

Even to this day, there is hope to have a world where equality is established and contempt, humiliation and destructivity are abolished.

PART II
INFANCY AND CHILDHOOD

CHAPTER 1:

A Psychoanalytic Viewpoint of
Illusory Omnipotence Starting With Infancy

Omnipotence is very commonly encountered in a wide variety of situations. We first came across it during the healthy development of the infant. Later on, in childhood, we see it in the form of magical and omnipotent thoughts, speech and behaviour. It is seen in everyday life in a transient mode in healthy adolescents and adults in their phantasy, jokes, dreams and parapraxis.

Omnipotence can also be a part of pathological conditions, e.g. we recognize that it is an integral part of narcissistic and borderline personality disorders. It is a part of the manic defence in all depressive states. It is present in obsessional neuroses along with magical thoughts, compulsive behaviour and ritualistic behaviour. In this case, aggressive thoughts and desires are seen to have the potential of being lethal. Hence, extreme ambivalence becomes intolerable and hence, needing to be repressed either through reaction information or manifested openly through obsessive compulsive behaviour. In the latter case, the compulsions are noisily displayed whilst the aggressive or hateful component of the ambivalence in repressed.

Omnipotence is also seen in a less inhibited manner in the culture of primitive races.

It is therefore of great importance for us to trace the origins of omnipotence as well as be able to work with various aspects of omnipotence, whenever it presents itself to us in our clinical work.

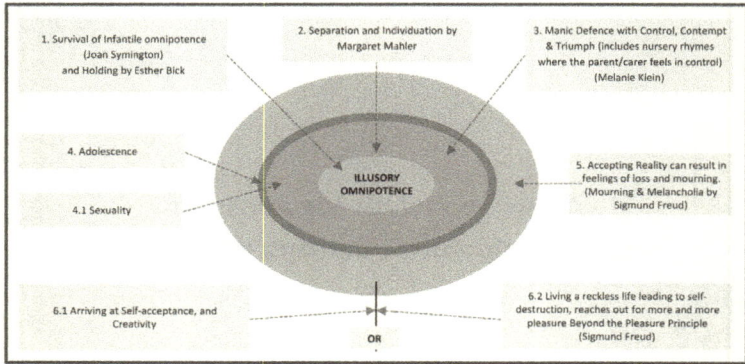

| 1. Survival of Infantile omnipotence (Joan Symington) and Holding by Esther Bick | 2. Separation and Individuation by Margaret Mahler | 3. Manic Defence with Control, Contempt & Triumph (includes nursery rhymes where the parent/carer feels in control) (Melanie Klein) |

ILLUSORY OMNIPOTENCE

4. Adolescence

4.1 Sexuality

5. Accepting Reality can result in feelings of loss and mourning. (Mourning & Melancholia by Sigmund Freud)

6.1 Arriving at Self-acceptance, and Creativity

6.2 Living a reckless life leading to self-destruction, reaches out for more and more pleasure Beyond the Pleasure Principle (Sigmund Freud)

OR

From illusory omnipotence in infancy to developing the capacity for individuation and separation leading to adolescence and accepting reality

The survival function of omnipotence starting from infancy, Esther Bick and Joan Symington

When tracing the origins of omnipotent behaviour in infants, Esther Bick (1968) and Joan Symington (1968) two well-known British child psychoanalysts, help parents to be attuned to their child and be aware of the crucial survival function of omnipotence. Joan Symington states, that "the primitive basis of omnipotence is the struggle in which the young baby engages in order to survive. It may even help the child to hold itself together by focussing on a certain object and steadying itself with various manoeuvres like writhing. However, when the mother has quietly left the room and gone to work, the child is unprepared for the absence and suddenly feels an unexpected loss of power and security". Sigmund Freud describes a child in a similar circumstance who played a game with a reel of cotton thread by herself. The child would throw the reel over the side of the bed and say "forte" in German, indicating that it is "gone" Then the child would reel in the thread, and say "dah" indicating it has come back to her. The reel represents her mother. The main difference is that the child feels in command of the reel.

Hence the initial unavoidable act of mother leaving quietly is brought to a happy conclusion by the child, being able to pull back the reel to be with her again. The passive position experienced by the child has now become active when she regained the reel. This healthy play overcomes the feeling of the child being at the whim of mother or whoever represents her mother.

Jacques Lacan (1981) perceives the infant as considering itself to being in bits and pieces and he describes how during the Mirror Stage it is the image in the mirror which gives the infant its identity. He says, the toddler, 'unable as yet to walk or even stand up and held tightly as he is by some support human or artificial, the 'trotte-bébé' nevertheless overcomes in a flutter of jubilant activity, the obstructions of his support and forcing his attitude in a slightly leaning forward position in order to hold it in his gaze, brings back an instantaneous aspect of the image of being a 'whole person' (without fragmentation).' In the theory of cohesion, Earl Hopper (2003b, p. 58), describes the stage of Oneness as part of the primary fear of annihilation.

The Oneness can also be considered as a person's development of total self-identity described during the perception of Gaze which includes Desire of the Object — 'objet petit a'. This is described further in detail in Section Three: 'Gaze and Perception'.

The importance of separation and individuation

STAGES OF EARLY CHILDHOOD

Childhood brings different stages of life for children to progress. This needs a healthy environment, where there is a capacity for voicing one's views of differences of opinion, without resorting to humiliation and aggression, resulting from competitive rivalry.

Parents need to take an active part in helping their child to attain separation/individuation and accepting new boundaries appropriate to their age. Unless mothers have had healthy separations in their own life, they find it difficult to help their children, who may feel unconsciously that they are needed by their mother and can develop school phobia and stay at home under different pretexts, rather than happily go to school without disruption.

Margaret Mahler – separation – individuation theory of child development

Margaret was born on May 10, 1897, in a small town in Western Hungary. She and her younger sister had a difficult childhood as a result of parental marriage problems. Budapest was a great influence in Margaret's life and career. In 1917 she reached medical school. Similar to other paediatricians she too realized how important it was to love and play with the infants for them to grow up mentally and physically healthy. She started her training analysis with Helene Deutsch seven years later and was accepted as an analyst. She worked with young disturbed children. Separation-individuation was her most important contribution to psychoanalysis.

Examples of individual omnipotence in the childhood

In these instances, it is clear to see how very fragile and illusory the infantile omnipotence can be. Whilst we recognise the importance especially for a young boy to get into the 'pretend mode' and play 'Batman' or 'Superman' in order to build his ego, it is also to be kept in mind how easily the child can feel shattered. Peter Fonagy and Mary Target describe how frightened a young three year old boy felt when his father actually bought him a Batman outfit which looked very realistic so that he very quickly reverted back to playing with his mother's skirt as a Batman's cloak. The necessity of gradual disillusionment to help the child cope with his/her loss of omnipotence is stressed by Winnicott.

Children may also learn to modify their subjective psychic reality so as to accommodate feelings of omnipotence which they may not be ready to yet relinquish. The example described by Romain Rolland in his novel, Jean-Christophe, is a lucid one. Jean-Christophe is described as a young child 'commanding the clouds go in one direction', being very angry with them for disobeying his command and finally, when he was faced with the realisation that the clouds were not going to change their direction, he then changes his own command for them to go in the opposite direction to which he had originally commanded them. They continue as before, but they are now seen by him to obey his last command. He is therefore, delighted with them as he is now able to feel that his belief in his own omnipotence is restored. As children grow older, we see that omnipotence is gradually abandoned and the reality principle is able to be accepted without the person sustaining a major narcissistic injury.

Illusory Omnipotence in Adults

An example of the survival function of illusory omnipotence in the adult is seen in the classic tale of one of Baron von Munchausen's famous adventures when his 'noble stallion' obeys his command, 'plunges through the bushes, but lands in the midst of a bog' and sinks downward at an alarming rate. Munchausen states, "dulled with fatigue though I was, my body responded. I felt a tingling at my scalp. My hair stood on end; my hand rose and took hold of my pigtail. Pulling it straight up, I found myself leaving my horse. Not wishing to abandon the hapless creature to sink in the bog and perish, I gripped my legs around his belly and with one mighty tug on my pigtail; I lifted us both out of the marsh".

Hence, an omnipotent thought, whether it be an illusion, a

delusion or part of a defence mechanism, is one endowed with a limitless magical power to produce the desired phantasised effect. Unfortunately, such an effect cannot stand the test of long-term reality.

The role of holding and containing in psychotherapy by George Christie

Holding and containing leads to surviving the eruption of aggressive primitive responses. The analyst knows and understands the deepest anxiety that is either being experienced or waiting to be experienced by the analyst. This leads to tolerance of the needs of love by the infant'. The infant learns that his distress and anger are not annihilating.(eg. Neville Symington)

Dr Christie and Dr Ann Morgan have worked with couples having longstanding unexplained infertility, despite artificial insemination.

It is usually the loss of a loved parent, sibling or friend that the infertile couple are experiencing. Discussing this in either individually or in group physiotherapy gives a fair reduction of their infertility. The management of these catastrophes can lead to the underline fulfilment of having a baby of their own.

The author as a young girl at the age of five needs no holding of parent or sister. She is starting to become self-containing.

Adolescence

During adolescence it is necessary for **infantile omnipotence to be gradually relinquished,** in the case of borderlines and narcissistic personality disorders, just as it is important to reduce splitting between good and bad, one needs to be able to differentiate between self and others, rather than exist in an undifferentiated state between 'me' and 'not me'. This, in fact, is not an easy task. The necessary disillusionment needs to be attempted very gradually and sensitively. Containment by relatives and friends need to take the place of being symbiotically attached to parents. When safe containment is not possible, then disasters are likely to occur, especially in those cases where insight is limited. Working with patients who take an omnipotent stance involves working with strong projective identifications, narcissistic injuries, without having the capacity to hold extreme ambivalences, denial and a constant breaking of limits and boundaries.

Adult life – Beyond the Pleasure Principle

At times, when the reality principle feels too harsh to bear, then the individual may turn to living life according to the Pleasure Principle in what appears to be a semi-permanent manner, demonstrating alienated omnipotent behaviour along with self-destructive desires.

Pathological gambling and addiction are such arenas where the thrill of the omnipotence and transient triumph experienced by the gambler or the addict is openly acknowledged. Sadly, triumph comes to a halt.

Fyodor Dostoyevsky author of famous books like 'Crime and Punishment' confesses, "The main point is the game itself, the thrill — I swear that greed for money has nothing to do with it although heaven knows, I am sorely in need for money".

Dostoyevsky also acknowledged his self-destructive desires by scolding and humiliating himself before his wife and invite her to despise him and to feel sorry she had married such an old sinner. When he had unburdened his conscience, the whole business would begin again, the next day writes Freud, Dostoyevsky's young wife accustomed herself to this cycle for she had noticed that his literary production never went better than when he had lost everything and pawned his last possession. When his sense of guilt was satisfied by his punishments, the inhibition upon his work became less severe and it allowed him to take steps along the road to success.

Most professional punters claim they follow their systems closely, work twelve to fourteen hours/day and never give into wild betting. They never admit that professional gambling can eventually prove to be a financial disaster. Instead they write articles full of denial, grandiosity and omnipotence like, "Yes, you can win", "Double your luck", "Pick 'em easy", etc. Their advice however, on reading the articles is to put aside personal whims, likes and dislikes and accept the harsh discipline necessary for punting success.

Hence, whilst following the pleasure principle themselves, they advocate theoretically a blind faith in strict adherence to the reality principle. In addition, a lifestyle of omnipotence as part of pleasure principle means the persons don't have to rely on anyone in interpersonal relationships, to have their desires fulfilled.

Guilt playing a major role in self-destructive activities is recognised by Sigmund Freud in his articles 'Criminals from Sense of Guilt' (1916) and 'Those Wrecked by Success' (1916), both describing clearly appeased inner guilt.

Here it is important to recognise that the sense of guilt was present before the misdeed and that the misdeed arose from the sense of guilt. The inability to work with such guilt can then lead to an illusory omnipotent attitude with underlying self-destructive desires.

We see similar behaviour in children too who often seem to be naughty on purpose, to provoke punishment and appear quiet and contented after the punishment.

At times, however, there can be no constructive outcome, especially where only guilt is never able to be acknowledged openly and instead repeated self-destructive behaviour results. This is similar to the gambler who whilst enjoying the thrill demonstrates totally insightless fatal optimism by crystallising moments of success and ignoring tragic aftermaths. Similarly, the borderline patient with whom reasoning is of no avail also leaves this total burden of tremendous responsibility to the caregivers and family to carry.

As desire and free will of any person will continue to be expressed with whatever strength and power is available to that person, in a particular society it is of crucial importance to mental health workers to study and be aware of the underlying predispositions and ego strengths of persons likely to lose control in a destructive manner. This may help towards understanding the reasons why a certain person is more prone to carrying out a particular action, which to an untrained observer seems to be purposeless.

Rhymes from the nursery

Herewith are examples of very early introduction to a variety of lyrics which may be sung to babies and little children in the context of them considered to be based on humorous backgrounds.

Sadly, these rhymes have often been accompanied with cruelty, unaware by tired parents. The meaning of the lyrics is camouflaged by the lilt of the soothing music. Moreover, the infant is not helped to understand the sadomasochistic and ambivalent feelings expressed in rhymes like 'Three Blind Mice' whose tails had already been 'cut off by a carving knife'. The innocent mice are instead lured to run after the sadistic farmer's wife, rather than go far away from such violence. Similarly, the child while growing up trusts the parents and teachers who wield power over them, regardless of the ruthlessness of such behaviour by any-one. Innocent children seem to enjoy the lyrics and the soothing rhythmic music while being totally unaware of the concealed cruelty in the meaning of these rhymes. Thankfully certain play centres have now banned this particular nursery rhyme.

A popular rhyme which sadly still exists is 'Rock-a-bye baby', where the bough eventually breaks from the dangerous tree-top, and baby 'falls down, cradle and all'. Humpty-Dumpty is also similar. In the first line, the child is encouraged to feel powerful, during the transition from birth to Primitive Omnipotence (with a toy having a huge round tummy, sitting on a wall as long as he/she identifies with Humpty Dumpty). This is immediately fol-lowed in the next sentence by 'Humpty Dumpty had a great fall'. No-one, even 'All the king's horses and all the king's men could not put Humpty together again!'

Hence the nursery rhymes described above, demonstrate the importance of respecting boundaries starting in infancy and childhood, protecting their children and themselves from all dangers, including death.

Cinderella is true to herself

Cinderella is a very popular fairy story written by many authors in keeping with their own cultural background. There are two versions, one by The Brothers Grimm, and the other by Perrault. The following is a combination of the above.

Cinderella's mother dies at a young age, and her father decides to remarry. One version describes two step sisters and the other describes six. Nevertheless, they all have developed intense sibling rivalry towards her. She is very beautiful and also each one thinks that she is father's favourite. Her step-mother's rivalry towards Cinderella consciously gives dirty chores for only Cinderella to do. Her outfits appear dirty and unbecoming. In contrast, the step-sisters are given beautiful dresses hoping they will outdo Cinderella. The King of the country in which they live, is looking for a suitable bride for his son, the Prince. There is a three day event arranged by him, where suitable marriage partners for the Prince are invited.

Cinderella continues to mourn for her dead mother. One day, their father decides to go by horseback alone to the fair. He gathers all his daughters including step-daughters and Cinderella and asks them what they would like for themselves, which he could give them as a gift. The step-daughters chose expensive attires with expensive jewellery. Cinderella said she wanted him on his return journey to bring her a fresh branch of a hazelnut tree, which she could plant and look after it well. Everyone was surprised. Father did the needful for his step-daughters. Then his hat touched the branch of a healthy tree. He remembered Cinderella cleaned his knife and cut the branch, covering it up with a fresh wet cloth, so it remained fresh till he gave it to Cinderella.

Cinderella was delighted and planted the branch in a very suitable area to become her mother's grave. Cinderella was now able to cry freely and feel relieved, that she could look after this area. The hazelnut tree grew sturdily. Birds sat and sang on its branches and the tree bloomed creatively.

The day approaches when the king would invite all suitable females who could dance with his son. Suddenly, there appears a Fairy Godmother in Cinderella's life. The Fairy Godmother encouraged Cinderella to go and meet the Prince, although she had not received an invitation. She sprinkled fairy gloss in gold and silver on Cinderella. A pumpkin was also carved out to be Cinderella's coach to take her to the party.

Cinderella's period of being demoralised is now over, along with her ability to be able to accept the love of both her parents. Her social life is no more unhappy. The compliments of the Fairy Godmother and the happy birds singing all around her tree, now allow her to feel happy and worthwhile. The depression concerning her mother's death is resolved. Her dignity and purity without aggressivity, have given her the capacity to help her step sisters. The Manic Defences described by Melanie Klein, namely to a) feel controlled, b) to be seen as an object of dirt by being surrounded by ashes in the cinder or succumbing to the triumph of her step-sisters, are now in reparation.

The prince falls in love with her and she responds lovingly to him and to all around her. She repairs all untoward feeling, which her step-mother and sisters had shown her.

The final test is the judging of a very small golden slipper lost at the King's ball. Some authors of this fairy story describe how the step-mother cuts off certain toes of Cinderella's step-sibs, hoping this would facilitate them fitting into the slipper. It fails the test and it is only Cinderella who is able to slip her feet into both slippers effortlessly. The Prince and Cinderella are declared suitable to be married and not only 'fall in love' but 'remain together in everlasting love'.

The uses of enchantment by Bruno Bettelheim

In Cinderella, the unrivalled tiny foot is a mark of extraordinary virtue and beauty. Perrault gave Cinderella the form which is now fully known. For example, initially she was described as only living among the ashes in her step-mother's house. Step-mother kept on giving her instructions on how to keep the house clean. She also put her own two daughters on a higher plane than how she considered Cinderella.

I believe in the fact that Cinderella's father asked all his three children, especially Cinderella and including his two step-daughters, what they wanted from him when he went to a Fair. This made Cinderella included and loved. She no longer felt degraded in the story. She was now able to receive the magic help of the Fairy Godmother who arranges for her to meet the Prince and eventually become a Queen.

The rejection fear compounds anxiety as soon as one sibling notices that others are preferable. The root of sibling rivalry reveals itself in the jealously and enmity of the two step-sisters. Cinderella's virtues become more prominent in that she does not ever take revenge on anyone for her own sorrow. (There is an absence of sadomasochism.)

In a fairy tale, internal processes are externalised. "The paramount importance of fairy tales results in something other than teaching about correct ways of behaving in this world". (p25)

Plato knew what intellectual experiences do for humanity. Even Aristotle, master of pure reason said "The friend of wisdom is also a friend of myth".

Fairy tales meet a strong need which carries deep meaning.

The myth is pessimistic while the fairy story is optimistic, no matter how terrifying some serious features may be.

The fairy tale allows fantastic events to occur. The happy outcome is due to the virtues of the hero, by chance, or by interference of supernatural figures.

The myth of Oedipus tells the child what happens if the dream becomes reality. Nevertheless, the child cannot give up the wishful fantasy of marrying the parent at some future time.

In childhood, more than at any other age, as long as security within ourselves is not established, fairy tales offer fantasy materials and guarantees a happy ending.

Inspired by an ideal, that no human can reach fully, is at least not defeating, but trying to duplicate the deeds of great persons. Hence, there is pervasive pessimism in myths and essential optimism in fairy tales. This book describes various combinations in relationships.

Unifying our dual nature

'The Queen Bee'; Here the nefarious doings of an evil spirit are turned into an animal, while the rest remains human. While the Queen Bee secretes honey one can also get bitten by the bee.

Two siblings may originally lack their differences. They live together and feel alike. In fact, they are inseparable. At a certain moment when growing up one begins an animal existence and the other does not. The child's personality is at first undifferentiated. Then Id, Ego and Super Ego develop out of the undifferentiated stage. During maturation in the Brothers Grimm story the little brother took his little sister by the hand and said "Come, we will go forth together out into the wild world to escape from a home depriving one at home". They walked the whole day over meadows, fields and rocks. When it rained little sister said "Heaven and our hearts are weeping together". Self-realisation requires leaving home and excruciating and painful experiences.

They keep wandering from one spring of water to another. The brother who is Id dominated wishes, immediate gratification of his thirst, but was warned that it would change the drinker into a wolf. The sister recognises the danger and helps to resist his thirst. This time they come across another spring from which the brother drinks and is turned into a fawn. She promises she will never leave her fawn brother. This symbolises Ego control. The story continues in a similar way, it reveals the battle that goes on in the children's minds related to desire, integration and victory. Finally, the vulnerable and disintegrated part of the children needs to be given up to achieve individuality and victory.

*Granddaughter exploring the world with grandfather
and enjoying his company.*

The World of AMAE

From the book — ' The Anatomy of Dependence ' by Takeo Doi

Herewith is a story told by Lafcardio Hearn titled "At the Railway Station". This admirably illustrates Japanese attitude towards 'Feelings of Guilt.'

A criminal who has been arrested for theft, killed the policeman who arrested him and escapes. He is however recaptured by another policeman and brought back to the entrance of the railway station. A crowd had gathered at the entrance.

The policeman calls to the widow of the policeman who had been murdered by the criminal. She was carrying a child on her shoulders. He tells the child "This is the man who killed your father".

The child bursts into tears.

The criminal then speaks in a passion of hoarse remorse, that made the hearts of all who heard him shudder. "Pardon! Pardon! Pardon me little one" the man says. "I did it not from hate, but in a mad desire to escape. It is a great unspeakable wrong that I have done to you. But now for my sin I go to die and wish to die. I am glad to die. Therefore, little one, be pitiful and forgive me". He is then led away.

The crowd and the policeman all break into tears.

The appeal with remorse has been made through the criminal's sense of fatherhood — that potential love of children, which is so large a part of the soul of every Japanese.

In Japan, an apology comprises what is essentially a child-like plea to the other party, which is always received sympathetically.

It is worth comparing this picture of events in a criminal, with the happy image in the previous photo, (page 35) of a loving grandfather and grand-daughter, walking hand in hand, establishing a normal relationship.

In the book 'Chrysanthemum and The Sword', Ruth Benedict shows that understanding of a different culture is hard at the best of times. She describes a tough/mindedness to recognise differences in Japanese culture, even when they are disturbing. This is also the opinion of Ian Buruma, in the foreword of the above book. He describes the difficulties that need to be overcome by the Japanese to either surrender, or fight to the last man, woman and child, which it would take to end the world war. However, Benedict also realises their deep sense of obligation to the emperor. The emperor had told his people to bear the Unbearable, surrender and build a new peaceful Japan. The Japanese owed the Emperor total obedience. If the world around Japan remained peaceful Benedict believed the Japanese would commit to pacifism. However, if the great powers started war again, Japan could resume militarism. Despite the Korean War, the Japanese economy benefited greatly, and remain stuck to the peaceful ideology. Japan has agreed since then that peace needs to be honoured.

Today there are many instances when the practice of AMAE remains acceptable internationally.

AMAE Reconsidered

Today there are many instances when the practice of AMAE remains acceptable internationally. However Amae is considered childish.

Amae is a license given to women rather than men, which results in a wish to be dependant, and seek the 'indulgence' of the other; eg. To snuggle up to the mother.

Dr Takeo Doi's basic mentality extended throughout the whole life of the individual and society in Japan. It takes care of the individual's needs in a warm and human manner. To some extent that it denies reality, objectivity and logic are sometimes ignored.

Amae is generalised and not localised.

Amae is considered by the Japanese to be a virtue of both eastern as well as western psychiatry, although it is strangely neglected by western psychiatrists and psychologists.

To most westerners it means "Please take what you want without hesitation". This can be seen as a lack of sensitivity to a Japanese guest.

Even a puppy follows the concept of *Amaeru*.

CHAPTER 2:

From Contempt to Regaining Dignity

Human bondage as described by Somerset Maugham and the background of orphan Philip Carey

A condensed account of self-contempt in an orphan Philip Carey born with a congenital club foot and how he regained his self-dignity

Literary writer, Somerset Maugham, in his book '*Of Human Bondage*' (1915), describes the book as being "not an autobiography, but an autobiographical novel, where fact and fiction are inextricably mingled". Maugham states that some incidents are related "Not from my own life, but from persons with whom I was intimate". After writing it he says, "I found myself free from the pains and unhappy recollections that had tormented me" (p. 3).

From my own experience, I have personally also known somewhat similar persons who had kept me puzzled and distressed for many years until I very recently read this book by Somerset Maugham. Since then, I too felt great relief at being able to apply the concept of contempt to those who had tried hard to devalue and betray myself.

The Background of Philip Carey

Both of Philip's parents died before he reached the age of nine. He had been born with one congenital club foot, which his father, a surgeon, had not rectified prior to his death. Philip's mother died soon after her second son, a dead baby, was delivered.

Fortunately, before his mother's death, she realised that her own life was limited. Hence, she arranged for a number of studio photographs done of herself, expressly for Philip to remember that she had loved him dearly and she never wanted him to forget how she looked and to always remember her.

It had been decided in advance by both his parents, that Philip would be sent to a religious boarding school shortly after his mother's death. She had trusted her brother, a vicar, and his wife (his aunt), as her next of kin. Sadly, not having had children of their own and being extremely rigid in the practice of their religion, his aunt especially realised they were not suited to take the place of Philip's parents. Nevertheless, his uncle kept forcing Philip to suddenly change the way he had been brought up. One rule was for Philip never to play on a Sunday. Moreover, his uncle absolutely refused to believe Philip, that his mother had never enforced this rule. This entirely incorrect judgement affected Philip greatly. He was still mourning his beloved mother, and in addition, was now accused incorrectly of being a liar. Philip was discovered hours later, by his aunt, sobbing inconsolably. That evening Philip sobbed and sobbed, feeling all alone in the world. His aunt did like him, but it took Philip a long time to realise it. This event precipitated Philip's starting at boarding school. In addition, during every visit to his adopted home, Philip realised he was not appreciated at all by his uncle.

Starting at boarding school was also emotionally very traumatic. Once the boys started undressing in their own dormitories to go to bed, Philip's clubfoot became obvious. The boys ruthlessly tried to tear off his bedclothes, saw the deformity and were contemptuous of him for it. Philip started crying softly without making a sound. He bit his teeth into the pillow so that his sobbing became inaudible (p. 47).

Another example from the life of Philip Carey was when a

schoolmaster lined him up with other boys to be beaten for what the teacher considered as a wrong doing. Philip was not able to defend himself verbally, but was devastated when the teacher noticed his club foot deformity and said "I would not hit a cripple". Philip felt worse hearing this (*Shame lurks unseen* as mentioned by Mollon, 2003).

Now that Philip's shame was brought to light, he could no longer protect himself in his dormitory at night. Other boys would forcibly strip his foot open to see it and follow it by scornful and contemptuous remarks. Although Philip would try his best to hide his foot in order to avoid being scapegoated, his limp was always visible, as was his slow labouring walk and inability to run.

Nevertheless, although his marks at school kept improving, no-one commented on it and Philip's self- contempt kept increasing. Finally, he could accept it no more. Sadly, his school principal's encouragement regards his scholarly achievements arrived too late. Philip felt he could not overcome his feelings of being a misfit wherever he lived. His boarding school students never extended genuine friendship to Philip. His club foot continued to make him feel totally like an object of contempt. Although Philip had every opportunity to stay at school and finally go to Oxford, he now rebelled against the values and wishes of his uncle and aunt, as well as his school principal. It resulted in him leaving England and moving to study in Germany.

Later on, he returned to London as a medical student. In the college café, he met a contemptuous, but attractive barmaid, Mildred. He fell in love with her, initially rationalising her contemptuousness towards himself, as being a result of her limited intellectual capability and financial limitations. He proposed marriage and kept taking her out to dinners and shows which she would enjoy. Nevertheless, she remained cold and indifferent to all his efforts to please her. He eventually became aware of the darker side of her personality and became repeatedly traumatised by all his failed attempts. She betrayed him repeatedly, by having sexual affairs with his friends, while openly rejecting him, even when he requested a kiss from her. Finally, her previous boyfriends left her and she went into severe financial difficulties. She then asked to share Philip's home as she had now become pregnant. Once in her envy and rage with Philip, she deliberately destroyed his home, including one of his most favourite work of art of a nude female, which he had painted during his youth. At long last, he finally realised, how devalued he had felt during this relationship with Mildred. He was now finally able to break away his emotional bondage as well as his financial generosity towards Mildred and her illegitimate daughter who was taught to call Philip, "Daddy", although she was not his child. Eventually Philip evicted Mildred from his home. She then turned to prostitution. Both Mildred and her little daughter eventually died of illness and starvation.

The human bondage between Philip and Mildred came to a final ending, following Mildred's death.

Philip's adopted father and maternal uncle, the vicar, also died shortly afterwards. This autobiographical account by Somerset Maugham once more demonstrates the serious lethal consequences, for those displaying considerable contempt and lack of empathy. Mildred's contempt onto others appears as a consequence of her own self-contempt which had never been resolved. She felt superior for those who could offer her sexual gratification. She was not in touch with the reality principle, but kept seeking pleasure from all available sources regardless of her future outcomes.

Philip gradually developed greater self-confidence, following resolution of both these deaths. He arranged for his club foot to be operated upon, which cured his congenital impediment. He completed his medical degree successfully and developed healthier relationships. He finally fell in love with a very suitable female, developed a mutually intimate loving relationship with her and married her.

Summary

In the novel '*Of Human Bondage*', Mildred, a single barmaid's own self-contempt drives away Philip Carey, a crippled medical student and the only person who ever loved her. She devalues him, driving him into a state of regression, and leading him to aggressive thoughts against her. She, in turn had destroyed his precious achievement, a painting of a nude, which he had done many years ago. This incident brought an end to Philip's genuine caring for her.

The thoughts of Confucius regarding self-assuredness

In the book '*Confucius: The Analects*' from the Folio Society, there are numerous words of wisdom, where the Master says to Su, "... only with a man like you, one can discuss the Odes. It is not the failure of others, to appreciate your abilities that should trouble you... To be able to appreciate one's own abilities is indeed a great asset".

"The greatness of a person lies in his heart, not in his head. This is intellect" said Mahatma Gandhi in '*A Thought for the Day*' (1945, p. 76).

An example of uncontrolled contempt

A hot headed, enraged father brought a limp little infant about six months of age to me, as I was the Emergency Doctor. He said very angrily, projecting his anger onto his infant, "I cannot make this child get into the jumpsuit!" The infant was screaming and totally out of control with pain. There was no need to ask any further questions. I did not blame him or ask obvious questions.

I introduced myself, told him that I was arranging for an urgent X-ray of the legs.

X-rays revealed exactly what was obvious visibly. During forceful pushing of the infant's legs into the jumpsuit, the father had broken both tibial bones! It was no surprise that all the child could do was to scream in agony.

The father then sat with his hands covering his own face. There was no more reason for the father to deny his own humiliation, rage and self-contempt. I expressed my sadness and suggested future plans for both father and infant in similar circumstances. The infant was admitted to hospital.

The X-rays had also shown evidence of previously broken bones. The outcome of the child's future, the reasons for father's intolerance with the capacity for him to change, along with closely involved family and medical help was discussed during family therapy sessions.

Self-contempt also contains a part of '*The Economic Problem of Masochism*' (Freud, 1924). Contempt by itself can lead to sado-masochist behaviour which is very destructive.

Discovering one's own identity through separation from malignant bonding

This needs to occur so as to develop a sense that one is the owner of one's own life (Klein, 1952). Theoretical aspects of Splitting, Individuality and Bipolarity are discussed by Zinkin, L. (1998, p. 104-106). Hence, allowing others to control oneself is not of benefit to anyone.

Jung believed in Bipolarity. He believed in one unit with two poles and two aspects of the archetype with one horn as seen in the unicorn. He disagrees that Christianity does not respect the primal unity of the archetype. Jung states that the Self is a union of opposites. This is where it differs from Freud's views on religion, unlike Jung who optimistically considers everything as being united.

On the other hand, Freud sees the Life Drive and Death Drive as being separate (McGuire, 1974). Freud also refers to the differentiating grade of the ego (Freud, 1921, p. 130). He believes this results from identification with a lost object, e.g. in Melancholia.

Daniel Stern's view is that one sensory mode, such as taste, can also be recognised in another mode, for example through vision. Bateson (1980, p. 16) believes that patterns can be recognised by babies. This corresponds with Jung's version of universality, innateness and numinosity which nevertheless shapes the baby's experience (Zinkin, 1998, p. 105) and also agrees with Jung's theory of Bipolarity, and that objects have different sides in them. The example is of a snake being restorative as well as destructive. Splitting occurring early in life is described by Bateson, as a term where one side of the split does not respect the other.

Sabar Rustomjee as a young teenager

Examples of social and cultural differences in various countries

Certain varieties of contempt are condoned or enjoyed, according to the custom of the place where parties, including music and dancing, are held. Invitees are usually close friends.

Here are two examples to the tune of a Sri Lankan party with dancing the 'Baila' which is a type of dance similar to a 'Kaffringha' rhythm. The words either contain a scene of violence among adults or show a combination of fun, envy and play among children.

Most Sri Lankans dance to it very happily, as they have been brought up in their culture to enjoy dancing, despite the words being either sadomasochistic or child-like. It is not meant to upset anyone. They are mostly held after dinner in homes of fairly rich, educated persons.

EXAMPLE ONE

The most popular dance, Baila, danced at most Sri Lankan adult parties. Mostly everyone is in fits of laughter all the time. The title is 'Kussi Amma Sehra'. When translated into an English version, the gist of which is the female cook Sehra, had a fight with one man named Pereira, who beats her up and smashes up her jaw. She begs the lady of the house by saying, "Oh my lady, I want to go home". Unfortunately, the so-called 'home people' don't know what to do. The rhyme repeats itself over and over again, while the guests dance, lifting their ankle length sarees to their knees and swinging their hips from side to side. So, the dancing and the music continues.

EXAMPLE TWO

The scene is a rural village, where nobody had seen a bicycle. So, everyone sings with glee; "Hi! Hoi! An elderly grandmother has brought a lovely bicycle. Look at it!" The boys are excited and dance around the bicycle. Then the girls do the same. Then both boys and girls join in a circle and dance round and round the bicycle. The climax occurs when they ring the bell. The same and similar Bailas get repeated.

EXAMPLE THREE

Indigenous Australians have a somewhat different story as in example two. An old man buys a brand new car and attempts to enjoy it by bringing it to the village square for everyone to see and appreciate. S. In a fit of anger, he burns the car. In this example envy prevails.

Overcoming contempt with oratory skills and humour

Herewith are some examples of oratory skills by various writers and deep thinkers.

John Ralston Saul in The Doubter's Companion (1955, p. 77), denigrates the person who initiated Contempt. The Sophist Antiphon says to Socrates "You decline to take money. If you believed anything you possessed was worth money, you would not part with it for nothing". Socrates replies "To offer beauty to all comers is prostitution… so it is with wisdom. Those who offer it to all comers for money are known as Sophists or prostitutes of wisdom".

Humour

After the Gestapo forced their way into Freud's apartment in Vienna in 1938, they ordered Freud to sign a document saying he had been correctly treated. Freud did so and added in his own writing "I can heartily recommend the Gestapo to everyone". The Gestapo left feeling very happy (Freud).

Examples in *'Plums of Woodhouse'* (1997) are numerous. The following is only one of them. Mrs Podmarsh embraced her son for winning a game and then said loudly and contemptuously "You are smelling of smoke!" Her son could only say "Well, the fact is…" and then the mother would keep interrupting to instruct him on the dangers of smoking. This went on many times before her son finally said triumphantly "Yes, I know mother, but the fact is Ted Ray smokes all the time and I thought I could win my game" (p. 129).

"Jokes produce freedom through hidden similarities. Jokes can have a contrast of ideas; sense in nonsense, bewilderment and illumination" (Freud, 1927). It is said, "That it helps lifting repression by modifying the super-Ego which in turn helps the Ego". It is also described that in order to play, we allow the unconscious to cross the barrier of resistance and become conscious. This brings about a stupid more human dimension. Play can then result creatively. Freud (p. 57) relates a 'stupid joke' said to an artilleryman by his superior, with a view to say the truth camouflaged in an equally stupid way.

Finally, I will relate a very commonly appreciated joke by Freud (p. 50) "An impoverished acquaintance borrowed twenty-five florins from a prosperous acquaintance". The next day they happened to see each other in a restaurant. The impoverished man was eating 'salmon mayonnaise' whereupon the so-called benefactor who had lent him the money, reproachfully said "Is that what you used my money for?" The other replied "If I don't have the money, I can't eat salmon mayonnaise, and if I have the money, I mustn't. So then, when am I to eat salmon mayonnaise?" Freud points out that the technique was in diverting the reproach. We can observe the similarity of the dialogue between the above example and the exchange between Socrates and the Sophist Antiphon.

PART III

GROUP THERAPY AND GROUP PROCESSES

A group at a seminar of the Group Analysis IOGAP held in Melbourne, Australia in 2012.

CHAPTER 1 (a)

Starting to Select your own Therapist/Analyst as Part of Personal Self-Awareness

I will start my own journey into Psychoanalytic Psychotherapy. When looking around for a suitable psychoanalyst for myself as part of my training requirements in the field of individual psychoanalytic psychotherapy, I obtained an appointment with a person whom I considered as being a very astute training psychoanalyst who may suit me.

I had already had an intensive group analytic experience 4/ week for a period of three years which I felt had been very useful and now wished for an individual psychoanalytic experience. During the interview I opened out to this person, and was quite shocked, disappointed and disillusioned when right at the end of the fist exploratory session the analyst said " I have decided not to accept anyone of Indian origin" and then went on to say in a couple of brief sentences, that some difficulties had arisen of a transcultural nature between himself and the last trainee of Indian origin whom the analyst had accepted. There was no apology given. We parted company politely, as there was nothing more to say.

I had not formed any clear idea of finding a suitable psychoanalyst for ¾ times a week of individual analysis. This analyst's **personal limitations** related to racial issues, were obviously well known to himself. So why had he given me an appointment in the first place? He could have spared me the insult by not giving me an appointment at all, or giving me a detailed explanation, which may have been easier to accept, rather than briefly bringing in a racial issue which was evident from the start. Moreover, I did not need to know that he had a failed experience with another Indian client. At another level I was also relieved that he did not accept me for a wrong reason, namely to prove to himself that he could help someone when in fact he realised from the first interview that he could not do so.

Over the years I have been very grateful that this incident had actually happened as I believe to this day that this led to my entering into and also appreciating an excellent analytic relationship with an English training analyst, a female who was not only astute but also gentle and warm with a great 'capacity for attunement". She was in addition very unassuming about herself. I asked her at the first interview which model of psychoanalysis she practised. She said something like "You know I cannot say I practise any particular framework. I learn as I go on". I was deeply touched by this It felt to me that she was saying that she was able with her enormous experience and expertise, to listen reflectively to her clients and interpret appropriately rather than be restricted by identification with any one particular frame. I expected her to say that she was Kleinian (most psychoanalysts in Melbourne were Kleinian at that time along with a few Freudians and Lacanians). Had she in fact said so, retrospectively I think I would have felt somewhat restricted myself, wondering whether everything I said would be seen by her in terms of only one model- meaning that the model would have been more important than myself, the person on the couch. All throughout my analysis she repeatedly gave **this same feeling of freedom.** Gradually for the very first time a realisation came upon me, that at least one other person (apart from my mother who had died many years ago, and my father who had died when I was five) was really interested in what I had to say and had my interest and wellbeing at heart. One could say I started this analysis with a feeling of idealization towards this analyst. I have realised her limitations many times, and her mistakes, and have accepted these as necessary in any work.

As I stated earlier, I had started in a training course in Group Analytic Psychotherapy. My **Group Analyst** was elderly and physically severely disabled. My work with him was initially of the nature of 4 days a week of group therapy which did not fully meet my requirements for the concurrent individual psychoanalytic psychotherapy I had undertaken. The training institute had agreed that if my analyst gave me an extra individual session weekly, they would accept this as adequate for my personal therapy. He did so, and although I mainly felt privileged and relieved at not having to change therapists, I felt considerable guilt at this frail elderly person having to get up an hour early just for me. Nevertheless, I coped with it, and benefited from his open and honest, confrontative style.

Then at one stage he made an error of judgement. He said very suddenly one day that due to his age and frail health he was giving the group, 9 months' notice of his retirement. Group members including myself felt shocked and deeply saddened and with some feeling of panic, started mourning our loss and started looking for other analysts. He then a month later changed his mind and said he would be continuing work for the present. He worked for a further 18 months before he died. However, once this momentum to leave him had started in the group, more than half the group left. As far as I was concerned, I also felt secretly grateful that an opportunity had come to leave him without undue emotional trauma or further analysis as to the real reasons for my leaving him and the group. It was a way of my avoiding facing up to his death, which was obviously around the corner, as he suffered severe ill health with frequent absenteeism.

My own father had died when I was five years of age and I much preferred not experiencing another death during my analysis, if I could possibly avoid it. My analyst had prepared the group, as best he could, as how we may react to his death. He would jokingly say quite often, that if we entered the group room, and found him lying dead, he had no idea what we may do. He did have a great sense of humour and would say, that for all he knew, we may gingerly step over his dead body and sit down at our seats waiting for the group to start. When he finally did die, I found my grief bearable, thanks to his continuous preparation. I knew from his dialogue with myself that he had no real religious or cultural prejudices, and this helped me enormously as a relatively new Australian. Following analysis with him, to this day I have never felt racial discrimination towards myself. He was so welcoming to people of all races and religions. I can now mainly feel some compassion towards the earlier analyst who had rejected me after the first session.

Towards engaging in a meaningful dialogue

1. The therapist needs to be in a **frame of mind with an underlying capacity for being objective, receptive, analytic as well as reflective.** This will then encourage the client to try to do likewise thereby creating a fertile climate for meaningful discourse. Free floating discussion and dialogue in an atmosphere of empathy and acceptance, is needed to promote trust, reduce inhibitions, resistances and explore the uncertainties of what is yet unknown. This can lead to working with sensitive and anxiety producing issues more productively. To be able to be both objective as well as subjective is a useful attribute in every therapist. It is a necessary **prerequisite towards developing a 'Capacity for Containment.'** (Rustomjee S from Containment and failures of Containment. GAS London.)

2. A psychotherapist also needs to be **without preconceived ideas** about what the client needs to discuss at any point

of time. Hence it is not advisable for the therapist to come prepared (armed) at any session with his or her own formulation of what has been discussed in earlier sessions and with what needs to be done now. The here and now of the session needs to be kept in mind A psychotherapist also needs to be **without preconceived ideas** about what the client needs to discuss at any point of time. The here and now of the session needs to be kept in mind. It allows the patient hopefully to arrive at the same conclusion in his or her own time and own way. This then produces a feeling of achievement for the patient, rather than a resentment towards the therapist for 'stealing the show' in advance. However, in spite of the therapist, sometimes doing the above, as long as it is not a routine occurrence, resentment does not usually build up. In fact, most clients do clam all credit for every successful outcome whilst temporarily denying all contributions of the therapist. The therapist like a giving parent may feel gratified at seeing a successful outcome, without needing to demand acknowledgement due to any personal insecurity or feeling overlooked or dismissed. **Premature Linking** on the other hand can only lead to in correct interpretations and only leave the client feeling he or she was left silenced and unheard. On the other hand, **well timed and well thought through comments or interpretations** once a theme has been fully developed by the client will produce lesser resistances and pave the way for ongoing exploration. Also having mentally prepared oneself not to entertain preconceptions will invariably lead to a more relaxed stance, e.g. Bion's concept of being without desire and without memory (Bion, W) (1970, page 41) if his mind is preoccupied with what is or is not.

CHAPTER 1 (b)

Fundamentals in working with groups

How does any group exist in our mind?

There is no such thing as an individual without a group. Just as we are not able to understand a melody if we listen separately to each note (Elias, 1987, p. 37). Similarly, we are unable to understand different aspects of ourselves if we allow ourselves to be mixed up with all our surroundings (Rouchy, 1995). The therapist needs to own whatever belongs to him and what the group is influenced by, its tasks or function. Without a task it remains a collection of isolated individuals. Hence group therapy in its various forms is vital to mankind.

Malcolm Pines, a great group analyst

Malcolm Pines was one of the first to discover and understand Group and Relational Therapy. He is a group and individual psychoanalyst whose pioneering work on circular reflections in group members has made him a leader in his field.

Countertransference has also been a critical area of work undertaken, studying the need to resolve personal resistances through self-analysis and supervision.

Group therapy

Group therapy focusses on interpersonal learning:

- It helps individuals get along in a more honest and authentic way with other people.

- It provides support network for specific problems and challenges.

Analytic Group Psychotherapy (as distinct from all other types of Group Therapy) provides the development of an awareness of both Conscious and Unconscious factors.

Users of therapy
It provides an opportunity to learn:
- 'With' and 'from' other group members and the accounts related by them.
- Moreover, that you are not as different as you had feared and are not alone in your thinking.
- A major part of certain groups can benefit from sharing thoughts and experiences.

Curative factors in groups through understanding oneself and our roles in society
''Universality is one of the most curative factors of group therapy'' (Yalom, & Leszcz, 2005, p. 272).

The following are adapted from Irvin Yalom, Claudio Neri and Others.
- Hope
- Universality leading to Normalisation
- Ventilation
- Developing a sense of self, of being a person with a right to exist
- To develop a sense of belonging
- To develop independent thinking whilst being in a group
- Developing spontaneity
- Learning from experience

- Learning through being exposed to a Corrective Emotional Experience where appropriate
- Psycho-education where appropriate in educational groups
- Altruism as applicable to the role of the conductor and the role of the group
- Understanding family dynamics and relating it to group interactions and society
- Analytically oriented groups understating the Freudian Unconscious and Social Unconscious
- Transference and Counter-transference
- Attacking Myths, Contempt and Shame
- Differentiating between the Public Face and Self-Contempt
- Working with Organisational Dynamics
- Leadership Skills including Negative Capability by John Keats
- Understanding Non-compliance.

It is amazing that members and patients with an inability to accept compliance, at times prove the opposite. There are examples in the text regarding longevity occurring when it was least expected in non-compliant patients. As described earlier, when reality is intact it is apparent that the Life Drive is at a satisfactory level.

When caretakers cannot differentiate evidence of Life Drive from a genuine wish to die by implementing the Death Drive, there occurs confusion. Fortunately, psychotherapeutically trained carers are able to distinguish these differences. The patients are encouraged not to go beyond the Pleasure Principle in an acceptable manner and caring manner.

Role of a Group Convenor

Selection of candidates as suitable group members

- To create a potential space with adequate containment
- Non-directive leadership leading to chaos.
- Encourage Objectivity
- Encourage every group to develop its own identity, uniqueness, focus and dynamics
- Provide guidelines for emergencies.

In a case of a young twenty year old boy, well known to me, was advised to live near the main hospital environment to be able to have easy access during emergencies. However, being grossly non-compliant he did not follow any boundaries and even changed residence out of reach of the hospital emergency services. It turned out to be a great surprise when months later I saw him looking hale and hearty with a smile on his face. It was obvious he has been lucky enough to be the recipient of a suitable transplanted kidney. He was feeling a sense of achievement and independence in himself. His parents too had been very encouraging to live a fulfilling lifestyle. They were keeping an eye on him and supporting him without making it obvious.

Foulksian group analytic concepts; resonance, mirroring

According to Foulkes, the Aim of Group Analysis is to establish harmony between the individual and the world, but not Conformity.

The group functions as a 'hall of mirrors' where resonance of thoughts occurs between group members. The thoughts of each group member in the group will reverberate/resonate with some aspect of the group there which is discussed in the 'here and now' of the group and becomes linked with what is uppermost in her or his mind. When verbalised in the group, by the member, it may be interpreted appropriately.

The Group Matrix is described by S.H. Foulkes as the 'hypothetical web of communication in a group'.

Basic Assumptions by W. R. Bion for groups (1961)

- Basic Assumption Dependency
- Basic Assumption Pairing
- Basic Assumption Fight Flight

Although there is hatred of learning by experience, the aim of groups is to work within a group and producing a work group where negative transference does not disintegrate the group. "The individual is a group animal at war, not simply within the group, but with himself for being a group animal and with those aspects of his personality that constitute his 'groupishness' (Bion, *'Experiences in Groups'*, 1961, p. 131).

The Fourth Basic Assumption of Incohesion: Earl Hopper

Traumatic Experience in the Unconscious Life of Groups

The Fourth Basic Assumption of Incohesion: Aggregation/ Massification or (ba) I:A/M

Earl Hopper states that "the fourth Basic Assumption is a manifestation of the fear of annihilation and its vicissitudes."

"Aggregates and masses are the two most simple, primitive social formations. They are not merely a collection of people or groups characterised by mutual attraction. They are not in sympathy with one another. In contrast mutual attraction and involvement among three or more people share an illusion of solidarity usually only for a brief period of time" (Hopper, 2003b, p. 66-67).

An aggregate is highly incohesive. A mass is like an aggregate masquerading as a group and should not be confused with a mob or horde. Metaphors for an aggregate are like a handful of gravel or a set of billiard balls. In contrast metaphors for a mass is a handful of warm wet sponges, stuffed fish or a lump of dough. A flock of flamingos reveals a pattern of being an aggregate. This is in contrast to a herd of walruses, which is analogous to a social mass (Hopper, 2003b, Figure 3.1 and 3.2, p. 69).

The Social Unconscious

Foulkes' concept of Social Unconscious is further developed by Earl Hopper, Malcolm Pines, Haim Weinberg and Farhad Dalal, among others.

Foulksian analysts state that the individual is "embedded in the social and that the individual is also permeated by the social". This they claim differs from the concept of the Freudian unconscious in the id, being both repressed and unconscious.

Hopper describes clinical work occurring in both Time and Space in four related areas, namely:

- The here and now
- The here and then
- The there and now and
- The there and then

Self-psychology in group psychotherapy: Walter Stone

Walter Stone, while practicing in Cincinnati, trained with many well-known psychoanalysts, e.g. Michael Baliant, Paul and Anna Ornstein and other faculty of the Chicago Psychoanalytic Institute where Heinz Kohut developed self-psychology. In 1977, in collaboration with Roy Whitman, he co-authored the initial paper "Contributions of Self Psychology to Group Process and Group Therapy". From that initial publication he continued to explore the concepts of self-psychology with particular emphasis on the need for empathy as a building block of the therapeutic process and some of the difficulties associated with group-as-a-whole interventions. He demonstrated how a group may be experienced as an object and/or a self-object. He utilized self-concepts in understanding the group self and application of the treatment of bipolar, borderline and narcissistic disorders and with the chronically mentally ill, including schizophrenic patients. This work resulted in publication of the book '*Group Psychotherapy for People with Chronic Mental Illness*' (1996). In collaboration with long-time collaborator Scott Rutan, he co-authored the well-received text book '*Psychodynamic Group Psychotherapy*'. In this book they integrated the various theories, with self-psychology receiving its share of recognition as a leading theoretical paradigm. He moved to San Francisco bay area in 2002 and worked at the University of California, Department of Psychiatry. His final paper is a sad one where he is saying goodbye to his final group of chronically mentally ill patients (2006). Many of his writings are published in 'Contributions of Self Psychology to Group Psychotherapy: Selected Papers' (2009).

I have witnessed him to be excellent in exploring and interpreting group as a whole intervention. He re-established a disorganised, unbalanced group very cleverly. He produced brilliant results in certain members during a weekend experienced in Melbourne (2014). This exposure to Walter Stone will remain in the minds of all who attended. It increased the level of functioning of groups as a whole in Melbourne. International Organisation of Group Analytic Psychotherapy (IOGAP) is deeply indebted to him. Despite Walter Stone having retired from mainstream self-psychology, I thank him most sincerely for his contribution to this book.

Two forms of group therapy in work related depression (Christer Sandahl)

Professor Christer Sandahl from Sweden has been very active

in forming a short-term focused psychodynamic group psychotherapy (FGT) which was evaluated in a randomized controlled
comparison with cognitive group therapy for work-related
depression. The study included white collar workers who had
been on sick leave for more than ninety days.

All patients were interviewed and responded to self-reported
questionnaires before the start of the treatment, as well as by the
six and twelve monthly intervals.

Work related depression was seen as being 'professional burn-
outs'. This needed rehabilitation interventions. "It has also been
stressed that burn-out is not a medical term nor a diagnosis."
Instead it's conceptualized as a 'psychological crisis' emerging
from chronic work stress. In 2003, the Swedish Board of Health
and Welfare diagnosed it as an exhaustion disorder and later
replaced it as being a burn-out in clinical context. It was this
present study that initiated the above.

In summary, this was finally evaluated as sick listed individuals with work related depression. The subjects were insured in a
large Swedish occupational pension fund. Clients had been on
sick leave from a period of six months to two years. In FGT a
focus for the treatment is decided in individual interviews before
treatment. It was decided that the focus needed to be expressed
both as a strength and a weakness. Initially they did not consider
themselves to be assertive in an actual relationship in a trustworthy group. The capacity to master challenges, as well as solving
problems, results in constructive outcomes. The patients gradually developed a sense of authority in the psychodynamic therapy
which helped to develop considerable self-confidence.

Seventy percent of the patients were female and had children younger than age fifteen. The pressure of teenage children,
including oedipal conflicts or sibling rivalry is not described in
the study. No significant differences and improvements were

detected between the two treatments. Nevertheless, it is encouraging to realise susceptibility of falling prey to high pressured working conditions. Moreover, these patients improved greatly in less pressured jobs.

It is possible that being out of work allowed them to be self-contemptuous. Following this when they regained non-pressured occupations their confidence rose to a happy working career.

CHAPTER 2:

Group therapy in consultation liaison psychiatry

A long-term analytic training group in a public teaching hospital

Background

This group was a weekly long-standing slow-open group (over fifteen years in duration), for treatment of chronic out patients, as well as for training and supervising students in how to use a Group analytic framework constructively. It was inaugurated by Dr Frank Graham pioneer of Group Analysis in Melbourne. It was followed by Dr Oliver Larkin and myself. Interested psychiatric trainees observed the group through a one way screen. Following the group, the same interested psychiatrists and the group conductor would have regular in-depth discussions regarding it. About four years after I first started working at this particular hospital, it was moved by the government, from the CBD to an inner suburb, to make it more available to the public and closer to Monash University. It also led many staff to move and live closer to their work or home. The group discussed below demonstrates the resilience and increased ego-strength of the patients. As I had already worked in Consultation liaison psychotherapy in Medical and Surgical units in the same hospital, I felt very much at ease as conductor of this slow-open group. I had often observed them from a one-way mirror (all patients had given their permission for observers as this was the routine in most public teaching hospitals).

The following example of Long Term Group Psychoanalytic Psychotherapy in a large public hospital weekly in a slow-open group, was being conducted by an experienced male group conductor, Dr X. As he was leaving the hospital, I was appointed to take his place. I hoped that I would be well accepted by the group which mainly comprised of patients with obsessional, phobic and psychosomatic illnesses. Dr X had given two months' notice. He was now changing from hospital practice to a private clinic, to which the patients did not have easy transport. This particular group was ongoing for four years. Group members were selected as being suitable, if they demonstrated ability for gaining insight. It so happened that all members worked in professional vocations and came directly after work. Members in this group were more sophisticated and fearlessly outspoken. Trainees who were mental health workers from other clinics were also allowed to observe the groups through one-way glass doors. They received seminars in the theory of Supportive, Individual and Group Analytic Psychotherapy at their own workplace. They were also encouraged to have individual weekly supervision.

THE SETTING

The group room had a one-way screen, so that student's in training could observe and hear the live group without being seen. After each group, there was a twenty minute discussion of major issues, with these regular trainees. Written permission for being observed had been taken from all participating group members.

Boundaries and guidelines

The importance of respecting boundaries has always been a core feature of Analytic Group Therapy. All members were encouraged not to be late to groups, thus reinforcing respect for themselves, as well as others who were invariably on time. Days which were stormy were considered an exception to being on time, as a matter of safety for members. Also, the issue of parking always being very difficult in this suburb was considered as being a reality factor. Mostly members found it easier to come by tram. However, this proved to have its own difficulties. Explanations of absences from analytically oriented groups conducted at this setting were encouraged. Advantages of being on time for the group was discussed. Missing out at the beginning of each group gives members a fragmented picture of the group interactions which does not prove to be productive. It also encourages dependency on other members to fill the gap for them.

I presumed that group guidelines had been previously explained prior to accepting each group member. However, I was mistaken and had to do so on the second session of this group. The following was discussed.

1. Strict avoidance of meetings outside the group was emphasised. If it was unavoidable, say if members worked in the same place or came into contact with each other accidentally, the meeting needed to be discussed in detail at the next meeting. This was an important group guideline. It was pointed out that informal discussions may have dangerous consequences, as the group conductor would be excluded from it. All conversations outside the group, between members, was the full responsibility of the group conductor and not of another group member.

2. No touching of members was accepted. Also, verbal dialogue encouraged members to develop their own individuality. Moreover, certain members may consider 'touching' to be indicative of seduction.

3. Absenteeism or lateness in arrival needed to be informed by phone to the conductor in advance. Any major emergencies need to be notified similarly. The conductor gave an emergency number for anyone who wanted to contact her urgently.

4. Truthfulness is considered to be the most important factor essential for the authenticity of the group.

5. Boundaries of the content of the group were totally confidential and were not to be discussed with family, friends or anyone outside group hours. For training purposes, identity of all members needed to be disguised.

6. Boundaries included 'no violence' as an essential feature. No one currently under the influence of alcohol or drug dependency was accepted to attend that particular group session. This is to reduce thoughtless or impulsive 'Acting Out' of frustrations.

7. Although time boundaries were recommended, no patients who arrived late were ever treated contemptuously.

8. Patient's dignity, including religious affiliation, was not to be attacked.

Members, who deliberately stated fictional experiences to impress the group, were empathically encouraged not to do so. Manic defences of Control, Contempt and the need for Triumph over others and their dangers were tactfully made overt. It was explained that these were 'defence mechanisms' so as to make the parents'/carers' own anxiety easy to manage (Klein, 1948 & Segal, 1987).

Further details for Analytic Group Conductors

Confidentiality is crucial to improvement. No intentional meetings outside of the group with other members are acceptable. Unavoidably, urgent issues which had arisen outside the group, needed to be first brought up with the conductor and followed up in the next group with all members.

This gave an opportunity for most groups to discuss the following issues openly and truthfully start to aim towards becoming a Work Group. This is always preferred, so as to encourage the group to relate truthfully in front of all members, rather than being unable to do so.

Hence Splitting, Dependency, Fight/Flight, Pairing,

Malignant bondage and Incohesion: Aggregation and Massification, as well as developing one's own group self can be explored as described by Wilfred Bion, Earl Hopper, S.H. Foulkes, Malcolm Pines, Walter Stone, George Christie, Ann Morgan, Felix de Mendelssohn, Bennet Roth and many others who are totally committed to Group Analysis.

Combined Group and Individual Therapy benefits members significantly, rather than group therapy by itself. George Christie and Ann Morgan, from Melbourne, brought the importance of treating groups of infertile couples, with combined therapy.

Dreams and Free Associations are important to bring out in the open during group analysis. Dreams were considered to be the Royal road to the Unconscious by Sigmund Freud. He also believed that dreams were connected with wish fulfilment. Dr Russell Grigg from Melbourne, in addition to Freud's views, believes in that dreams repeat issues which have not been worked upon at a conscious level successfully.

Both Transference and Countertransference are considered an integral part of an analytically oriented psychotherapy. This is discussed further in later Chapters.

Contempt, Shame, Narcissism, Grandiosity, Envy and Arrogance and Malignant Bonding are important issues which need in-depth work later in this book. Similarities and Differences need to be clarified. Patients may prefer to discuss shameful incidents in Individual sessions initially prior to opening up their own core feelings in a group.

All boundary violations need to be openly discussed analytically without offending the group members.

Three weeks' notice is essential to give the group prior to any member's intention for termination. This helps to open out difficulties and as well as prepare the group for the potential loss of the member. It also allows the members to appreciate the contributions made by each other for the healthy functioning of the group.

Selection of patients

It is advisable to initially assess all patients prior to accepting them. This may entail a number of individual sessions before introducing them to the group. Group guidelines can be clearly explained prior to accepting a group member. An example of this is Dr Tom Main's paper *'The Ailment'* (Main, 1957), where there were serious difficulties in the process of selection. This is discussed later.

Herewith, I am explaining the thoughts of outspoken group members who have just had a change of group therapist. They all suffered from psychosomatic disorders and a number of them had been hospitalised in psychiatric units in the past.

The First Session

After welcoming me, there was total denial of loss of Dr X, the previous therapist who had left the group after giving the necessary notice.

Member A: (twenty year old single male diabetic) "I'm glad to have a new doctor — a woman." He did not elaborate why.

Member B: (twenty six years old depressed male with obsessional behaviour) "Things are closing in on me. I'm angry, but I really don't know why" (continuing 'unconscious denial' with 'repression' of loss of Dr X.)

This is typical of obsessional patients, as they have difficulty in accepting changes in their environment. After exploring this for a while, the group is able to help him come to the point. He then says:

Member B: "I'm wondering how I'll cope — I have never let my mother have the final word" (the group laughs). "I can't even think — the anger stifles me — I want to do something".

80

Once again, I interpret the helpless rage of the group at changes and coping with the loss of Dr X leaving. He continues:

Member B: "I remember when I was in hospital, I thought I may as well kill myself, I felt I am a burden on you, mother. I've wanted so much to be perfect. Instead I've likened myself to a machine. I've become rigid". He is almost in tears by now. I say his tears show his warmth and his depth of feelings.

Member C: (24 year old single female — is able to bring out her own anger at not being able to resolve issues about her mother with Dr X.) "Dr X sucked me in and then went off. He wasn't even here when my mother died and I missed the last session he was here".

The group was sympathetic, helping Member C to ventilate her grief. They gave her time to discuss her feelings of loss, without changing the theme.

The group was facing reality. The mother of Member C dying was accepted with genuine sadness. The group was able to help Member C by listening empathically to her fears of loneliness and difficulties with current rigid male partner.

It was clear, the group was able to be cohesive, but the loss of Dr X was being felt by the majority of members.

The Second Session

The weather outside was stormy. As the Psychiatric Unit overlooks part of the CBD, I saw certain group members get out of a tram and chat with each other while entering the hospital.

Although they were all on time, I realised Dr X had not been aware that at least the majority of the group had been having a pre-group chat on the tram.

I felt it was an appropriate time to discuss group boundaries and guidelines after they had settled in.

The group first discussed Member C — how she was feeling

following the last group. She was very realistic, that her mother's death would take her a long time to get used to it. However, she was pleased she had managed to go with her siblings to a house-warming party of mutual friends.

There was a lull in the group then. I thought this was an appropriate time for me to explore their aims in coming to the group, as well as know their current pressing issues.

However, prior to that, analytic group guidelines needed to be discussed. Hence, I opened the topic and introduced certain analytically oriented guidelines for the group to follow. How to leave messages if not coming — with whom — my beeper numbers — no socialising with each other outside the group, etc. The guidelines were evidently there before, but I had found they were not being followed, with socially isolated members chatting away to each other in the waiting room, walking together to the tram stop after leaving the group. I explained that the aim of this group is not to provide friends for them, but to help them make internal changes which will free them of conflicts which have prevented them so far in getting the best in their lives, from both themselves and also from the outside world. I did not defend my thoughts. It demonstrated my own freedom of speech and my individuality. As the majority of group members worked in institutions, hospitals as mental health workers and school teachers, they were able to accept the boundaries fully.

> **Member D,** thirty one year old female with problems in her marriage — started questioning the importance of being on time.
>
> **Dr Rustomjee (R):** "Otherwise you miss out on whatever has already been discussed and start by relying on other member's impressions. This can become a disadvantage for you."
>
> **Member A:** (continues) "By the way, I can't remember your

name" (and most apologetically), "It often happens to me with foreigners."

Dr R: (smiling) "Perhaps it's similar to forgetting guidelines which also were known once, but now forgotten."

Member C: (female — with annoyance) "Your methods are so different from Dr X's. You are more laid back", after a few minutes she continued, "But we talk more with you around" (quite grudgingly).

Dr R: (bringing in their loss of Dr X) "If Dr X and Dr Rustomjee were both identical, the group wouldn't have to bear the loss of Dr X or need to adapt to any change at all."

Member A: (angrily) "I've had this fantasy of killing someone … perhaps it's Dr X" (long pause).

Member A: (continues quickly) "Did you all hear of the change in the gun laws and the guy who shot his own mother?" (he seemed to want to scare me).

Deathly silence followed.

Dr R: (it felt extremely hilarious to me and I could not stop smiling) "Oh! How interesting — I am still alive!"

The group now laughed happily (most members realised I was not upset at all and they felt very relieved). I did not say anything about transference, knowing that accepting guidelines was plenty for the present.

Member E: (male school teacher with difficulties in relationships at work) "I'll wait and see how this all works."

Member D: (through gritted teeth) "I'm trying hard not to rock the boat."

Member C: "I feel safe with Dr Rustomjee around and having her phone numbers too."

In later sessions they continued tremendous opposition to the guidelines followed. All felt very restricted and controlled by them. Thankfully, they were able to explore and verbalise their feelings.

Member F: (a male mental health worker) "What happens if we break a guideline?"

Dr R: "We will all try to understand the reasons why it happened."

Member D: (in a rage) "We'll look like zombies going to the gas chamber if we don't talk on the tram!"

Member D: (some weeks later) "Now I am glad you mentioned guidelines — it shows you care and you believe in what you are doing. I hate to admit it, but I have made a new friend at work."

The group was delighted.

Member F: (said to him) "If it was not for the guidelines, I would give you a hug."

Everyone smiled or giggled. I felt part of the group now too and looked forward to every session.

Member G: (female who worked as a school teacher) "I'm still working on how I will cope with the death of my parents who are elderly."

It was three months after I started conducting the group that **Member A** related he had a dream in which his father had died, but he got up feeling better. The material he presented regularly showed renewed growth and creativity. Most members gave their own interpretations regarding how much he had developed.

Dr R: (after everyone had stopped their interpretations and there were a few minutes left) "Maybe he was now close to letting go of unhealthy dependency on father and Dr X in his transference. He is now enjoying doing creative work!"

Member G: "I hope I can come to that stage too."

Member A: (very softly and gingerly) "Thanks".

That was the end of the session. The group continued to work till the hospital site was changed to the inner suburbs. Only one member could not attend due to transport difficulties. The others continued to work. This being a slow open group as one member leaves the group, the vacancy is filled by another suitable member.

Being a Member of an Analytic Group and overcoming defence mechanisms between group members and staff

In conclusion, our pathway in life does not need to be either one of ceaseless yearning for an unattainable love, whilst remaining in a passive dependent position or one of continuous rebellion, especially fight/flight against the one occupying the position of authority. By enduring ambiguity, especially where unresolved conflicts had already produced severe neurotic disorders it would help the group member to regain his/her individuality. Analytic group psychotherapy with or without individual psychotherapy and combined with appropriate medication, where necessary, is one such modality which can help achieve this aim.

Summary

I have intentionally not enlarged on any theoretical issues in depth so far. Accepting the sad reality of life through the unavailability of Dr X when Member C's mother died, and voicing ambivalence towards Dr X and myself, seemed very relevant for the present. The anger and realisation of the limitations of Dr X not being around and no-one similar to him in his place felt really sad for everyone. My empathy towards all members I felt was being accepted and seemed a reasonably appropriate start for a new group. At times, prolonging a natural mourning process is not beneficial. The differences between mourning and melancholia will be discussed at later training sessions.

Psychoanalytic containment for overcoming defence mechanisms among consultants, group members and staff

Restoring hope, faith and desire to be alive, by working through early life traumas, mourning, adolescent issues and reaching creativity

Schopenhauer wrote of the beginnings of the history of development. World War Two led to the development of Group Psychotherapy. The understanding of group morale became a critical factor in being successful in winning or losing. Wilfred Trotter believed in the herd instinct in peace and war. Leaders can sway the feelings of crowds of people.

When the aim is conformity, there is a contagion of minds. A mind can be primitive, childlike, expressive and impulse-laden or reality based.

Investigators of two types of conflicts and tension are Whitaker and Lieberman who works with Focal Conflict Theory and Henry Ezriel using the Common Group Tension. Ezriel worked as a psychoanalyst with groups. The two diagrams below demonstrate Henry Ezriel's Focal Conflict Theory from the side of the patient, as well as that of the staff. When staff insist on conformity, it is very difficult for an anxious patient already in acute mourning to comply with the hospital rules.

Diagrams of Henry Ezriel's Focal Conflict Theory from the side of patient and that of the staff

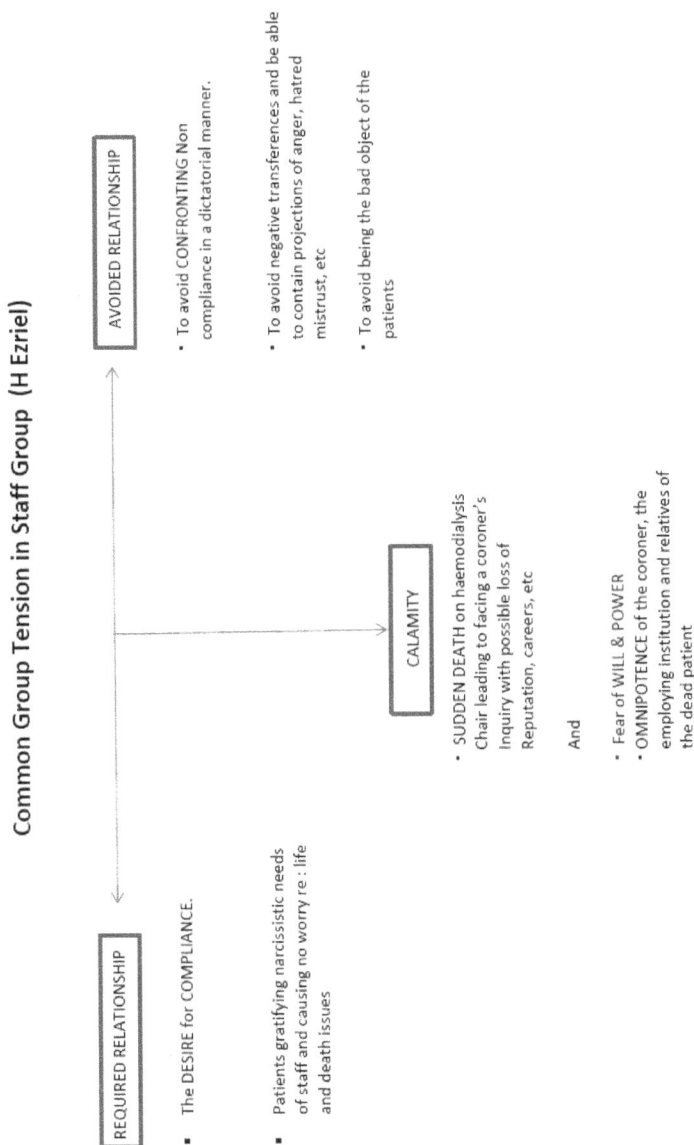

Common Group Tension in Staff Group (H Ezriel)

REQUIRED RELATIONSHIP

- The DESIRE for COMPLIANCE.

- Patients gratifying narcissistic needs of staff and causing no worry re : life and death issues

CALAMITY

- SUDDEN DEATH on haemodialysis Chair leading to facing a coroner's Inquiry with possible loss of Reputation, careers, etc

And

- Fear of WILL & POWER
- OMNIPOTENCE of the coroner, the employing institution and relatives of the dead patient

AVOIDED RELATIONSHIP

- To avoid CONFRONTING Non compliance in a dictatorial manner.

- To avoid negative transferences and be able to contain projections of anger, hatred mistrust, etc

- To avoid being the bad object of the patients

Combined Individual and Group Psychotherapy

Common Group Tension in patients' group (H. Ezriel)

REQUIRED RELATIONSHIP

With the
Convenor / Group

1) Initial 0-8 sessions of Defensive
Material revealed
- Passivity,   ) with the
  Dependency,   ) false image
  Outward Over-) of an "ideal"
  Compliance   ) patient

These lead to :
- Rationalisations and masking of
  Internal conflicts

Splitting of good/bad – (Convenor
and patient being the good ones)

and lack of authenticity

2) Later sessions revealed
THE DESIRE FOR A
FUNCTIONING KIDNEY
Expressed through Magical Expectations
From Group leader eg. To get a kidney
Transplant or a 'miracle cure'.

Self-consolidation with avoidance
Of expression of feelings of rejection
"my husband offered me a kidney but..."

CALAMITY

Fear of TOTAL ABANDONMENT
similar to childhood experiences of
deprivation. Fears that it will be
repeated in the 'here and now'

Fear of fantasised OMNIPOTENCE
OF THE STAFF in taking them off
the transplant list and stopping
dialysis, leading to their death

AVOIDED RELATIONSHIP

With the
Convenor / Group

- To avoid Ext. Reality with LOSS OF
  CONTROL and feelings of
  helplessness

- To avoid experiencing of negative
  transference with feelings of
  rejection and aggression towards
  staff and partners

- To admit there was no outward
  expression of a kidney transplant
  from relatives or staff

- TO ADMIT TO REBELLION AND
  NON COMPLIANCE

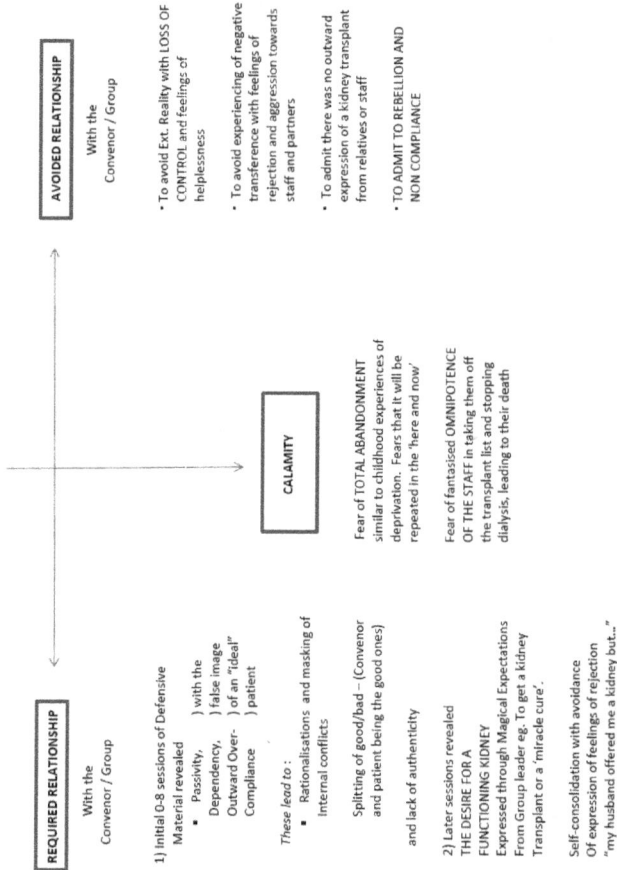

Psychoanalytic psychotherapy in a renal unit – Example: Andrea and her kidney transplant

Herewith is the case of a young single orphan, **Andrea,** in her early twenties who has arrived for an urgent Kidney Transplant. As this particular transplant met all her requirements very well, there was no time to give her any notice.

I got an urgent and irate call from a senior nurse from a Transplant unit one morning. It was described to me that a certain patient who will be referred to as 'Andrea' was due for transplant in the next couple of days. According to the nurse, Andrea was 'upsetting the whole ward, and causing chaos'. The nurse was even considering discharging Andrea. Firstly, she described how Andrea's parents had recently died in a car accident. Andrea was still in mourning and said she was cross she had to enter hospital just at the same time she was planning to see her favourite TV program! Secondly, she refused to wear hospital garments, but insisted she wore a silk nightdress all day instead. Thirdly, she did not want to discuss anything about her transplant. Finally, both her parents having died two months ago, all she gave as next-of-kin was a girlfriend's details. The friend had dropped her off at the hospital entrance and gone to her own work!

I was by now looking forward to seeing Andrea, as the history given by phone from the ward situation seemed crystal clear to myself as being in keeping with the dreadful traumas she was still unable to overcome. I felt attuned to Andrea's own fears. I realised that Andrea was terrified to allow herself to undergo a very major operation without any kind and caring relatives and friends around her. She was also trying to cover up her severe mourning for both her parents. The nurses misunderstood her underlying fears, and instead, described her as being "A self-centred spoilt brat who refuses to do anything she is told to do." They treated her as such, without having the ability to place themselves in Andrea's position and understand Andrea's own fears of her own possibility of impending death.

I knocked gently on the door of her room, introduced myself, and asked if I could come in to have a chat. She said that I could, as long as we discussed only where she could go for a holiday after the operation! I agreed and did not force any questions on her, but simply helped her to relax and feel optimistic. She gradually told me her life story of her own accord. My transference feelings towards her were to soothe her anxiety verbally and relax her, so as to gain her trust in myself. My verbal reassurance was directed in giving her recognition of her courage and making it obvious that myself and the medical staff were in full admiration of the fact the she had already taken a huge step in agreeing to the operation. This helped her greatly. "Only brave and trusting persons would do what she had done." I said that the rest of the work left to be done now belonged to the doctors and nurses. All the staff had excellent reputations and everything was expected to go well. My analytic framework by 'respecting all boundaries' and reassuring her the ethical way was the obvious way to proceed. No matter how sorry I felt for her being an orphan, I did not bring her gifts or give hugs like any loving mother would do. She did not need any more losses in life.

Patient Andrea's life story, as expected, was very tragic. Her grief was intense. She was suddenly informed with no notice at all, that a transplant organ was now ready and waiting for her. It was because of her very young age and the sudden availability of a very well-matched transplant, which matched her as a recipient, that she had been put forward on the transplant list. I said I would introduce her to some staff who would be right beside her all throughout the operation. I kept my word.

I also reassured her that by her very quick arrival to the ward and the expertise of the doctors and perfect match of the transplants, all was really the best anyone would wish. After a period of IV drips etc., a new and healthier life would be right in front of her. She would have lots of happy places and a bright future ahead.

Her anxiety reduced, and she now started to trust me, especially as I reassured her that I would be in the ward when she woke up after the operation. Very luckily all went well. She did end up wearing hospital clothes without any further non-compliance. However, she did not quite forgive the original ward nurses who she said were very rude to her. Once she recovered sufficiently to walk freely, she would paste messages and lists on her ward door as to which particular nurses and doctors she was willing to talk with! After another couple of weeks, she became friendly with most of the staff. At times a humorous atmosphere prevailed even with the nurses she had initially disliked intensely. Her friends from work also came regularly to visit her. She rang me the day she was discharged from hospital and thanked me very sincerely. I was informed from the ward that she had made a full recovery. She then regularly visited the out-patient clinic, without further worries.

In retrospect, my work was mainly to listen to Andrea, to give her reassuring, supportive and sustained empathic visits. It actually was much more difficult to help the nurses to be aware of Andrea's courage in agreeing to have a major operation all alone, as she really had no parents or siblings anymore. In addition, at the time of her admission, she was in mourning for both her parents and siblings' tragic deaths. It was Andrea's main desire to meet her close relatives who lived abroad after her operation. Closing her room doors to some of the nurses in the ward and browsing through travel magazines, may be partially her own way of denying facing her fears of dying during the transplant operation.

The main question from the nurses at the time of her sudden admission was:

"If she is that depressed, after her parent's and sibling's death, why is she behaving as a spoilt brat?"

My answer was,

"She is presenting with the three well acknowledged features of a Manic Defence which are Control, Contempt and Triumph."

This surprised the nurses as they were not used to recognizing Manic Defences. Details of Manic Defences, leading to transference and counter-transference reactions will be clarified in detail under separate chapters (Klein, M.; Segal, H., 1967).

I hope the reader is now able to resonate with other persons similar to Andrea whom they have known to demonstrate Contempt for similar reasons. Rather than openly being able to share current fears of operations being unsuccessful, they prefer to live in denial of their basic needs, withdraw from intimacy, put on defence mechanisms filled with airs and graces, wear expensive clothes, silk nightdresses and read travel magazines.

From the point of view of my own counter-transference towards Andrea I was feeling very relieved and delighted seeing the bunch of travel magazines she was carrying with her all through the interview. To me it seemed apparent that she was looking forward to going to foreign places and a possible brighter future with her relatives.

These inexperienced nurses had only felt insulted by misjudging that she has developed a negative reaction towards them. Once Andrea's operation was successfully completed, there gradually grew a more amicable and relaxed ward culture. The nurses began to feel warm towards Andrea, as well as being more motherly and caring. Her non-compliance was cured with regard to her kidney transplantation. They realised Andrea's limitations and her sadness regarding her major losses at such a young age. One could now say that self-dignity was restored by all involved.

CHAPTER 3:

The Median Group by Patrick de Maré "Koinonia"

The theory of the median group reflects S.H. Foulkes' attitude that this is a new stance in our thinking about groups as a result of an increase in size of about twenty members and the cultural dimensions that this entails. It handles frustration and hate which engender negative or anti-libidinal energies with their transformation into psychic energy through dialogue.

The Median group leads from hate to the establishment of **Koinonia** or **impersonal fellowship** that promotes rather than inhibits communication (Reference Group Analysis Sage London V 23, 1990 p. 113-127). During the invitation of Patrick de Mare from UK to St Vincent's Hospital in Melbourne, we were hoping to learn how to keep aggressive interchanges at bay. Patrick by this time was an elderly gentleman with a good sense of humour along with entertaining musical abilities on his piano accordion. The latter was only brought out by Pat at the termination of most sessions. His main guideline to us was "Keep all your clubs and spheres outside the group and use your own psychic energy through dialogue to bring out peaceful resolutions". As we had already experienced a week's theoretical exposure to him prior to his starting to teach us large group therapy, we had arrived at an understanding, his way of thinking.

Those who are accustomed to work in a contextual void with the analyst standing in for reality find it difficult initially to focus primarily on family constellations which often occur in median groups. The median group also approaches new thinking about cultural context.

Median groups handle the anti-libidinal (energy) forces of frustration and rage by structuring them through dialogue. It is mostly in a larger context that multi-cultural structures are capable of emerging out in the open in a median group.

Median Group Principals

1. Face to face single circle seating similar to Foulkes small groups (1964)
2. Regular meetings
3. Free floating discussion
4. A non-directive convener who encourages impersonal fellowship (Koinonia).

The groups are not communities nor are members dependent on each other. Contact outside the situation is minimal and should be discussed if it occurs.

Purpose

To enable people to learn how to talk to each other — learner dialogue. This can occur not only in psychotherapy, but also social therapy, schools, hospitals, industries, trade unions etc.

In the median group we have moved beyond the personal and the familial. We enter the social domain where we explore social myths, i.e. the social conscious.

The aim is not to socialise the individual, but to humanise society.

The process of the Median group

1. The individual member is in a mutually frustrating structure with others. He/she either stays and hates or panics and runs away.
2. If he/she stays long enough, he/she becomes a membership

individual and dialogue ensues. More dialogue therefore continues transforming hate into energy, which in turn mobilises further dialogue.

3. The mind diffuses hate and transforms it into the super-ego of abandoned and lost objects. Hence it enters a stage of mourning and ends up not in love but in friendship.

William Blake wrote "For the bird it's a nest, for the spider a web and for the man friendship" (W Blake, 'Proverbs of Hell' C1793).

Specific features

1. Context is paramount.
2. Process. Being a learning situation, frustration is a place for learning membership of a median group. It has two dimensions, the vertical and the lateral.
3. Content. Group bonding and Koinonia could be interpreted as the transformation of sibling rivalry and competition. Group culture is group minded.

Median group creates a post-oedipal approach. Genitality is inevitably both biological and social.

CHAPTER 4:

"The Ailment" by Tom Main –
Difficulties in Creating a New Special Unit

This well appreciated article came into being following unresolved problems during hospitalization of severely traumatized patients whose ailments ended with tragic outcomes.

Dr Thomas Main was born in 1911 and has been well known as one of the earliest founders of group analytic work in Britain. He is often mentioned along with the pioneers, S.H. Foulkes and Wilfred Bion, all of whom worked at the **Northfield Military Hospital** in 1943. Tom Maine's best known article 'The Ailment' was published in the British Journal of Medical Psychology-Wiley Online Library in 1957. He was also the Medical Director of the Cassel Hospital in London for thirty years. He was a psychiatrist, a psychoanalytic therapist and a well acknowledged teacher. He worked for many years with combat troops. He was also a founder of the Tavistock Institute of Human Relations. Tom Main looked up to John Rickman as a most prestigious member at Tavistock. He believes that Rickman recognized the importance of giving the group space during silences in order to encourage spontaneity. He also respects many other analysts, including Harold Bridger, who taught us in Melbourne during his many visits.

Main starts by describing how reassuring it is for the treating staff of hospitals, when a patient is totally cured from the gravest of illnesses and 'makes a miraculous recovery'. Moreover, that this is especially rewarding when there are no relapses. Main, however, also believes that any mental health worker who really thinks and believes in the above process is being 'idealistic, unrealistic or even omnipotent'. He then examines the opposite extreme, namely that a patient who worries us too savagely can be impossible to maintain. Main refers to the latter being a part of 'primitive human behaviour' (Main, 1989).

Herewith is a summarized account given by Main, regarding 'a dozen inpatients' who were hospitalized. He describes the referrals for these patients came from his close, fully trained and respected colleagues. Obviously, he trusted them and the advice they gave him. Their advice was to treat the patients very sensitively, as they had gone through severe traumatization and were helpless and very vulnerable. The referrers had suggested 'intensive psychotherapy' and for 'the patient not be judged' unfairly. Different agencies who had been involved with their treatment in the past had not communicated freely with each other. This leads us, the uninvolved reader, to recognize that perhaps 'Splitting', along with a degree of lowered Self-Esteem leading to Self-Contempt of the staff, may have occurred during the treatment of these cases.

This first group of patients who were highly recommended by their own doctors, were introduced as if they were **Special Patients**. Their history given during their introduction to Main, was that some of them were neglected by previous caregivers. Hence, Tom Main and his nursing staff got the impression that these patients were to be now treated as being Special. He divided the nursing staff into an inner group who had individual interviews with these Special patients, and an outer group of more senior nurses. The Inner group of nurses initially felt what Main termed as an Arousal of Omnipotence which was rewarding for them. They attended to the Desires of these Special patients.

His very important paper 'The Ailment' was now widely published in the British Journal of Medical Psychology in

1968, The Ailment and other Psychoanalytic Essays in 1989 by Free Association Books, London, and other journals, namely Psychoanalytic Psychotherapy in 1990.

As time went on, the current carers, namely the 'chosen' nurses did not interact closely with the outer group of senior nurses. Nurses who were especially chosen for looking after these patients also found it best not to get too close emotionally with their counterparts who were not chosen. Hence, sub-groups appear to have started. Possibly rivalry and envy may also have begun between the subgroups present. It now also began to be apparent, that the total burden of getting these very sick Special patients to a healthy frame of mind, was going to be very difficult.

In my opinion, these staff were expected to be endowed with having the 'caring' and 'mirroring' ingredients of Irvin Kohut (Kohut, 1979) and his followers, e.g. Stone (1977). The patients on the other hand were expecting to be cured of their long-standing vulnerability following early and later life traumas by mainly a supportive and caring environment. These same patients had been transferred from one unit to another leading them to project all their hopes on the new treatment team.

Past History. Dr Tom Main unfortunately had not gone into great detail with the referring doctors, as to why they thought the patients had not improved under their own care originally. What impressions did the referring doctors have regards the resistances of the Special patients they referred? Had there been any Negative Therapeutic Reaction and knowing what the precipitants were would have helped the chosen inner group to have some idea without disclosing any details to the patients.

Tom Maine had initially regarded his chosen team to be very suitable for these Special patients and they all had appeared to start optimistically. Sadly, the final outcome was poorer than what everyone had hoped. Main considered two features were in action from the start. One was a constant 'Sentimental Appeal' from the patients not to be abandoned by those who looked after them. The other feature of importance was that these patients contributed towards starting an 'Arousal of Omnipotence' in the chosen nursing staff. This was ego — building for these nurses, at first. When no improvement was evident, they kept trying harder and harder to appease the traumatized patients and many suffered from burn-out.

From a Lacanian point of view, the Sentimental Appeal was an insatiable Desire for endless attention which was soon changed to a Demand. If the desire was not attended to exactly as the patient requested, the arousal of Omnipotence was revived in the nurses whenever the temporary needs of the patient were fulfilled.

The continuation of these two sad subgroups of longstanding patients and worn out nurses, being placed in a group of a Special category, without improvement. Both inner circle subgroups could not accept the strain that they were going through.

The diagram in this book in Section II, Chapter 1, clearly demonstrates, the importance of there being in every infant a core of Illusory Omnipotence. The other areas of growth may then develop, namely Separation/Individuation and dealing with the Manic Defences of Control, Contempt and Triumph, eventually leading to development. Hence there are two possible reactions.

a)   Growth and individuality as part of the Life Drive; or

b)   An inability to accept that both the nurses, as well as the patients were going through their own incapabilities. Especially when this leads to going 'Beyond the Pleasure Principle' leading to the Death Drive as described by Freud.

Repressed trauma is also described by Freud in his work on 'Remembering, Repeating and Working Through' (Freud, 1914). This could help to overcome the traumatic events of one's life.

I agree with the conclusion stated at the time of referral that the distress suffered so far needed psychoanalytic psychotherapy. If it had been closely supervised by Tom Main himself or other staff, the progress and outcome could have been to the benefit of the whole unit.

Working with patients who give a clear history of earlier painful traumatic experiences need to be taken very seriously and different measures used. However, this is all in retrospect.

Final outcome as given by Dr Tom Main

It appears that in Tom Main's unit, the outcome was deemed unsatisfactory for more than half of the patients. Out of twelve patients, one was given a leucotomy, seven were treated with continuous narcosis, one had a short course of ECT, four were discharged to closed hospitals, out of which two died within two years. Two patients committed suicide (in one case the relatives refused to let the patient go to a mental hospital).

Five patients were sent home from Dr Main's unit. Three remained in analysis and are leading stable lives. One needed no further treatment.

Effect on Tom Main himself

He sets a very brave example of admitting his personal massive disappointment for not observing a number of things which he admits "happened under my nose" as he puts it in the article. He had explained the difficulties of treating similar patients, at the start of the article.

Effects on the chosen nurses

They were not encouraged to set boundaries with what they could do and what was impossible for anyone in their position. Instead they took full responsibility for managing extremely difficult patients by themselves due to arousal of their own omnipotence by the patients. These nurses did have breakdowns, experiencing the very sad outcome of patients they once had liked. Also, as Tom Main describes it, he himself has experienced situations where patients had poor outcomes. Maybe a supportive group for debriefing the chosen nurses in a group may have led to better results.

Results regarding the rest of the nursing staff who were not chosen

This would depend on their own training, and their capacity to bear a trauma of this nature. They could have initiated say a social activity with the patients. They also needed a safe space to voice their own feelings of hurt. In fact, a Supportive debriefing for the whole Treating team, including nurses who were not chosen, would have restored the original trust of containing the team together. An external group conductor from another training unit would have been very neutral and hopefully provided a more satisfactory outcome.

Everyone is aware of the harsh reality of life and death, but no-one confronts the reality and disappointment on a daily basis. Why?

Is it because there is the aura that everything is able to be contained and there is a denial of the failures of containment (Reference. Containment and Failures of Containment (Rustomjee S. 2007, Group Analysis Vol 40(4)). Main describes, in detail, the disastrous end that befalls a number of patients as well as staff.

On admission, the patients were declared to be Special even before they came into hospital. Hence it was presumed that they were so-called 'best type of patient'. This seems to be the first evidence of both staff and patients being duped. The patients also would have received the same message that they were very special and were given feelings of entitlement. This was reinforced by the nurses, running to their every wish and demand. They could even be described to be treated as belonging to a separate elitist category.

It seemed that the culture demanded the following:

- It was expected that this brand new unit had to show it fulfilled all its expectations, no matter how unrealistic these may be. Failure of the Psychotherapy Unit to fulfil all of its aims was an unthinkable calamity.
- The 'inner circle, viz.' the immediate treating team was expected to cope, without complaining, no matter what the consequences were to their own health or that of the patients they treated.
- Perhaps (this is my thoughts only) that the Outer Circle, viz. those working in the hospital, but not chosen to treat in the team, were expected to be silent and not discuss their feelings. These feelings may have ranged from hurt and disappointment at not being chosen, to envy of the Inner Circle, and anger to the chosen nurses (displaced from anger to the staff who made the decisions). Maybe they even felt helplessness to go against the wishes of the administrators of the Unit, Tom Main being one of them.
- Unusual circumstances are vulnerable for whoever starts a new unit, ranging from the administrators to all working in it.
- Main refers in the Ailment to "Primitive human behaviour".

Main also describes the evasiveness of the younger medical staff e.g. they avoided attending a group of all interested staff to help the nurses who were already traumatised. One medical officer lost a patient file.

Main, then decides to continue with his work of discovery, as to how things went so wrong. What, besides shame, were these young medicos avoiding? It is possible that they also may have felt ashamed of their own behaviour which they didn't want to admit in front of everyone. Could it be their rage perhaps at not being invited to be a Special and integral part at the start? The Shame/Rage cycle is a well demonstrated feature, in certain instances (Reference; The Solitude of Unbearable Shame.2009. Group Analysis. Vol 42(2)).

This article has led to a better understanding of a vulnerability of human nature.

Rice, A.K., stated, "Since each part of any enterprise has its own primary task, it needs an organisational model for itself" (Rice, 1969, p. 569).

GROUP PSYCHOTHERAPY

HISTORICAL OVERVIEW

BY DR GEORGE CHRISTIE

Comments by Sabar Rustomjee on "The Ailment" by Tom Main — Difficulties in Creating a New Special Unit

First page

Trying to understand what Tom Maine is saying is noteworthy, and may be explored at a further level by us:

He is painting a picture of how delighted he believes all medical practitioners and hospital workers feel, when he describes the so-called **"best type of patient"** who from the gravest of illnesses makes a miraculous recovery , and that too without any relapses!

At this point he refrains from saying openly that anyone(doctor, nurse, group worker etc.) who really thinks and believes in the above thinking process is in analytic terms very idealistic or unrealistic or even omnipotent(word used by Main .We all know there is no such entity as" the best patient," because there are numerous reasons for not getting better quickly in any hospital. In fact Main being the authentic person himself, comes to this conclusion very much later in the article . He then sets an example of admitting **his personal shame** for not observing a number of things which happened ' **under my nose'** as he puts it in the paper.

So then , despite the **Arousal of Omnipotence** in the Doctor and carefully selected Nurse team, augmented by the **Sentimental Appeal/seduction by the patient**, why does no one from the outside circle of the unit,(ie those not directly involved with the treatment of the patients) point this fact out without wearing rose coloured glasses ? We are not priviledged to the motives of those in this outer circle. **Everyone is aware of the harsh reality of life and death, but no one confronts the reality and disappointment on a daily basis.** Why?

Is it because there is the aura, that everything is able to be contained, and there is a denial of the failures of containment(Reference .Containment and Failures of Containment.(Rustomjee S. 2007,Group Analysis Vol 40(4).) Main describes in detail, the disastrous end that befalls a number of patients as well as staff .

Could we examine the situation differently from Main and see the pitfalls which were not seen, and hence not avoided? In my own training of students, I highlight the importance of the very first sentence spoken by whoever. **Here the theme was set by the Referring doctor.**

These were **conflicting statements** made about the patients

a) **The patients were declared to be Special** even before they came into hospital (page 4). Hence could we presume that the hospital staff considered them on the one hand **to be the so-called best type of patient**? This seems to be the first evidence of **both staff and patients being duped.** The patients also would have received the same message that they were very special and were given feelings of entitlement. This was reinforced by the nurses running to their every wish and demand. They could even be described to be treated as belonging to a separate elitist category. A place where all previous mistakes made by others would be corrected by the present hospital unit.

*It seems to myself as if the **workers and patients behaved reactively to the culture of the place.***

It is as if the culture demanded the following:

- It was expected that this brand new unit had to show *it* **fulfilled all its expectations, no matter how unrealistic** these may be. *Failure of the Psychotherapy Unit to fulfill all of its aims was an unthinkable calamity.*

- The' **inner circle'**, viz.' the immediate treating team' *was expected to cope*, without complaining no matter what the consequences were to their own health, or that of the patients they treated.

- Perhaps (this is my thoughts only) that the **Outer Circle**, viz. those working in the hospital, but not chosen to treat in the team, were **expected to be silent** and not discuss their feelings. These feelings may have ranged from hurt and disappointment at not been chosen, to envy of the Inner Circle , and anger to the chosen nurses(displaced from anger to the staff who made the decisions). Maybe they even felt helplessness to go against the wishes of the administrators of the Unit, Tom Main being one of them.

Issues which could have been explored more in the paper are:

- 1.The vulnerability of whoever starts a new unit, ranging from the administrators to all working in it

- *2.A point of great interest in Main's reference to "Primitve human behaviour"*

What qualities of human nature does he include in it?

- He also describes the evasiveness of the younger medical staff ,and finally an important patient file was lost by one medico .Main, then decides to continue with his work of discovery, as to how things went so wrong. What, besides shame, were these young medicos avoiding? Could it be their rage perhaps at not being invited to be an integral part from the beginning? The Shame/Rage cycle is a well demonstrated feature, in certain instances.(Reference; The Solitude of Unbearable Shame.2009.Group Analysis.Vol 42(2))

- Whose Shame was the whole treating team carrying?

- Carrying the Shame and Blame and becoming burnt out by Projective Identification is the most important factor in the article.

All reading this article needs to define all areas where this is seen to happen

Areas which needed to have been done before patients were accepted

Criteria for selection should have been clearly defined

1. Observing closely, it is apparent that Objectivity in making an initial Assessment with each individual patient was absent .

Sabar Rustomjee

MBBS;DPM; FRANZCP

CHAPTER 5:

Supportive Expressive Group Therapy (SEGT) for Women with Multiple Recurrences of Breast Cancer and a Limited Life Expectancy

This method was initiated by Dr David Spiegel and his associates at Stanford University School of Medicine, starting in 1979. Spiegel researched women with recurrent breast cancer whose average life expectancy was up to eighteen months without psychosocial treatment. Dr David Kissane, Brenda Grabsch, David M Clarke, Graeme C Smith, Anthony W Love, Sidney Bloch and others participated in the project. I was also assigned to a newly started team with a co-therapist.

Spiegel found that the type of group most suited to his patients in USA encouraged increased openness to feelings and thoughts along with expressions of affect. Nothing was forbidden to discuss. There was an atmosphere of acceptance and a suspension of direct confrontation. The groups were cohesive and respectful with problems starting from early life to the present, were encouraged. Unlike psychoanalytic groups there was an encouragement of relationship between group members, rather than forbidding contact outside the group. Coping with illness and dealing with issues with death and dying were encouraged.

This is a newly started Australian Research project comprising a random choice of Breast Cancer patients with less than ten months to live.

In everyday life we come across numerous experiences of Supportive Expressive Group Therapy (SEGT) working within an appropriate framework, held together in a group matrix of well selected members. Interpersonal verbal dialogues arising within these members find it possible to create a 'Safe Space' and arrive at 'Human Dignity' not only for themselves, but also for others. On the other hand, we are also made aware of various episodes of Social Disintegration. The causes of these may be due to natural environmental disasters or may be deliberate and pre-planned. The origins of both need close examination in order to create a 'Safe Space' for mankind to survive and lead a creative life. It is vital to help parents, teachers, leaders, employers and others to identify *Anti-Group activity arising from destructive Anti Group forces* (Nitsun, 1996).

This chapter starts with Clinical Examples of groups, where experience in conducting therapy groups, using an Expressive Supportive framework, has helped the group and its conductor considerably in overcoming various unconscious resistances in difficult settings. These groups were conducted in both an in-patient hospital, as well as outpatient clinic setting.

Example: Group Psychotherapy with terminal metastatic breast cancer patients

''Hang in there, we will see it through.''

These were the words of a group member suffering metastatic breast cancer who had stopped chemotherapy and now had less than two months to live. She was a member of a research-based breast cancer Supportive Expressive Group, which met once a week, and was conducted by a co-therapist and myself. She had attended this group for the previous six months.

The words embraced three main themes:

Firstly, that of survival in the present;

Secondly, a hope that she will be able to successfully traverse her forthcoming last journey into the unknown of death and finally that she wanted to give courage to the rest of the group who would in their own time be making the same journey.

Finally, in the story of Pandora's Box when all else had escaped, only 'Hope remained'. Annihilatory moments cannot lead to survival without there being any hope. Just as where there is a desire, there is life, similarly one also needs to say that where there is hope there is also life.

It is usually one of the functions of a good enough group conductor to instil hope in group members (Yalom, 1975). However, in a well-integrated and well-functioning group, one encounters group members able to do that for each other and for themselves.

This group member had entered a palliative care centre at that time and missed attending the group for a couple of weeks. It is in this context that she expresses her innermost feelings to the group. The Palliative Care Centre appeared to symbolise for her a safe transitional space in which to experience her feelings of grief. The space lay between the objects she loved on earth and peace in death beyond.

Working with depressed patients within a group of members with metastatic breast cancer necessitates the group repeatedly experiencing loss, mourning, reparation and magical expectations, idealisation, persecutory anxiety, feelings of helplessness, worthlessness, abandonment by people who have loved them, fears of being forgotten after their death, being replaced by a more worthy competitor to meet the needs of those left behind and above all feelings of uncertainty both about the near future and of the process of dying itself. When these conflictual feelings are able to be experienced and finally worked through in group psychotherapy with a supportive framework, the member is able to not only regain their own feelings of self-worth among family, friends and community, but also as a result of an enriched ego to rediscover hidden talents leading to the emergence of very creative aspects of themselves. Those whose metastases have not progressed very rapidly are able to start on a much more productive lifestyle than they had been able to previously. Moreover, some may wish to leave behind their own footprints as a testimony of their personal struggle in life.

In the words of Longfellow (A Psalm of Life) — it could be:
"Footprints, that perhaps another
Sailing o'er life's solemn main
A forlorn and shipwrecked brother
Seeing, shall take heart again."

The reader could imagine that a group talking constantly along the themes of life and death would be morbid. In reality, the opposite was the case. Humour along with creativity emerged within this particular group in the first two years. There also emerged feelings of relief from carrying burdens from the past. At an individual level, it was clear to see that most, if not all, the members had made astonishing progress.

One member started a tertiary course in Real Estate training along with another family member who had given up studies. She was also able to establish a much closer relationship with those friends and family with whom previously she had an embittered relationship.

Another elderly member, who used to come with an oxygen cylinder to group, started making teddy bears for her grandchildren, grand nieces and nephews. On one occasion she brought a basket full of teddy bears she had sewn to show the group. It was a new creative outlet she had discovered, that served as both a joy for her and her family.

Two members who had lived very enmeshed lives within their families went on holidays without their grown-up children. She and her husband actually went overseas on three separate occasions for a few weeks each time. One member not only passed her Bachelor Degree, but also organised and attended the wedding of one of her children prior to her death.

In addition, another two members continued to work part-time, one in a sales position and the other as a hospital nurse till a few months prior to their deaths.

All these results occurred within a time span of two years of commencing this slow-open. A slow-open group is one which is not time-limited or closed to new members. It was undoubtedly the creativity in this group was a very rewarding experience for all members, as well as the staff.

However, following this period, a large number out of the twelve that made up the initial group members had died or were too sick to attend regularly and there was a period of many months during which recruitment of new members was very difficult. The pool of suitable members appeared to have run dry.

Difficulties in adapting to the death of a group member
Herewith is the example of the very first Breast Cancer Group to which I was allocated. Our group training course had thankfully recently discussed Morris Nitsun's work regarding Anti-Group (1996) on the topic 'Destructive forces in the group and their creative potential'.

Coping with the unexpected death of a new member
As the members started to sit down, a very sad and unexpected message was conveyed to myself by the secretary of the department. A telephone message had been sent around to all group members too, informing them that a certain group member had died that week. Although the group had only started two weeks ago, the atmosphere felt very heavy to bear. In case anyone wanted to attend the funeral, all details had been given. She

had been the youngest group member, married and had a young child. Neither she nor anyone else, had expected her to die so suddenly, as there had been nothing to warn anyone. Everyone, including my co-therapist and myself, were totally shocked and felt flat. No-one could have foreseen such a tragic occurrence in advance. Nobody gave any indication of intending to attend her funeral. It all seemed impossible even to visualise.

Obviously, there was no Container to reassure us (*Second Thoughts*, Bion, 1967) regarding the future of our group or how to contain our grief. We were now, face to face with Reality. We remained in this state about ten minutes. Our main task now was obviously to group ourselves together and speak when we felt able to verbalise our thoughts and our feelings. This is similar to the recommendation of S.H. Foulkes, the pioneer of group analysis. His words were "Trust the Group". All members were requested to feel free to say whatever they wished. As the more experienced conductor, I put this proposal to the group.

From my previous experiences, I had realised that for patients who had been given a probable time limit for their own life, they found it very difficult to accept someone else leaving them suddenly, without any prior indication.

John Keats's advice of considering 'Negative Capability' and patiently, 'enduring ambiguity, without irritably reaching out for fact or reason' was the obvious way to proceed. We shared the mourning silently like equals.

Then, one member, seething with rage, said with sheer contempt in her voice, that she could not bear the reality of the sudden and unexpected death.

"Doctors have just no idea how we feel!"

I felt reassured that she had broken the silence and spoken her own feelings truthfully. I realised that this was a moment for me to be gentle with her and understanding, as well as being authentic in my reply. I was hoping to restore trust, reality and stability in the group once more. I also wanted to 'stop the splitting' between 'we', the patients who feel the pain, and "You doctors", the ones without any 'feelings'. At this moment, my dearest mother came to my mind, similar to me having a 'free association' (Bollas, 1983; Freud, 1961). I remembered the numerous times I would visit her oncologist with her, as she had cancer too. At those visits, somehow, I endured the sadness and so did my mother. We were also given the very best of treatment, always taken in from the queue first. The senior oncologist was a relative of ours too. The treating oncologist after having known him many years, all through my mother's numerous operations felt like a very kind and trustworthy friend. I was also respected for being a medical student. Hence my own experience was that of going to visit a kind and caring oncologist. My family realised how serious her condition was and all we could do was to make her life as comfortable as possible.

I now replied to the group with genuine feeling. "Maybe so, between certain persons and their doctors, but as a matter of fact, I care deeply for all my patients." This group member was now shocked hearing the warmth in my feelings, both towards herself and all those close to me, who were now suffering. It quickly dispelled the 'anti-doctor' feeling and brought back the 'group-as-a whole' atmosphere. Their angry, contemptuous feelings about so called 'all doctors', faded away. A more human, cohesive, empathic and caring 'work group' was now growing. No further mention was ever made of my mother. All personal details and boundaries were respectfully kept in place. It felt that the group was finally in a Safe Space in which to verbalise honest feelings openly and express emotions without erupting into uncontrolled anger, rationalisation or denial. They could see and accept my authentic feelings for all of them. After all, the human part of me was no different from their own. (Maybe a couple of members felt sad for me too.)

This group continued in terms of the research with a Supportive Expressive Psychotherapy framework. Unresolved grief of losing their previous member would suddenly erupt from time to time. As new members were gradually added, the group became more acceptable of the transience of life. The group now had become primarily empathic towards each other as well as myself. They had witnessed the human part of myself, which in the past had previously been split off and denied.

A Supportive Expressive framework is very different from other Group Analytic frameworks. In Supportive Expressive groups are clearly more supportive and empathic. Analytically orientated groups are composed of members where confrontations often take place, helping members to explore their own shocked responses, with repressed self-guilt, leading to projected anger towards both co-therapists in their unconscious transference. SEGT is more empathic. Group members now, with my acceptance of their sudden loss, gradually became able to acknowledge the unforeseen situation that had arisen. They were able to accept their own unknown future with tragic reality-based events, rather than project their own anxiety onto myself. I needed to explain that it was the 'position' of the doctor/group leader or oncologist which was attacked, regardless of the person herself or himself towards whom it was directed. When this was explained to them carefully, they calmed down. I explained that it was my freedom to decide the technique which I considered would help the group the most without being offensive to anyone (Symington, 1983). I added that it had been an example of my trust in the group regards my sharing an important event of my life, with all of them.

Existential anxiety of living in a space between life and death is not easy for anyone, but it is certainly worse for

patients who have to bear it on a more acute daily basis. My own attunement in recognising their anxiety and being able to share it with them in a dignified manner proved to be certainly helpful to all, including myself and the co-therapist. This incident helped to integrate the group, rather than divide the group.

The group member, who had initially voiced contempt in this group, gradually became an involved, helpful and active member. This session and future ones were often expressed in a cohesive, friendly, safe and caring manner. The absence of further contemptuous and harsh judgemental responses promoted greater trust and self-dignity within the group. The group was now acknowledged as a 'Safe Space' for ongoing clarifications and integration of the group culture. My appropriate countertransference was not analytically oriented either as I had revealed a personal issue. It was geared towards giving reassurance to the group by demonstrating that myself as leader would have no exemption to the reality of experiencing life and death issue.

CHAPTER 6:

Anti-Group: Morris Nitsun (1996)

Some of the new group members exhibited strong resistance to being in a group and started displaying Anti-Group phenomena (Nitsun, 1996).

I will now give some examples of potential anti-group interactions and how they were worked through satisfactorily. One instance was when a patient challenged me angrily with …

''Do you know what it is like to be dying of breast cancer and what it is like for our families to live with us?'' I answered calmly "Why would you want to believe that my immediate family or myself haven't been through the same?"

It was the honest and genuine answer that I had given with respect to the members that immediately rang true to the patient that I too must have undergone at some part in my life similar feelings to what she and her family members were going through now.

I thus prevented her from her unconscious attempt to split the group with the conductors separated from the rest of the members. Such an interaction could be the start of undermining therapists and reducing them to the level of being unsuitable for the task at hand. In a 'them' versus 'us' pattern from which no party can emerge as victorious.

Conflicts in family and other relationships following one member developing breast cancer

A group member's marriage had broken up when her husband left home with his young secretary as soon as the diagnosis of breast cancer had been made for her. She had then started years of bitter battles with him, which she had recently ceased altogether. "I don't hold anything against him anymore" she would say. Similarly, she was unaware of the intensity of her rage to her GP who had failed to diagnose her cancer earlier. She said almost apologetically and with a laugh "He is a very good man, but I must say he/knows absolutely nothing about cancer". Instead she directed her rage to her oncologist, "He must be a very good oncologist, but he looks at me with such pleading eyes. I can never tell him anything that's wrong with me". It was the same with her children. No-one could win. Her son, after a lot of hints from her (made at the persistence of the group), finally came one day to do her garden. She then told him he should be at home because his wife was ill that day and sent him off, feeling guilty. Her repressed anger that he had not been available to help her for so long contributed to her not being able to accept his help now and be grateful for it. "No-one can help me now. What can this group do?" I gently pointed out her enormous hurt, her repressed rage to her husband and her GP, which was now possibly contributing to her rage towards her family, her oncologist and the group. At a conscious level she had been until then unaware of these dynamics. The group also helped her greatly to mourn the loss of her marriage, which she described had been a great source of satisfaction and stability for her.

In conclusion, I wish to state that I have personally found the experience of being a group conductor with metastatic breast cancer members a very enriching and enlightening experience. I believe I have helped my fellow group members and myself to appreciate the meaning of life. In the words of Mathew Arnold after all -

"Is it so small a thing

To have enjoyed the sun

To have lived life in the spring
To have loved, to have thought, to have done?"

Rivalry in Co-Therapists

My own response was a mixture of feelings. It was obvious in cohesive groups that we, as co-therapists working together to help them, were very sincere. None of them would ever admit that openly, but whenever one of us co-therapists went on leave, we were unconsciously avoided for many weeks until they forgave us re-establishing a caring relationship with us. Quite often we would go to their funerals too which showed our genuine affection for them.

The supportive Expressive framework, like the one described above, is very different from a group analytic framework, where in the latter there is no fear of death. The patients were hardier and could express their harsh judgemental responses if needed. It helped them to be open without fear of retribution here to humour often followed when appropriate without ill feelings. Similarities and differences were able to be cleared up openly as seen in the first example of long-term analytic psychotherapy.

Summary

There were three replication studies of SEGT from Canada, USA and Australia failed to show an increase in survival of life as an advantage of pursuing with SEGT. However, there was a distinct advantage in the quality of life. This is described in an earlier chapter. My main query now is that if both the therapist and the co-therapist had training in analytic supportive therapy how much greater advantage would that have been to the patients? In my opinion, the negative therapeutic reaction between client and therapist and vice versa would have been reduced greatly. In conclusion, assertiveness, humour, creativity, altruism, truthfulness

and cohesiveness are major issues which produced a more satisfactory lifestyle.

There are two recommendations I wish to make on the basis
of the above:

i.   A 'creativity scale' can be compiled so that not only the
     duration of survival is measured, but also levels of creativ-
     ity attained.
ii. The intake for each group should be so that even if only
     60% attend at any one time, there would be at least five to
     six members present in each group.

It is important for therapist and supervisors to be aware of
what exactly is an 'Anti-Group'? All groups have in-built creative
and destructive tendencies of which society is well aware. It is the
limited exploration so far of the potentially destructive tendencies of certain groups that has contributed to the limited use of
group therapy in general as a therapeutic modality. If both constructive and adverse effects of any treatment modality are not
clearly spelled out along with techniques of overcoming these
— why would entering such a group therapy program attract
potential new members? Moreover, it is not until such splitting
occurs in a previously stable group, that newly arisen group
anxiety can be suitably addressed. All group conductors need
to address this by being able to deal with both overt and covert
expressions of aggression, distrust and hostility. They need to
be able to reinstate a "Safe Space" within the group and regain
trust in the leader(s). There also needs to be the conviction in
the leader that constructive forces within a group will be able to
overcome the destructive ones so as to promote the emergence
of a well-integrated group. A 'work group' is aware of both its
potentially constructive as well as destructive tendencies.

'Reassurance as a means of Analytic Technique' in therapy, had
been described by Melitta Schmideberg (1935), who very correctly

points out that although traditional analysis is conducted so that the analyst is allowed to experience frustration, so as to experience her individuality, at certain times reassurance leading to allaying of anxiety and guilt may at times be very much more appropriate. This is especially applicable to the management of breast cancer group members. Schmideberg (1935) describes how initial reassurance makes it possible for the patient to accept interpretations which may have otherwise been perceived to be hostile. It may also well be the first sign of trust when a group member is able to express his/her mistrust. In a Breast Cancer group all members are already so greatly traumatised that any further frustration introduced even through introduction of routine guidelines can be experienced as too persecutory at times. This was especially so at the time when Anti-Group destructive phenomena was developing. At times this was so called the 'second group'.

An adherence to strictly ethical behaviour on the part of the group leader(s) and members, as well as the emphasis on confidentiality could be the only guidelines applicable. Even the latter basic guidelines were not always acceptable. These could be to encourage members to arrive punctually, the need for the group to end at the appointed time, a discouragement of outside group activities which could potentially lead to a rupture of confidentiality of personal matters raised in groups were all usually met with extreme resistance and anger in the second group. Statements from certain group members were: "Don't treat us like schoolchildren — We can do what we wish. We are all adults". This actually was accurate as the group members were helping research and had not come as patients.

The techniques used by the co-therapist and myself were firstly not to feel annoyed with these members. We realised how helpless and fragile they must feel and that all they wanted was a locus of some control in their lives which was anyway so full of uncertainty. However, we did not feel guilt laden either. Instead, I firmly stated that it was quite OK if they decided not to come on a particular day, but we needed to be informed in advance so we did not need to wait in an empty room for an hour and a half! This appeared to work. Any discussion even about pointing out their need to control the therapists would have, I feel, met with more anger. Merely expecting them to take some responsibility for their decisions at a factual level seemed to turn out best.

David Spiegel, in his pioneering work with breast cancer sufferers, in his book *'Living Beyond Limits'* shares with us the importance of realising that these patients are already suffering from high levels of guilt by nature. I fully agree with him and hence I realised that interpretations ordinarily given to neurotic patients did not produce the same results in these groups. Instead it felt like a double blow to these members who found it difficult to accept any limitations to their behaviour.

I also wish to highlight the importance of being vigilant and following the course not only of their outrage and persecutory anxiety, but also of their excessive helplessness, especially when this is related to personal and family conflicts. It is this inner feeling of helplessness that contributed to their intense rage which appeared unbearable at times and greatly increased the person's vulnerability.

Donald Meltzer (1973) describes four varieties of internalised maternal images namely the 'good breast', the 'bad breast' which frustrates and destroys the 'idealised breast' which is fantasised as all powerful omniscient and immortal and finally the 'primitive toilet breast' where the function of expulsion is primary and contributes to the earliest representation of mother as part object. This function has also been attributed to the role of the group conductor.

With regards to the handling of the hitherto repressed rage, I am of the strong opinion that allowing/encouraging group members, especially those with metastatic breast cancer to keep on simply venting this without any understanding of the context and using the group as a 'toilet breast' is not beneficial and, in fact, it could be quite harmful as these members are not as well equipped to handle the full intensity of such emotion at this stage in their lives. Their underlying personalities have been described by some authorities as being 'patient, repressed and strangely devoid of anger'.

On the other hand, when this repression is worked through with the aid of supportive and reassuring interventions, there emerges insight and along with it the capacity to deal with impact on the current issues, e.g. a group member who had gained considerable insight at this stage was able to say: "It is difficult to be alive and dead at the same time". In the transference, these words also reflect the difficulty in coping within a group where known and loved members die and new ones come in.

This, of course, applied not only to the group members, but to the co-therapists as well who cannot tolerate the strain of repeated deaths. The usefulness of having co-therapists in such groups cannot be minimised. It avoids unnecessary breaks in therapy when one is on leave. Each therapist may be able to reveal blind-spots of the other and to compensate for these when applicable.

CHAPTER 7:

Group Therapy for Latency Aged Children and Their Parents

Jan Smith, Psychologist and her Therapy Group at the Royal Children's Hospital in Melbourne

The Royal Children's Hospital in Melbourne has a high standard of education, treatment and training of all disciplines of Mental Health. A psychiatric clinic was first established in 1923. Dr Winston S. Rickards was the head of the department when I was still in my final year of training in psychiatry. I continued working in the field of paediatrics for many years, concentrating mainly on training students, in a median group psychotherapy setting as well as working with in-patients in the hospital as a Consultation Liaison Psychiatrist.

Short Term Group Therapy for Latency Children and their Parents was started by Jan Smith, psychologist, at the Royal Children's Hospital and the structure was followed by many others including myself. Each program was conducted for ten consecutive weeks. Mothers and children attended for a session of two hours. The first hour was an activity group for the children, in a playroom with a pair of co-ordinators, one male and one female.

Concurrently the mothers participated in a separate room for the mother's therapy group with two different co-therapists, one male and one female. Refreshments were then given to the combined children and parent groups.

In addition, on two evenings there was a parent's group to include all available fathers. One was midway in the program and the other at the end of the program. Parents were then encouraged to attend three months later and followed up individually if needed. Six monthly and one year review programs were continued.

Evaluation of thirty-four families is reported to have improvement for twenty-eight of the children and their families (84%) by the end of the ten week programme. One child with organic brain damage was withdrawn and five remained unchanged. Twenty-six children maintained their improvement at the end of six months. A year later twenty-two of the twenty-six (87%) were symptom free. No child was adversely affected.

The lasting effects demonstrate the benefits of a time-limited, group based programme, *which involves family members.*

Family involvement

Co-operation of parents is a vital factor in improvement.

I believe a few words regarding Jan Smith and her tenacity and dedication to the task she undertakes, is relevant. She is well known around the world as the female who climbed to reach the top of Mount Everest three years ago with limited resources. "Congratulations Jan!"

CHAPTER 8:

Assessment of difficult patients for individual and group psychotherapy

Arrogance – Grandiosity – Personality Disorders

ARROGANCE

"Arrogance may be combined with Stupidity and Curiosity." (Bion, 1990, p86)

"Arrogance where life drive predominates, Pride becomes Self Respect." (Bion, 1990, p86)

"Arrogance where death drive predominates, Pride becomes Arrogance." (Bion, 1990, p86)

"The very act of analysing makes the analyst an accessory, in precipitating regression and turning the analysis into a piece of acting-out. Analyst and patient together can form a frustrated couple." (Bion, 1990, p87)

GRANDIOSITY

A Grandiose Person never really feels free as he or she is excessively dependant on those from whom she/he has chosen to obtain admiration and become involved (Miller, 1993). It is difficult for them to even admit the above to themselves.

A clear feeling of illusions of omnipotence with warm and loving contact with one of the parents, usually mother, is often described. The other parent is often felt to be critical and rejecting. Psychosomatic illnesses for example, Asthma, Psychosis and Irritable Bowel Syndrome are seen frequently, mainly with unhealthy grandiosity. Sibling rivalry is naturally intense as when one child is treated as being Omnipotent or near perfect. My personal view is that empathic long-term psychotherapy can be a great help those with a grandiose image. The therapist needs to be aware that at no stage any humiliation needs to be directed towards the patient.

The Myth of Narcissus

The myth of Narcissus is one of the most known Greek Myths, due to its uniqueness and moral tale; Narcissus, was the son of River God Cephisus and nymph Liriope. He was known for his beauty and he was loved by the God Apollo due to his extraordinary physique.

Narcissus and Echo

The tale of Narcissus is entrenched in mythology as a fable establishing the moral teaching of the age. Narcissus was the son of the

River God Cephisus and a nymph named Lynope. His beauty was admired by the Gods and renowned after his death.

The tale hails its roots from both Greek and Greco-Roman origins; with differently emphasised elements appearing in the literature of the Greek poet Conan and the Roman Ovid.

Greek

Conan illustrates Narcissus as a beautiful man who spurned all his male suitors. Aminias, another young man appeared to Narcissus and was also spurned by him, but left with one of the man's swords. Aminias killed himself with the sword and called a curse upon Narcissus for the pain and anguish he caused.

Clouded by the death of Aminias, Narcissus appeared by the edge of a lake and became infatuated by his own reflection. Unable to obtain the beauty which he saw, he died on the banks of the lake from the pain and sorrow, never able to fulfil his desire.

Greco-Roman

Ovid describes an altered tale. In his version, Narcissus' parents become worried of the exemplary beauty of their son so they appeal to a prophet, Teiresias about what lay in their child's future. The prophet told that the boy would grow old only if "he didn't get to know himself".

Later, the Nymph Echo saw the boy and fell madly in love with him. After following him for many days, Echo showed herself to Narcissus who rejected her, telling her to stop following him. Heartbroken, Echo spent her life wandering glens; till only an echo of a sound remained.

Seeing the pain Narcissus had inflicted, Nemesis, the Goddess of Revenge punishes Narcissus for his actions. She curses him to develop a desire of unattainable beauty, which he perceives in his reflection in the lake. He now falls in love with his reflection, wallowing in sorrow and ultimately killing himself.

This is a popular story about Narcissus and whoever has a narcissistic personality.

In our everyday lives we do come across many narcissistically inclined persons. They may have antisocial features, paranoid traits, absence of conscious and pathological need for power. Malignant narcissism is a term used as an alternative to narcissistic personality disorder. It reflects nastiness and destruction. They can be intelligent and high functioning, but go to great lengths to achieve their aim.

Personality Disorders e.g. narcissistic personality disorders have non-psychotic presentations. Narcissistic or character disorders are described by Rosenfeld (1957) and Bateman (2002) as two separate aspects of Narcissism. There are the thin-skinned narcissists who are difficult to treat because they become offended very easily and maybe susceptible to self-trauma. Those belonging to the thick-skinned category are not so vulnerable but can be verbally very aggressive (Bateman & Rosenfeld).

Narcissistic Personality Disorder treatment seeks to guide their clients to important self-realisation without totally alienating from the therapeutic process. Yeomans describes a case of a patient who was arrogantly superior over him. Yeomans replied gently "It must be difficult to have a therapist with so many limitations". He was trying to demonstrate that she was projecting her own feelings of inferiority masked by a superior exterior and projecting it onto the therapist. There is lack of empathy for self and others, but there is a clear tendency to protect themselves at all costs. There is lack of intimacy in making friends and healthy relationships with family. Years of abandonment are frequently encountered. Obsessional tendencies are sometimes to an extreme degree and control the rest of the family. They prefer that others in their family go for therapy rather than accept that they themselves have a problem. They may respond marginally to anti-depressants, but can also take overdoses with them. Sibling rivalry and jealousy of those in a better materialistic position is very common. Their children can also be at risk as they may not be as appreciated as they need to be. Separation individuation is very difficult in children. However, when it does occur there is very little support given to them while they are attempting to live independently (Bateman 2002, Yeomans. F.E, Rosenfeld, 1957 and Symington, N., 1993).

Narcissism and its management

The Mason Wasp: Henri Bergson — "Creative Evolution" (1919)

French philosopher Henri Bergson in his book '*Creative Evolution*' (1919), describes the Mason Wasp which stings a caterpillar at a precise point in its body, paralysing it. The wasp then lays eggs in the paralysed body and the eggs hatch in three days in the flesh of the caterpillar, which is alive, but paralysed. It provides food for the little grubs. If the wasp stings one millimetre away from the right point it kills the caterpillar and the exercise won't work. The wasp knows how to sting in the right place through a type of sympathetic communication between the two insects, which enables the wasp to feel where to sting. This is similar to us making contact to other human beings either by projecting ourselves into their world or by introjecting them into our world. Here within as an Example of a patient whom Neville Symington looked after during a colleague's absence for twenty sessions once a week. As soon as Symington was about to give expression for a thought, it went out of his mind and he lost it. He then started concentrating all his psychic attention and made an interpretation in words. This was followed by silence. The following week the patient and her husband were able to make love, as a change had occurred between them which helped her husband's capacity to become intimate with her, which had not happened for a long time (Symington, N., 2006).

Working with borderline patients (Malcolm Pines and others)

Malcolm Pines describes using fundamentals of object relationships between the id and the ego. Pines understands that borderline patients are very centred around themselves and their own hurt which may well be at most times derived from transference from another person important to him/her in life.

Pines treats borderline patients very effectively in an empathic manner which acknowledges real trauma and a reluctance to become trustworthy of the group and the therapist. Pines accepts the need for containment and boundaries. This is a very difficult area as the borderline patient may well interpret it adversely as an attack on herself or himself.

The more disturbed borderline patients live with primitive rage and destructiveness. They may attempt to project their feelings onto others leading to paranoid behaviour. These forces are not used to attack other people's resistances as they have an inability to realise the depth of difficulties others in the world have.

Borderline patients do not behave as relatively separate, independent and autonomous persons, they tend to merge or fuse with other members. The ones I have come across have had a very pampered childhood before the age of two or three years of age, followed by illnesses in other siblings or parents. The older child then yearns for a return back to her/his omnipotent state and falls down flat, when the realisation comes that this is impossible, it can lead to overdoses and long hospitalisations. Self-mutilation for example, coming close to hurting the cornea of their own eyes or threatening sharp cuts around the carotid artery areas. These thoughts and actions of the patients make it obvious that they often need hospitalisation for many months. Group therapy with these patients needs intensive supervision, despite the length of time these symptoms persist. The patient does often improve with Pines' understanding of their own particular trauma. The precipitating factors of similar traumas is very difficult to isolate and understand. It certainly has a negative influence on the rest of the group. They need to be seen as regressed psychodynamically. Therapists have to be aware not encouraging adverse transference interactions. In Australia we have a special well-trained unit of inpatients suffering from borderline disorders.

Pines describes the clinical profiles of two patients with borderline tendencies in a twice weekly slow-open group. Only after about a year's therapy the patient improves and is able to trust some of those who look after and shelter her. Borderline features are possible to be contained under a caring environment which leads to reduction of regression. Countertransference is a very important factor in the therapeutic relationship between the patient and the therapist.

Example: A case history of a grandiose and omnipotent young man and his battle to overcome Contempt

A handsome young man, aged nineteen, presented to myself over fifteen years ago with a history of ongoing mild somatic symptoms, considered by his physician to be psychological in origin. When asked regards his personal issues, he said he actually wanted to see a psychotherapist, as he realised his symptoms were related to relationships and work problems. He had walked out of numerous jobs when he could not get along with the workers and the managers would not support him. He was an only child, worked in the building industry and lived alone in a large rented house. He had a nephew who sometimes stayed with him, for a couple of months, when out of a job. Neither had steady girlfriends at the time. His history revealed that he was very regularly in conflict with the law for speeding, fearlessly weaving in and out of lanes of traffic and shouting abuse at other drivers. Nevertheless, he was an experienced driver and managed to avoid accidents or even minor dents to either his own or another person's car! What he seemed to enjoy most was convincing the police that the other driver was always at fault. He also often used physical violence at roundabouts with male drivers on motorbikes who abused him. Somehow, fortunately he succeeded almost every time and so never received any significant penalty. We came to a decision at the first interview that it was very necessary that the boundaries of our work be kept intact and not violated by him. Hence, I clarified that I would not give him any medical certificate related to his culpable driving or physical aggression. He was agreeable to take all consequences for his own actions. We established a good working relationship from the start.

Being an analytical oriented psychotherapist, I asked him to remember if he had experienced situations where he had felt he was treated with Contempt. He came up very quickly with the memory that as a very rough boy, probably aged three, his father always forced him to stand on top of a box and read the time from the clock on their wall. Out of sheer fear of making a mistake, he would become anxious and read the time on the clock of their wall wrongly. His father would then become furious and hit him saying "Repeat after me big hand is at…, small hand is at…" This would be repeated numerous times daily. My patient would feel very humiliated and crushed by his father's loud booming command accompanied by the physical abuse. He felt that his father was belittling him, by using the words 'big' and 'small'. He disliked being alluded to as being 'small'. He wished to identify with his tall and strong dad although he was ambivalent in his own feelings about him. There was a clear inequality between both his parents' perceptions of himself. This was highlighted by the fact, that when he was a little child, his mother often used to sing to him a song related to Jesus Christ, like "Away in a manger no crib for a bed. The little Lord Jesus lay down his sweet head". Hence, he had one parent, his father relating to him as a boy of limited intelligence, whilst mother sang songs to him, as if he actually was her 'Little Lord Jesus'. The latter gave him a feeling of Omnipotence.

One day when he was a child, aged four, he woke up to find his mother, who he thought was next door. He climbed over the cot and went onto the main road. He then started walking down Nepean Highway. The Police saw him and as they were on a motorbike, they put him in the passenger sidecar of the bike and asked him where he lived. They brought him safely home. All the neighbours have gathered around him and gave him a cheerful welcome. This made him feel very much like little Lord Jesus in his own way. His mother had a limb deformity, but still used to run after him with a feather duster if he was extremely naughty. At school he was bullied a lot as he had blonde hair. **However, many girls found him very attractive and often asked him for a lock of his wavy hair.** He was a very honest person, never told me a single untruth. Of his own accord he asked me whether he can join a group. **The only vacancy that I had was in First Episode Supportive Expressive Group. He became the 'Star of the Group', to the extent that all the psychotic patients brought their problems for him to solve.** Similar to his mother, some of them worshipped him too.

However, at one stage an older gentleman joined the group. He had a huge bunch of keys on his belt like a prison warden which he kept jiggling around. This was as much as our Group Star could tolerate. He picked up his own bicycle helmet put it on the ground and challenging the newcomer, he said, "Let's go to the park outside. I'll show you who is boss". I immediately stood up myself and said quite clearly, but without any emotion, "If either of you take just one step towards the door you will no longer be part of the group". Aggressive actions are not acceptable in the group. The group had been previously aware of this restriction. Our Group Star then started laughing and said, "Oh doc, we were just teasing!" The whole group started giggling and the attention wore off. He did not try that with any more newcomers. He used to frighten his medical practitioner's secretary a lot if she didn't take him in within five or ten minutes. He would threaten her that he would burn the surgery down. I was well aware to be fair to him and all group members equally without giving any preference to anybody. He accepted that very well. However, he sometimes did bring up a story of having bashed up a cyclist and that a policeman saw him and the cyclist and gave a verdict in favour of our group member. All this was hard to believe, but it was part of his Grandiosity. I was aware never to humiliate him like his father has done. Humiliation causes violence (Gilligan, 2000). He improved rapidly, went abroad and returned after five years. He said his mother was dying and he came to see her.

After her death he wanted to join another group. However, there were no suitable groups available at that time and so I continue to see him individually. He married a suitable girl and had a son. He was in awe of a beautiful present which his son gave him at one of his birthdays. In view of the fact that he had obsessional traits he never opened the present and liked to keep looking at it every day. He and his wife travelled abroad and enjoyed life. The last I heard of him was a card, from Europe, where he was coping well in life.

Envy, Jealousy, Contempt and Arrogance

ENVY

Melanie Klein considers "Envy" to be oral sadistic and anal sadistic with expression of destructive impulses operating from the beginning of life. It may be associated with a 'constitutional basis' according to Klein.

Karl Abraham also considers an oral sadistic nature to be an important component to envy. This is a similarity between his views and that of Freud's on Beyond the Pleasure Principle (1920). Abraham also considered exploring destructive impulses in envy.

In this chapter I would like to verify similarities and difference between envy, jealousy, contempt and greed.

'Envy is the angry feeling that another person possesses when someone else demonstrates having accomplished something desirable.' The impulse being to take it away and spoil it.

In Jealousy, although the other person feels the same as above, there is no destructive element attached to it.

Contempt is when a person often is locking up his true feelings and only has the time perhaps in the next session.

Elements in which the recipient is meant to be scornfully degraded in public. Contempt is not associated with the intense degree of the death drive as compared to envy. In Envy a very good example of the death drive is Shakespeare's Othello who describes envy and mistakenly refers to it as jealousy when he says "Oh beware my Lord of jealousy; it is the green eyed monster which doth mock; the meat it feeds on ….."

Klein sees the feeding breast as the baby's first envied object and considers it to have unlimited flow of milk.

Envy leads to the baby considering that it has the ability of scooping out the contents of the breast and feels very disappointed when it is obvious that the baby cannot control the milk flow of the breast.

This primitive envy is observed in the transference relationship of both individual and group psychotherapy. Envy and the defences against it play an important part in negative therapeutic reactions during the transference as described by Freud. It is further developed by Joan Riviere. This can prevent the building up of a working relationship in the transference. The infant shows this by producing difficulties during his/her feeding.

Excessively anxious mother relates to the child feeling anxious.

Envy spoils the good object and the capacity for enjoyment between the parent child relationship.

Gratitude is evident when the mother is the one and only object in the infant's life. With repeated positive interactions occurring the infant feels totally gratified. Gratitude is closely linked with TRUST and is the basis for trust in one's own goodness.

In both child and adult, the feelings of persecution and dis-integration occur during the child paranoid-schizoid position. Certain infants can have a flight into genitality. (p.195)

Freud's explanation of penis-envy in women and its link with aggressive impulses is a good example of when the female realises that she has to accept not having a penis. This changes her atti-tude to her mother and father. Later in life during adolescence the female/daughter can develop homosexual feelings and can turn away with hate from her mother and father.

If identification with a good and life-giving internalised object can be maintained, this becomes an impetus towards creativity. The spoiling of creativity implied in Milton's 'Paradise Lost' is similar as the child feels that Satan is envious of God.

Goethe said "He is the happiest of men who can make the end of his life agree closely with a happy beginning".

Klein often describes her approach to anxiety as a focal point of her technique. Or working with the focal point of her anxiety. (p.217)

JEALOUSY

A lot of people confuse envy with jealousy.

Even Shakespeare in Othello as stated earlier, describes Iago as saying "Oh, beware, my lord, of jealousy! It is the green-eyed monster which doth mock the meat it feeds on. ..." Shakespeare continues to show how the destructive element of Iago encouraged Othello to murder his ever-loving wife Desdemona followed by Othello's suicide. This reveals the evilness and envy in Iago.

Iago's envy is due to the great achievement of Othello by his military success, as well as marriage to his ever loving, trustworthy wife Desdemona. In addition, he did not feel sufficiently recognised by Othello.

Eventually, Iago suffers the same fate of being condemned to death.

CONTEMPT

Contempt occurs in those who already have feelings of self-contempt and have not worked psychoanalytically to openly overcome them. *Contempt is one of the defence mechanisms already described by Melanie Klein where scorn is directed at a person in public without any compunction.*

'Of Human Bondage' by Somerset Maugham is the best example of self-contempt I have come across. The medical doctor, Philip Carey, was born with a club foot which was not corrected in childhood. His parents had also died during his early childhood. He was sent to a boarding school by his religiously oriented uncle and aunt where he was treated very contemptuously as a result of his disability. His academic achievements were not highlighted which led him to leave school prematurely.

However, by then it was too late and he left for Germany. He returned to follow medical studies and fell in love with a good looking, but arrogant, waitress Mildred who was materialistic and kept following her pleasure principle without considering reality factors. Once more he was not given the respect he deserved. He tolerated all her insults. This included her flirting openly with his friends and trying to force Carey into being the father of her illegitimate child. This was followed by an episode of rage leading Mildred tearing up a treasured hand painting which he loved dearly. It is only after the death following prostitution and illness of Mildred that Philip was able to give her up. His colleagues actually had to physically hold him back from seeing her dead body.

He then gets himself operated on for his clubfoot, which he had from birth, and finally feels confident to marry a very suitable partner.

ARROGANCE

Arrogance, as described by Wilfred Bion in '*Second Thoughts*' (1957), is as follows. He details the appearance of a certain class of patients who also demonstrates Curiosity and Stupidity. Due to the distribution of these scattered symptoms their relatedness often fails detection. Bion consolidates the above by concluding that such a case is indicative of a 'psychological disaster'. He summarises arrogance by considering that in a personality:

- Where 'life instincts predominate, pride becomes self-respect'
- Where 'death instincts predominate, pride becomes arrogance'

He compares the above with the Oedipus myth making the sexual crime a peripheral element whereas in the story it is the arrogance of Oedipus who vows to lay bare the truth at no matter what cost.

Bion points out how the 'scattered references' of curiosity, arrogance and stupidity point the way to disaster that has occurred. Hence an analyst treating a neurotic patient needs to be aware that a psychological catastrophe may be underlying at the outward appearance of curiosity, arrogance and stupidity. This may indicate that by analysis there may be regression in the patient.

Wilfred Bion feels that one may need to accept the acting out and regression as an inevitable part of the process. Splitting, projective identification, and confusional states on related symptoms had been described by Melanie Klein, Hanna Segal and Rosenfeld as part of the analysis of psychotic patients.

In my own experience, if initially the relationship between the analyst and the patient has started in a containing manner and full awareness of the above frigidity of the patient, the result can be that of mutual trust and recovery. The analyst should not expect miracles. The therapy will not be according to boundaries set for most analytically oriented patients. At times when there has been a crisis in the life of the analyst, the true feeling of warmth and understanding by the patient is often verbalised and sympathy in a professional manner is genuinely expressed by the patient. I have described this in cases where very early life crisis in the patient needs to be avoided until the patient is fully ready to deal with whatever material is willingly provided. I am aware of cases where the patient has suffered greatly by the sudden death of the analysand. In my opinion every effort should be made during the inability of the analyst to meet the expectations of the patient in a containing and caring manner. In the alternative, the patient of the dead analyst suffers greatly wondering why he/she was not given any notice of the severity of the analyst's health and impending death.

Features of Hidden Contempt	Symptoms In one's self and others	Results
Occurs openly without shame	Pain and Scorn	Unconscious devaluation of Self and Others
Lack of empathy	Demoralisation Lack of faith in one's self	To understand feelings of personal shame. To recognise negative capability as expressed by J. Keats and be able to work with mystery, ambiguity and doubt.
Consequences	A lack of intimacy	Possibility of improving relationships.

Features encountered in groups

	Symptoms of Noncompliance	Psychosomatic Illnesses Psoriasis, Irritable Bowel etc.
Starting Point Self-Contempt as part of three Manic Defences described by Melanie Klein & Hannah Segal	Needs an analytically oriented background provided by the leaders of the group.	• Can improve with psychoanalytic psychotherapy by understanding of neurotic problems • Unsupervised work leads to delay of both neurotic and psychotic problems • Major Depressive Illness can be uncontainable at times.

141

	Symptoms of Noncompliance	Psychosomatic Illnesses Psoriasis, Irritable Bowel etc.
	Example: Freud's case of the Female Homosexual. As the father's look was very angry towards his female homosexual daughter, Freud needed to explain to the father, the current difficulties his daughter was going through (she was being dismissed by the female she felt attracted to). The daughter improved with features of understanding around her.	CAN BE LETHAL LOOKS CAN KILL

CHAPTER 9:

Transference and Countertransference

A brief introduction to the concept of transference and countertransference Definition

HISTORY

The term 'Transference' was originally founded by Sigmund Freud in his Studies of Hysteria (1893-1895, SE 2). It was described as a false connection, where feelings belonging to one's early life regarding certain very important person/s were deflated later on to a number of others, at an unconscious level. Relationships with an earlier parental figure were disconnected and believed to be now recognized as being linked to someone in the person's current life. Hence feelings and attachments to persons get displaced. The subject continues to believe that the feelings are totally belonging to the present, without the slightest doubt at a conscious level that its origins were from way back in the past.

Moreover, the patient living in the 'here and now' may present as being regressed and confused from time to time. This may be also related to an inability to connect a past traumatic event to a current recurrence of feelings of depression, mourning, anxiety or even psychosomatic symptoms. For such patients, a very patient, well supervised, and at times, a long-term psycho-analytic psycho-therapy is needed. The analyst needs to be aware of the possibility of there being a link from what had remained unresolved in the past, with whatever is occurring in the 'here and now'.

Margaret Little's Transferences with Ella Freeman Sharpe and D. W. Winnicott

I will be starting with Margaret Little's psychoanalysis with Ella Freeman Sharpe. Little starts in 1940 when she found herself emotionally involved with a patient and could not go with untreating him. Freeman Sharpe had a vacancy for her to undergo personal psychoanalysis so that she could understand her transference and countertransference that was going on between herself and the patient.

In the first session she started on the couch, but found herself unable to speak or move. Ella Sharpe encouraged her to sit up and talk. Little felt a total annihilation which was transference psychosis based on her childhood and early infancy. It is very sad to read her interactions with Ella Freeman as the latter seems to be talking almost in different languages. They were both using analytic terms and both felt misunderstood by each other. The ambivalence was very great. Nevertheless, Freeman Sharpe would have seen Margaret Little's potential for the future as a psychoanalyst. She encouraged Little to apply for training. Little's father died in 1945 and she was refused entry at her father's funeral. Obviously, Little had great ambivalence towards her father as well. A further calamity happened after Little retuned from a European Congress. She was given the news of Ella Sharpe's sudden death. Fortunately for her, Winnicott had a vacancy and took her for treatment from 1949 to 1955 and 1957. Little was aged forty-eight at the time.

She was once again terrorised during her first interview. Winnicott interpreted that Little was shutting him out 'for some reason'. There were episodes of violence on Little's part by smashing a large vase. The next day he replaced it. However, he did not reprimand her at all. Little felt guilty and repeatedly mentioned she was aware that she hurt him. She would sometimes get spasms during which Winnicott would hold her head. This holding and facilitating environment had a very helpful and safe feeling for her. He would always try to make very appropriate places of residence where she would be safe during his periods of holidays.

Her younger sister died in 1934 at the age of twenty-eight before her parents arrived in Australia. All these losses to anybody would be massive and extremely difficult to overcome. However, with her analysis with Winnicott she was able to confront her mother some years later. Her mother's reply led to Little stopping outside on wet grass and breaking her ankle. Many people were very kind to her at this stage. She related a lot of material from her childhood to Winnicott who was very helpful to her. He encouraged her to voice her feelings rather than supress them. He also saw her once weekly for eighteen months during which time she improved remarkably. They stopped therapy by mutual consent in 1955. She felt her identity had been recognised. Winnicott was never afraid to react or be spontaneous. He often explained what he was saying. He then supervised her in her treatment of other patients. This was a very valuable experience as he had known her so well as a patient previously.

Even in this day and age I doubt if anyone would be able to replicate the form of therapy that Winnicott gave to Margaret Little. It would be very reassuring for him that she had made excellent use of the work done together and became a well-known psychoanalyst. She clearly points out the differences she had between transference neurosis and transference psychosis.

Harry Guntrip's unsatisfactory analysis by Fairbairn and Winnicott as described by Padel (1996)

The only person who could analyse Guntrip was Guntrip (p. 87).

Guntrip (1975) wrote about his analysis with Fairbairn (1952) and Winnicott (1963). He sought analysis for 'symptoms of unreality and schizoid isolation'. In this day and age, it would have been diagnosed as 'chronic fatigue syndrome'. He also complained of neurasthenia.

He had been told by his mother at the age of three, that he had walked into the room and seen his younger brother Percy lying naked and dead on his mother's lap. He felt devastated and fantasised that his mother had some responsibility regarding Percy's death. Observing Guntrip's reaction she sent Guntrip out of the room. He continued to feel very ill with various serious symptoms. He was thought to be overflowing with grief for his brother. He realised his mother had always been a very cold person, as in her early days she had always needed to look after her own siblings after her mother went to work. Guntrip's mother has always resented this greatly. Having two sons of her own now, she was even loathe to feed them.

Horowitz (2004) reminds us of the sufferings of early traumas, as well as deprivation in the past, in children whose cases were similar to Guntrip's symptoms. These children saw themselves as victims of their mothers' coldness and combined it unconsciously, with a need to punish themselves for free-floating and disowned torment, which they were undergoing.

At the age of eight Guntrip left home and stayed in a more suitable environment. He now began to thrive. Moreover, his mother too became less depressed and angry.

Guntrip, and others similar to him, wondered if their cure was based on reparative re-parenting to overcome their mother's previous coldness. This is what led Guntrip to seek psychoanalysis with Fairbairn and with Winnicott. He had been wondering whether he was punishing himself by thoughts of evading guilt. Sadly, both analysts could not give him a definite answer. Guntrip's symptoms remained static and did not improve permanently. However, it led to Guntrip's inability to form a positive therapeutic transference relationship with both his analysts.

Abraham (1919, p. 85) also writes about narcissistic patients who feel they are better than their analyst.

Interestingly Freud (1913) also believed in totem and taboo. This is described as the dead having a lust for murder.

Transferences

Sigmund Freud (1905) wrote, "Psychoanalysis does not create transferences. It merely brings them to light". This is similar to other hidden factors.

Heinz Kohut's version of Transference (1979) is considered to be in a position where the therapist is idolised, as if he/she was totally an omnipotent being. This transference is termed as an 'idealising and mirroring transference' by Kohutian analysts. This omnipotence resembles the phase in Winnicott's modified diagram, where Omnipotence is the original and main survival function for every infant. (Symington, J., 1968)

Transference and Countertransference are important issues regarding the management of psychotic illnesses and their differentiation from non-psychotic personality disorders. (Bion, 1957, pp. 43-64)

Stages of contact with reality

Bion approaches the subject in a series of stages, the first is recognising 'contact with reality'. This is evident by listening to the patient and observing evidence of 'omnipotent fantasy which is intended to destroy the awareness of reality'. However, the reality is never entirely lost. It's living in a labile state which is neither life nor death. The Ego retains contact with reality, but the patient can be undergoing a psychotic personality disorder (p. 46). The second stage is when it is recognised that the trauma the victim went through was not a mere illusion, but it was an actual fact which had occurred in reality.

During Transference, the psychotic patient splits his objects and becomes aware that the reality he hated can be fragmented and projected onto others, including the one with whom the psychotic patient is conversing. Due to the psychosis the patient realises he now can't restore the fragmented objects and restore his original personality. The example given earlier regarding Margaret Little's analysis, with Ella Freeman Sharpe, is very relevant.

Each split up due to fragmentation, is felt to consist of a real object which is encapsulated in a piece of personality that has engulfed it. Bion gives an example of a gramophone which when being played is felt to be watching the patient and even listening to the patient. Hence it controls the object.

Bion puts forward his final question "How does the thing become conscious?" The answer can be "By coming into connection with verbal images that accompany it". A trustworthy colleague may help to overcome some of the projected identification at times, but this does not always totally overcome the paranoid component in chronic cases.

In fact, it is not only the primitive thought attacked, because it links sensory impressions of reality, but splitting processes are extended to the links within the thought processes themselves.

Marrone, M., (p. 181) describes that both negative and positive transferences are equally central to psychoanalysis.

Countertransference

Heinz Kohut's example is that the narcissistic structure is an attempt to deal with the wound created by an unempathic caretaker. Hence the analyst's role is to work towards being as empathic as possible at all times which is often best discussed in one's personal therapy.

Jacques Lacan does not recognise countertransference, as

emerging only from the analyst, as a reaction to their analysand's responses. Lacan's term is only to consider all responses as 'transference', despite these arising from the analyst or the analysand.

It is acknowledged that non-supervised transferences, and those trainees prematurely ceasing personal therapy, are likely to suffer disadvantages. Countertransference too, similarly needs to have the capacity to be experienced and have close examination with their supervisors.

Transference and Countertransference are the most vital and important issues during therapy of every patient. It relies on one's recognition of issues which arose in one's personal therapy which were repressed earlier. Freud's chapter on Remembering, Repeating and Working Through, as well as Beyond the Pleasure Principle, are vital in understanding the intricacies of psychoanalytic treatments. The book, 'The Freud-Klein Controversies 1941-45' with various scientific controversies, edited by King and Steiner, is invaluable.

The art of music and the art of painting convey very important additional perspective to the verbal discourse between people.

Transference interactions between therapist and patient

Why some female patients do much better with female therapists?

In my second analysis, I benefitted greatly with a female analyst. Why?

She was not theoretical. She followed my trend of thought, by mainly pointing out why I did some particular event. There was never any reproach. It was left open for me to work on it there and then or come back to the same event another time. If the subject was too difficult, while I tried to consider why she thought I had kept on taking an inappropriate course of action, she in her own way, showed extraordinary patience. Sometimes, I would simply fall asleep on the couch. She never disturbed me by waking me up. Throughout that time, I felt totally understood. When I brought back the subject, there was never any reproach.

In turn, when I saw her teenage daughter look jealously at me at a road crossing, I too remained silent and showed my dignity, without bringing ill feelings into her or her mother about me carrying tales. Sometimes I felt jealous of her daughter too, but also pleased that her daughter accepted reality, that many trainees now had time with her mother!

Only once I identified with my analyst, rightly or wrongly. We both had too many books and letters on a table in our respective consulting rooms. Apparently, neither of us needed to put on an air of perfection. I know nothing about her own upbringing, but her honesty in what she said, always provided food for thought.

Patient transference can lead to illusions of mutual consent

This theme is well described by Dr Robert L. Simon in Psychiatric Annals 24 Nov. 1994

Lawyers, judges and the jury often find it difficult to differentiate Romantic Love from Sexual Exploitation. Love in a psychoanalytic situation during a Transference, is different from love between two persons who did not know each other before any therapy starts. Transference Love is less worried about consequences which can result of it being unethical. Simon says it is different from two strangers meeting each other at a supermarket!

Robert discusses whether both parties had the capacity to make such major lifetime decisions, simply by saying, "I Do", in order to get a legal marriage licence, without being under duress. Hence both parties need to be capable of making suitable decisions.

Robert concludes that it is immoral ethically and professionally. Hence it cannot be professionally defended.

CHAPTER 10:

Supervision — The Art of Introducing Reality in a Culture of Containment

Supervision is a journey of three or more participants, filled with emotions, feelings, knowledge and ideas. It needs to accommodate oscillation between knowing and not knowing, periods of discovery and periods of darkness.

The origin of negative capability

This reflects the wisdom of the famous poet John Keats' thoughts regarding Negative Capability which came to Keats' thoughts in 1817. He was walking home after a Christmas pantomime with two friends who disagreed about certain issues.

Keats then realised the importance of being capable of being in uncertainties, mystery and doubt without reaching after irritability and doubt. His friend and poet Samuel Coleridge agreed it was better to break away from relentless search. The importance of Beauty and Truth, along with Independence leading to Freedom became more essential to living a healthier life.

Supervision is one of two essential clinical training experiences in psychotherapy. This applies to both individual and group psychotherapy. The other experience being participating either in personal individual therapy or as a member in an experiential, therapy or training group depending on the reasons for such a choice.

Both supervisor and the supervisee may never have met before. Hence accepting each other's views can be difficult. However, it is a requirement of the experienced supervisor to reduce any tension during the supervision. The most important ingredient is to have trust on both sides. Here John Keats' negative capability using is an important method of being able to appreciate different points of you without coming to harsh conclusions. Contempt is both audible and visible and can be taken with humour rather than seeing it harshly. In my experience of the long-term analytic group (Please see Part III Chapter 2) taken after the original therapist (Dr X) had resigned and it was my very first group with these patients. I had treated some of them in individual therapy earlier in the hospital wards, hence I felt friendly towards all of them. Sadly, they had been without a therapist for over a month. There was an episode of mild contempt towards me which I quickly turned into a joke. The group settled down feeling relieved. I also set all boundaries and gave all of them my contact phone numbers to reach me in case of any further problems.

Differences between Psychotherapy and Supervision

During psychotherapy, the therapist works with conscious and unconscious issues as they unfold in the patient/client. In contrast, although during Supervision, the personal weaknesses or problem areas in the supervisee trainee do become visible in a clearly identifiable manner, the task of supervision does not allow the supervisor to work on them. The reason for staying within the boundaries of Supervision is that otherwise the Supervisor is caught between the two roles, namely:

a) Providing therapy to a trainee supervisee; and

b) Providing Supervision to the trainee supervisee regarding the patient of the trainee.

Providing supervision is also different from giving seminars. In the former, the clinical aspect of the interaction between the supervisee and his/her patient is of main importance. In giving seminars, theoretical issues are explored in greater intensity.

The Frame of Supervision needs to be preserved and respected. This comprises:

- Time of the Session, along with lack of major interruptions through absence;
- Venue which provides privacy; and a
- Means of encouraging Trust and Confidentiality

The above are pre-requisites for creating a 'safe space' in which work can be done. Details follow later.

Issues concerning the supervisor

Relative Neutrality and Anonymity. These in psychoanalytic work need to be similar to treating a patient in analytic psychotherapy or psychoanalysis.

Models in Supervision

By their fruits shall ye know them, states Dorpat in his Forward to R.D. Lang's book 'Doing Supervision and being Supervised'. (1994)

Regardless of the model used, there are certain components which are considered as Essential ingredients of Supervision. These are as follows:

1. Supervision among other components needs expertise in 'Trigger decoding'. This means isolating the precipitating factor or the factor relevant in producing the current problem or area of resistance that has arisen in the narrative of the ongoing work produced by the supervisee of the patient.

2. The supervisor may also need to explore whether or not 'frame violation' has occurred, that is, whether unknowingly some action or inappropriate intervention resulting in boundary violation has been given or transmitted by the supervisee/therapist to his/her patient. At the same time, it is mandatory for the supervisor to explore himself/herself if a parallel error has been made during Supervision.

3. There may also have been an 'absence of validation'.

Nevertheless, all experienced psychotherapists re well aware that regardless of how appropriate an intervention may be, it is not necessary that it will be of any major significant help to the patient/client, due to the multitude of conscious and unconscious resistances that are involved.

Techniques of Psychotherapy and Therapy/Therapist Variables

All therapists are not experienced to practice all types of psychotherapy. Every supervisor may not be able to help every supervisee and most importantly, every client is definitely not suited to being under the care of every therapist.

However, it is the work of the supervisor to help the supervisee to make appropriate choices of the type of psychotherapy for the patient/client.

The theoretical basics, indications and contraindications of the different types of available treatments need to be explained and discussed by the supervisor with the supervisee and by the supervisee with the patient treated. This needs to be followed by arriving at a decision with the supervisee regarding the best possible type of psychotherapy for the patient or group.

Once it is agreed that supervision will take place, details of the framework or structure of supervision are discussed.

It is worth noting that even during these straightforward discussions there are both conscious, as well as silent unconscious, processes operating so as to gage.

The fit between the supervisor and supervisee

Both supervisor and supervisee are assessing each other at the same time that they are discussing supervisory details. Each will wonder about the knowledge, the expertise, the ability for commitment, how seriously the work will be undertaken, the personality of both — especially with regards to any criticisms exchanged, the maturity and tolerance of both etc., as has been outlined earlier.

Both supervisor and supervisee need to be able to be reflective and open in their discussions regarding work. Their thinking needs to be unsaturated and not rigid or fixed. They should not be preoccupied with other matters during the Supervisory time allocated. All this is so that new experiences for the supervisee can unfold and new techniques can be put into practice.

When there is no choice of selection of supervisor or supervisee, both parties need to be aware of their unconscious feelings towards each other, so that this does not prove to be a significant resistance to the supervision.

Other venues where both meet

E.g. seminars, social occasions etc. need to be another important issue of awareness. Neutrality and Anonymity need to be observed as far as possible in all settings for better results.

The Setting — providing a stable structure

As far as possible the setting, i.e. the venue, should be suitable for total privacy where confidential material can be discussed without fear of intrusion. It also needs to be soundproof as far as possible.

The setting should also remain constant as far as possible. The analytic explanation for this is that while certain things in the outside world remain constant, there is greater possibility for internal movement to happen. Otherwise both parties have to constantly spend energy in adapting to new places and different times.

Details of the framework

The following needs to be discussed well in advance and agreement reached, namely:

- Time of the Supervision. How any changes of time will be negotiated?
- How changes in the venue, if necessary, will be negotiated.
- How material is presented.
- How and when notes are written.
- What are the goals or requirements of the supervision?
- The fee structure for sessions and involving absence of the supervisee. (Payments a month or a semester in advance may be appropriate in certain circumstances.)

The frame needs to be consistent and fixed. All planned vacations and procedure for emergency interruptions should be discussed.

The writing up of sequential process notes needs to be done immediately after the therapy session, so as not to be distracted by writing during the session. Notes need to contain the precise words spoken and not the understanding reached by the supervisee.

The supervisor's conclusions need to be gathered only from the material presented.

The timing of the interventions by the supervisor is an art.

Issues of responsibility

A frank discussion about to whom the supervisor has a primary commitment e.g. to the supervisee, the client being supervised or the 3rd party needs to be clear from the start. For example, the hospital in which the patient is being treated.

What is expected from each other? E.g. if either is regularly late in arriving or if either one has to attend to outside telephone calls during the session, e.g. if the supervisee or supervisor is on duty for outside calls at the same time etc. — would apply in a hospital setting.

How vacation and other breaks will be handled e.g. the length of time that notice is given in advance. What responsibilities both take for such absences, e.g. cover arrangement for the supervisor's leave.

How long supervision will last under ideal conditions.

How supervision may have an effect on concurrent personal therapy and how and when to bring these issues to the supervision arena.

Finally:

- What are the limitations of Supervision?
- What are the differences between Therapy and Supervision?
- Ideally how and when supervision will end?
- The procedure of how complaints against the supervisor; and
- Complaints against the supervisee are appropriately reported.

Details regards Boundary Issues

NEED FOR ABSTINENCE

In any analytically orientated psychotherapy, any form of physical contact, except for a handshake at the time of leaving the session is considered inappropriate. Abstinence from all forms of contact, as well as up keeping the anonymity of the supervisor are considered to be helpful.

This is because familiarity or over familiarity or an active friendship with any person in the role of therapist, educator, mentor or supervisor often leads to loss of respect, due to doubt as to the authenticity, dedication or conflicts of interest of the person involved, with regards to the task at hand.

The supervisor also needs to either abstain from using, get

written permission or distort any material presented by the supervisee, so that confidentiality of the patient/client under treatment is maintained.

Painful as it may seem at first, the results of abstinence are invariably well worth the pain.

The Work of Supervision

1. Definitions of Holding and Containment and how it applies to the supervisor/supervisee relationship and the patient or client and therapist relationship.
2. Interventions by the supervisor — When to be listening to sequential process material and how and when to intervene.
3. How Reality is introduced in both the above parallel processes.
   - The task of recognizing individual, group and subgroup themes.
   - To be able to recognize Anti Group development and use it to advantage.
   - To be able to be aware of Transference and Countertransference occurring between the trainee supervisee and his/her client.

The work of holding and containing

This lays the foundation stone of trust. Through holding and containing, fears related to anxiety and depression are reduced. There is no component of judgment during containment. Instead there is 'attunement'. During the process of attunement, the supervisor tunes in, not only to the 'triggers' presented by the patient and the supervisee, but also to the affect which is unfolding in each. Validation of affect is an important aspect of attunement.

During holding and containment, splitting between who is the 'good' one and who is the 'bad' one, of the supervisee/patient dyad, needs to be recognized by the supervisor as a defence mechanism by the supervisee, which can only lead to projection of shame and blame and non-resolution of the conflicts/resistances.

Gross emotional deprivation in either of the three participants, supervisor, supervisee and/or patient usually presents with material soaked in 'repressed fears of abandonment'. This type of presentation is commonly seen in borderline patients where acting out behaviour is the outward symptom, with fears of abandonment being not easily located due to their repressed location. This is also due to the fact that fear of intimacy of the borderline, tricks the novice supervisee, into believing that the patient is independent.

There is an excellent example given by Robert Langs (1994) of a supervisor/supervisee crisis after the supervisor advises the supervisee to increase sessions of a difficult borderline patient. The patient then promptly takes an overdose. I would see this as a result of fear of intimacy between the patient and her therapist (the supervisee). In this case, there was obviously poor trigger decoding by the supervisor, of all the material presented and the lack of acknowledgement of the visible affect conveyed by both the client and the supervisee. In these cases, the patient relies on the therapist worrying about the patient's life and death. This is exactly why a therapist seeks supervision, so that the supervisor helps the supervisee to hold and contain the anxiety, rather than advise action resulting in a premature changing of the frame. In this case the supervisor had also changed the time of the supervisee's sessions as she had a personal job promotion. Hence, we see the parallel change of frames and parallel stresses that all 3 parties were going through.

Timing of Interventions by the Supervisor

As stated before, this is an art. Questions for purposes of clarification, can be asked at any time. The time for substantial intervention ideally is usually after the supervisee has had an opportunity to present his/her account to the extent that the supervisor has a clear conception of what has transpired. Here it is vital that the anxiety or over enthusiasm of the supervisor does not produce premature interventions, which may or may not be accurate. The parallel process consciously and unconsciously occurring between the supervisor and supervisee can transmit a totally wrong model to the supervisee, who then during therapy may well intervene inappropriately or prematurely.

The introduction of reality in the supervision

This is naturally essential in real life. However, it can be the turning point in one's life or one's therapy, depending on how this is done. It is this moment when utmost empathy and sensitivity is essential by the treating team towards the client. However, it is also the same moment when the therapist and supervisor feel most anxious, especially when it affects life and death decisions to be made by the patient, with possible repercussions on the reputation of the supervisor and supervisee. It is also this moment either supervisor/supervisee may also regret having taken the patient on in therapy.

Obviously, at such a time both supervisor and supervisee can be most vulnerable and need each other's trust and goodwill and maybe also the same from the family of the patient.

The Advantages and Disadvantages of Group Supervision with a supervisor or a Peer Group Supervision setting

The expertise, authenticity and trustworthiness of the group members, as well as group cohesion and goodwill are some important factors in ensuring satisfactory group supervision.

Nevertheless, it needs to be kept in mind that group supervision is often insufficient to provide satisfactory supervision, in depth, to each and every group member. Obviously, the same client cannot be followed through during every session and neither can transference and counter-transference issues be explored in detail.

Hence group supervision can be most useful either for experienced therapists or those who for whatever reason cannot have access to weekly personal supervision. In situations where there is ongoing, say monthly group supervision, the supervisor needs to be clear to the third party/employer of the supervisees, that he/she cannot take any responsibility for patient health and safety, as intervals between the supervisions is too long.

Assessment of Supervision

According to the AGPA manual on Supervision (2006), this can fall into the categories of a) Clinical competence as assessed through progress of the patient, b) Emotional difficulties, such as over identification with the patient/client, difficulty in confrontation with reality etc. and finally, c) Ethical concerns and the gravity of this. It is usually the report given by the supervisor that determines whether or not the supervisee is able to practice as a therapist.

Supervision of Co-Therapists conducting Group Therapy

It takes considerable expertise to be a competent supervisor of co-therapists.

A supervisor needs to initially establish what is the natural form of presentation between these two co-therapists. For example, one of the co-therapists may be much more forceful, always wanting to present first, wanting to take longer, wanting to be heard, in other words, one with narcissistic traits and/or with inner feelings of emotional deprivation where he/she has been overlooked in life.

How the other co-therapist deals with this is another issue worth noting. It may be with relief, that the co-therapist does not have to worry about any mistakes made etc. It may be with envy or it may be with great generosity. On the other hand, it may be with suppressed or repressed rage.

Here, in addition to the routine supervision, the supervisor also needs to make overt the difficulties experienced by the co-therapists, as well as strengths between them.

Issues of attraction between the co-therapists and the effect it has on the group members. I have come across group members who regress markedly when there is subtle flirting between the co-therapists. The members may be enraged too, that the co-therapists have a conflict of interest, but in the absence of inner strength to verbalize this, they regress.

On the other hand, we also see very successful co-therapist teams and even husband and wife co-therapy teams. Good supervision, especially during the early years, as well as authenticity, as well as the ability to voice openly any dissatisfactions are key ingredients.

What Transpires during Supervision

Firstly, it is the greeting between the supervisor and supervisee. It may become apparent from the start as to whether or not and to what extent the greeting is friendly, apprehensive, has a worried air, has hostility, hidden or open, feels competitive etc. It is now up to the supervisor with his/her greater experience to see how this needs to be addressed. A containing reply to an obviously worried or preoccupied supervisee can be "How are you today? Do sit down and relax". This may imply, without it being said, "I am in tune with how you are feeling and I think I can be of help".

I usually have a cup of tea or coffee or a glass of water ready nearby for the supervisee, according to whatever the choice may be and start in a relaxed and reflective way. The supervisee would be free to have it or not. It would be a mark of respect, given by myself that the supervisee is in the same occupation as myself.

I am fully aware that a lot of analytically orientated supervisors may frown on this ritual. I realize this welcome is totally different from that given to a client in therapy. In the case of a client, I would simply smile and say "Good Morning" (or whatever is appropriate for the time of day) and let the session unfold. There would be no ready access to tea, coffee or even water. However, water always needs to be provided on request.

Role of the Supervisee as Facilitator of the Group

Resistances regards being a member of a Group (adapted from AGPA manual):

1. 'A key concern for new members of any group revolves around what to expect from the group leader (or group facilitator in Foulksian terms). Many people have never been in group or individual psychotherapy before and share common myths, fears and misconceptions that surround group therapy. One critical point in this regard is in the area of what role the group leader will assume. Will the leader be an ally or an adversary? Will the leader protect me if I come under attack?'

2. Will the group leader or group members put pressure on me to stop medication?

3. Contact out of group hours. There is considerable diversity about this issue. When I conduct analytically orientated groups, I make it crystal clear that I strongly discourage meetings or any contact with each other outside the group room. In case of chance meetings, I encourage members to bring the details of the meeting into the next group, I

do so myself, if I happen to notice a group member in any presentation of mine.

I point out that if we had groups as split off entities from the therapy group, we are going to have a fragmented experience of what it is like to be a group member.

Moreover, if a member say felt suicidal and rang another group member due to being shy to speak with myself, then the suicidal member may well (due to transference feelings towards myself) be expecting the other group member to have similar experience and expertise as myself so as to be able to prevent suicide. This is not the duty of any group member.

Also, aggressive or romantic attachments can result between group members, which can feel too difficult to overcome.

Reporting of sessions by the Supervisee

The supervisees reporting needs to be as outlined in the initial descriptions.

I always advise my supervisees to present from verbatim material as far as possible and to write all notes immediately after the session.

This gives a clear overview of how the exchanges in dialogue are occurring, how much time the supervisee is taking to get to the point, the anxieties of both supervisee and patient and how transference and counter-transference interactions are taking place. The disadvantage is that the supervisee can become ritualized into every minute detail which becomes time consuming, so that not enough time may be left for obviously major interactions.

In cases where supervisors encourage supervisees to be self-selecting as to what part of the material is chosen for supervision, it is possible that a supervisee may select areas in which she/he thinks great progress was made. The supervisee may also omit certain areas of dialogue which were felt to have been a mistake.

Taking a History
Details of this will be in Appendix A.

Arriving at a Diagnosis
Certain hospitals where group therapy is being done may well insist that there be a Psychodynamic Formulation as well as a DSM diagnosis. This helps considerably in providing a clear framework in which work can proceed.

Ensuring a Safe Space for Group Therapy
The AGPA manual on Supervision highlights issues related to the creation of emotional and physical safety within the group, as described below.

A 'sine qua non' in all therapy groups is the assurance of the emotional and physical safety of the participants. This includes group leaders as well as group members.

Supervisors must review the contingency plans for managing potentially dangerous situation within the group sessions, as well as fall out from group meetings that may occur between meetings.

Specific foci in supervision include scapegoating of a group member, verbal threats to anyone in the group, suicidal potential of group members and behaviour that threatens the viability of the group (i.e. Substance abusing members who come to sessions under the influence of drugs and/or alcohol).

Ensure that the group is sensitive to gender, cultural and religious issues.

Some of the more commonly encountered differences among members include gender, ethnic, cultural and religious factors. Supervision should include an appreciation of how best to utilize these issues in a respectful manner that is also maximally conducive to the attainment of the individual and group goals.

"If someone other than the group leader is prescribing

psychotropic medication for a group member, the leader has to be knowledgeable about the drug regimen."

I believe that those who have a prejudice towards a group member taking psychotropic medication should not pass this onto the patient/client, as they may well endanger the life of the patient/client by doing so.

Patient safety issues — High on the list of supervisory priorities is the supervisor's awareness of the risk of potential self-harm or harm to others presented by group members. In the case of self-harm, groups that include depressed patients dictate that supervisor and supervisee assess suicide risk and the need for medication and/or hospitalisation. This is done initially and is reviewed throughout the course of group treatment.

One popular tool for assessing suicidal potential is the use of a structured factor analysis. Less formal methods may also be employed to evaluate the depth of depression, but regardless of the method employed, the supervisor is charged with the responsibility for ensuring that adequate steps have been taken to diagnose and treat any potentially life-threatening circumstances emerging from group members.

Similarly, since group therapy, by definition, involves more than a one-to-one therapeutic relationship, supervision has to include the potential for harm, emanating from multiple member-to-member levels of the group. Verbal attacks, threats from one member to another or any other potentially injurious behaviour have to have the highest priority in group supervision.

PART IV
GAZE AND PERCEPTION

CHAPTER 1:

The Gaze

Sabar Rustomjee — looking into the future…
what will the future be?

In our relation to figures of representation, something slips, passes, is transmitted from stage to stage and is always alluded to, is what we call the GAZE.

The notion of Gaze is illusive. It slips forever from our grasp, similar to *Desire. i.e. the object a or petit à (Lacan, J., 1973, pp. 91-104).*

The Gaze is distinguished from the conscious act of Looking. It is marked with the deceptiveness of *mésconnaissance*. The Gaze surrounds us on all sides even before we are born. It is always connected to the look. (Lacan, 1979, pp. 67-104)

Freud refers to Gaze as the difference between perception and consciousness. It is also the site of repetition.

Some would term it as part of Object Relations and elaborate it through Desire and its interpretation (1958-1959). It also contributes to Transference (1960-1961) which can include extreme Anxiety (1962-1963) on the part of the recipient. The Gaze is about other people. The Gaze integrates the domain of vision into the field of desire.

The voyeur is in command of his own subjectivity, but is caught out in the act of looking. It is reduced to shame as a subject carrying out the function of his own desire. The function carried out is his own desire.

Lacan refers to Anamorphosis, so as to be only recognisable when looked at from a certain angle. An example is the picture of the skull at the base of the portrait of the ambassadors. It needs to be held at a particular angle for it to be recognised.

Vision

The vision is itself illusory. It is totally dependent on light (Lacan, J., 1978, *The Line and The Light*, p. 94).

The screen is the mediation between the Gaze and the picture. It is the locus of the stain which is the focal point of desire.

Lacan refers to the Gaze as coming from outside. What we

notice is that it is not only a two sided photograph, we see it from all sides and angles by moving around the picture. An example is the virgin and the child by Leonardo da Vinci where we see numerous angles of the same picture.

It makes the subject a picture in the Gaze of the other. "I am looked at — that is to say I am a picture… and I am photographed." (Lacan, 1978, p. 106)

Envy

It is the sort of envy that is aroused by *witnessing another person satisfaction, even if it is no longer desired by the envious eye, e.g. an older sibling looking at his mother feeding a new baby.*

Lacan takes pleasure in pointing out battle scenes. Gaze is always behind the picture. The Gaze of the other is the spectacle that draws the crowd.

S.H. Foulkes's Curtains

S. H. Foulkes and his wife Elizabeth went shopping to buy curtains for his rooms one day. They chose a beautiful curtain which had specks of red, black and white on a background of ochre.

At the following session a group member was aghast. The curtain at close quarters, demonstrated "Persian soldiers in their turbans and tunics capturing, tying up, striking and beheading their captive prisoners". (p. 91)

"Yet, at first glance the overall impression of the curtains is a pleasing one of colour and harmony." (Nitsun, 1996, p. 22)

The curtains were later used for training purposes at Daleham Gardens NW3, where they hang in the front group room for business and training purposes.

What lies hidden is the truth. 'Negative Capability' brings awareness to ambiguity and mystery. (John Keats. 1988.)

CHAPTER 2:

Paintings Awaken the Soul

The Ambassadors (1533) by Hans Holbein the Younger

In this painting we see two extremely wealthy, educated and powerful young men. Jean de Dinteville on the left was the French Ambassador to England in 1533, was aged twenty-nine when the portrait was painted. On the right is Georges de Selve, an imminent scholar who had recently become a Bishop, aged twenty-five and later became French Ambassador to Venice at which time it was ruled by Spain. Between the two Frenchmen stands a table that has an upper and lower shelf.

Objects on the upper shelf represent the study of the heavens. Objects on the lower shelf represent educated pursuits on Earth. At the left end of the upper shelf is a celestial globe, a map of the sky in a frame used to calculate astronomical measures. Next to it is a portable brass sundial. Next to it is a quadrant for navigating the position of a ship by measuring the apparent position of fixed stars. Next to it there are other astronomical instruments for measuring the position of heavenly bodies.

In the top left corner, almost unnoticed, is a silver crucifix. It represents the goal of salvation (not forgotten amidst advanced scientific knowledge).

On the lower shelf at the left is a book published in 1527 which is a guide to arithmetic for merchants. Behind it is a globe representing geographical knowledge. Next to it is a square emerging from the book which probably represents the skill of map making.

The lute, the chief courtly instrument at the time, stands for Earthly love of Music. One string can be seen to be broken representing the sudden breakage of death. Beneath the lute next to a pair of compasses is a copy of a Lutheran hymn book. There are flutes beside them which were popular instruments for all levels of society.

Holbein has placed across the foreground, a reminder of human mortality. When this is viewed from a certain angle it is a human skull which has been distorted by stretching it sideways in an anamorphic projection.

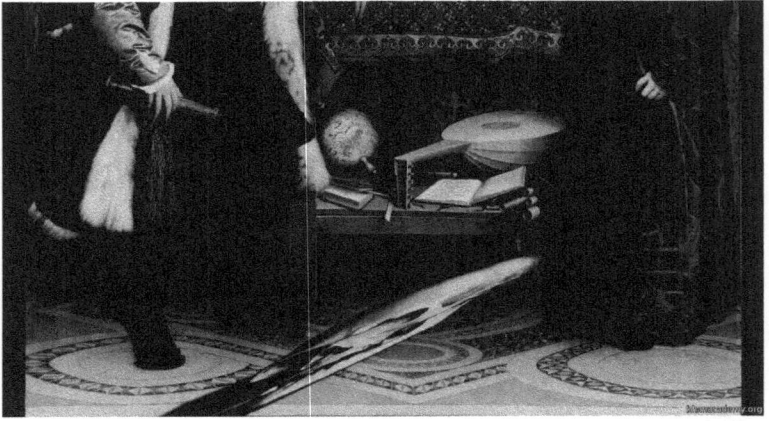

Anamorphosis reveals the skull when held at a particular angle to the line of light

CHAPTER 3:

Gaze is born from Desire (Objet petit à)

Leonardo da Vinci and his three famous paintings of women

LEONARDO DA VINCI

Leonardo came from an insignificant background and rose to universal acclaim.

Leonardo da Vinci was multi-talented himself. He was an illegitimate son of a lawyer, who gave him every encouragement to further his talents. It is said that he had a magnificent singing voice, great physique, excellent at mathematics and with a scientific mind. Nevertheless, often, he did not complete all his paintings.

Ginevra de' Benci (1474) by Leonardo da Vinci

Ginevra de' Benci with an element of self-contempt, withheld identity with half closed eyes gazing over her shoulder.

Ginevra de' Benci was painted by Leonardo da Vinci (1474-1478). She has been considered one of three most beautiful women painted by Leonardo da Vinci; the other two being Mona Lisa (1503) and Cecilia Gallerani (1489-1490).

Ginevra's name is related to the Italian word 'Ginepro' meaning Juniper. His painting of her is truly beautiful, set in a background of shiny juniper leaves, and landscape of distant trees in between hills and valleys.

Her face and neck reveal her pale pink, delicate smooth skin. He describes her as having a 'proud and perfect head'. She appears to 'withhold her identity', along with concealing her innermost thoughts. She lures the viewer's gaze. There is a slight downcast look in her left eye which accentuates a lack of focus. Her gaze is directed over the viewer's shoulder. Her heavy half-closed eye lids cast a shadow.

Leonardo has made an inscription for Ginevra, which reads, *"She adorns her beauty with virtue."*

Cecilia Gallerani: The Lady with an Ermine (1489) by Leonardo da Vinci

Carrying an Ermine with Dignity

Leonardo's third greatest portrait is that of Cecilia Gallerani, whose portrait reveals a gentle and dignified female, who is holding an ermine in her hand very lovingly. Both Ginevra and Cecilia have been recognised as talented women in their own right.

Mona Lisa (1503-1506) by Leonardo da Vinci

Mona Lisa's beauty and fame has spread throughout the world of art. Her painting in the Louvre is surrounded continuously by silent admirers, following her capacity to keep her viewers within sight at all times.

The gaze from her eyes allows each viewer to perceive it as if it is directed solely to him or her is object petit a.

Mona Lisa (1503) has been reproduced in every conceivable

medium. Nevertheless, it remains intact in its magic. It is a work that we can only gaze at in silence. Mona Lisa is stationary in the painting similar to the sun. We people from the earth walk around her from different angles to appreciate her beauty.

Edvard Munch
The contemptuous face/Edvard Munch — Self Portrait

Puberty — long black hair reminds
Munch of his mother and her death

The Scream, Edvard Munch (1893)

CHAPTER 4:

Perceptions Portrayed by Master Painters

The life of Edvard Munch

Edvard Munch was born in 1863 in Adalsbruk, Norway, and was christened at the age of two. His father Christian Munch was a qualified doctor in the military garrison. He had a keen interest in practising their religion, as well as studying literature and history.

Edvard had four younger siblings. After his mother's death, his aunt Karen looked after their house. Karen taught Edvard and his siblings how to cut silhouettes out of paper and also how to draw. Their work was taken very seriously and preserved. Munch has remembered every single drawing even as an adult! Edvard worked systematically drawing items from around the house.

The early death of Edvard's mother

Their mother Laura constantly grew weaker with tuberculosis. She was not even expected to survive her last childbirth. She wrote a farewell letter to her family addressed to their eldest daughter Sophie. The letter was often read aloud with the family and became a guide for their father in bringing up his children. It felt as if their mother was with them all the time, both in life and in death. Mother expressed hope in her letter. "We all who God has so carefully bound together may meet in heaven never to part again."

Edvard describes his life quoting the following: "When I cast off on the voyage of my life, I felt like a ship made from old rotten material, sent out into a stormy sea by its maker" with the words "If you are wrecked it is your own fault and then you will be burnt in the eternal fires of Hell".

Munch then painted the picture of the Endless Scream. His courage, creativity and talent in staying alive and to keep on painting is admirable. I agree with Marit Lande (1998) of the Munch Museum in Oslo, that Munch was affected intensively between the two opposing social and religious forces from birth onwards. These were the priests and the seafaring folk in Norway. Both his parents would sit with the family each evening and solemnly read the Bible. The Norwegian fishermen also regularly battled with the stormy weather to make a daily living for their existence. Although Munch's father was a medical doctor, he could not help Edvard, as tuberculosis was incurable and rampant at the time. The majority of Munch's family died from it, starting with his mother in 1868 and followed by his beloved sister Sophie nine years later in 1877.

Edvard Munch got engaged in 1899 to his fiancé, Tulla Larsen, aged thirty. Sadly, the relationship broke up and both were traumatised by this. She was the daughter of one of the city's largest wine merchants. It appears that Munch still had great difficulty in overcoming the mourning of his mother. He blamed himself often for it. Munch felt as if it was like an unspeakable 'Nameless Dread' (Stephen, K. 1941 & W. Bion, 1962).

It is no wonder his paintings of '*The Sick Child*' of his sister, Sophie (1885-1886) and his world famous masterpiece '*The Scream*' in 1893 depicts his extreme anxiety and fear of a horrible death. These paintings are part of his finest collection known as '*The Frieze of Life, A Poem of Life, Love and Death*', which includes numerous aspects of human existence.

Edvard Munch's painting of the Scream demonstrates Munch's inner dread. His concurrent creativity can be admired from his great collection of work which depicts his love as well as his suffering. The various stages of his life come alive in his works.

From my own experience, when treating a teenage patient who had grown up in Norway, she said that her mother would threaten to send her to live with rough fishermen, if she was naughty. It was implied that the weather being icy there and her being without anyone to help, there was every possibility she would die too. Death was considered as an ultimate punishment even for any misdemeanour. The only way Munch expressed his fear of the intensity of being unforgivably punished during life, was through the vivid expression of his art. His painting 'An Evening on Karl Johan' depicts himself as a shadowy outline of the back of a man, walking away from a crowd of bourgeois well-dressed people wearing coats and top hats. Moreover, the crowd all have rounded spectral eyes and a fearful look. The painting is also cropped at their waist. Munch looked down on the bourgeois. There was moreover a vague rumour that Munch was having an affair with a married lady in an apartment on that street and did not want to be recognised by anyone in the crowd. In analytical terms, if this rumour is correct, he had unconsciously projected his own fears regarding his affair being discovered onto the round fearful eyes of the cropped crowd of Karl Johan, who appear very anxious.

Munch's painting of the 'Sick Child' (his sister Sophie) had also unfortunately brought up enormous anger by his critics. Apparently, they felt that the subject of the painting drew its power, as emerging from the luminous large pillow on which the sick girl was resting her head. It reminded his critics of his dying sister having a halo around her. He painted numerous versions of his dying sister, some of which were claimed by him to be 'a study' and hence incomplete. His first version was in 1885-1886. Eventually, the painting of 'The Sick Child' was appreciated.

In 1892 he was treated very contemptuously with his show

at Oslo being closed after a week! In the rudest possible terms, his critics attacked Munch describing the shape of the sick girl's left hand as appearing ugly and deformed. "It seems to myself a disgrace, to repeat the exact words used, especially as the painting appears obviously incomplete even at that time" (my words). We can only imagine the demoralising effect the critics had on Munch! His previous shows in Oslo had honoured him by giving him second and third scholarships in 1890 and 1891 which helped him to persist with his art.

This painting of his sick sister Sophie was displayed at the Tate Gallery via Oslo in 1939. Surprisingly it provoked a violent and angry response from the viewers. A magazine wrote ironically in 1886, "Surely that can't be a hand. Can it? It looks like a stew in lobster sauce!" Munch suffered greatly from this unnecessary criticism and spent two months in hospital. He gradually recovered and sold a large number of paintings. He began with murals for the Great Hall of Oslo University. In 1944, Munch died peacefully at Ekely leaving his estate to the city of Oslo which opened the Munch Museum in 1963 to mark the centenary of his birth.

The masterpiece of his work was first recognised from 1893 when he presented The Scream. His next masterpiece was Puberty in 1894. Here he draws an innocent young girl with dark black hair covering a considerable part of her face. The clearest painting of his own Self-Portrait is with Burning Cigarette (1895) which hangs in the National Gallery in Oslo. Another masterpiece was Madonna, which was painted in the year 1894-1895. Munch considered it as one of his best renditions.

Munch's feelings about Adolescence, while describing Puberty, describes what he sees and what he feels. He says "I am frightened of my own shadow; my own ghostly face. I lead my life in the smallest of details in my memory return to me". Puberty is that difficult phase of transition from childhood to adulthood. In the painting of 'Puberty' he says "We perceive sexuality and a sense of being at the mercy of the unknown".

Munch's other masterpieces are far too many to comment. The most relevant ones related to the topic of this book are the ones depicting the depth of his Contempt (Munch, 1926); Self Portrait with Palette (Munch, p. 313). No literary work by itself could possibly describe the depth of his feelings on these vital issues. His own autobiography, combined with his paintings, in my opinion, give a very impressive multi-dimensional outcome.

PART V
THE STUDY OF CRIME

CHAPTER 1:

Martin Bryant, Port Arthur, Tasmania and Anders Behring Breivik, Utøya, Norway

Martin Bryant

A glimpse of Martin's omnipotence while (probably) watching the cameraman

Bryant's Life and Consequences of living with a low IQ

On 28th April 1996 Martin Bryant, aged twenty-eight, was imprisoned for having committed a massacre. He was the eldest of three children, having two younger sisters. A coloured photo of him when the first sister was born shows him having large light blue eyes, taking the attention of his father and the photographer, with the baby ignored totally by him. This demonstrates his Omnipotence as well as sibling rivalry.

There are many theories of why the massacre occurred.

As a boy at junior school he could not read or write. He was assessed as having an IQ of sixty-six. It was difficult for him to cope, as a large majority about eighty percent in his class coped well educationally as well as with regards to forming relationships. If the boys teased him, he would cry. Nevertheless, he would hide and then pounce on them to frighten them. Everyone saw him as not being age-appropriate. He always said "All I want is for people to like me". Sadly, he received no ongoing psychotherapy and did not learn social skills.

However, his behaviour drove other people away from him. This, in my opinion, was the appropriate time he desperately needed treatment by a child psychotherapist. In addition, there needed to be a different family therapist for the parents, to help them to hold and contain the family, including his two younger siblings. In addition, there needed to be joint sessions, conducted by both therapists for Martin and his whole family. His father may not have suicided had he be given sufficient support from psychoanalytically trained workers. Sadly, this avenue was not offered to the Bryant family. Obviously, the above technique was not practised by those who diagnosed his IQ to be sixty-six and were aware of the hidden despair his family and Martin were going through. Maybe everyone put out a brave front, to the world outside. Apparently, Martin's father presented him with an air rifle on his fourteenth birthday. Martin used it to frighten away birds mostly, but also shot a parrot. He then walked around the parrot and shot him a number of times to be sure the bird had died.

When he was a teenager, he was taken to be seen by Dr Cunningham Dax, a highly reputed Australian psychiatrist to determine if he qualified for a disability pension. It was affirmed that he was able to apply for one. He did not complete his schooling. Dr Dax wondered if he was schizophrenic, but that was never considered seriously as being a likely diagnosis. He praised

Martin's parents and said that without their support, life would be difficult for Martin to survive.

His father found him a job as a gardener for a middle-aged single female, who was a millionaire and heiress to the largest lottery company in Australia. They suited each other and started living together, although there is supposed to have been no sexual interactions. She was very close to him and he also often said that she had been his only friend.

They would go shopping very often. One day, while she was driving her car an accident occurred. Martin said that as they had taken three dogs with them in the back seat and he was trying to stop them from becoming too distracting. Sadly, the heiress, Helen, died as another car hit hers. Martin's neck was badly injured, and needed medical care. This was a huge blow to Martin. He always said she was his best friend. Whether or not he mourned for her adequately, is not known.

He then went back to his family home. His father cleaned up the two-storey house, which was in a total mess, with about forty animals. Helen's aged mother is said at times to be propped up and tied to a chair when Helen and Martin were not with her. After Helen's death, Martin's father helped greatly, by filling up about twenty skips to throw away the rubbish that had been collected. Helen had already made a will giving Martin Bryant all her assets.

Martin's attachment apparently remained at a pre-sexual level with Helen. After she died, however he did make friendships with certain girlfriends from time to time.

Martin's already shattered life, suddenly took another tragic turn for the worse. Nobody noticed that Martin's father appeared suicidal. However, he committed suicide and his body had been found in a shallow dam under water. He had written a suicide note to everyone except Martin. We do not know how Martin reacted to this. His father had always been there, throughout his life, to help him out of all his external troubles.

It is said that on the 28th April 1996, Martin Bryant and a girl spent some time together, after which he told the girl he had work to do. After she left, he prepared himself for a journey. He bought a new, long bag with a zip which could fit three semi-automatic guns. Apparently, he then drove to Port Arthur. His mother, however, now claims that Martin has no recollections of driving to Port Arthur. (It needs to be noted that often those who commit serious murderous activities repress these in their conscious thinking.)

The rest is the most gruesome massacre in recent Australian History. In a certain family the mother and her two children were killed, although the mother begged him not to kill the children. Within ninety seconds twenty people were killed and twelve severely injured. This went on and on ruthlessly. Many people even now state that they cannot forgive him for killing innocent children.

He contemptuously referred to foreigners and Protestants as WASPS. He looked down on them. He ruthlessly killed thirty-five lives; twenty persons suffered attempted murder and three grievous injuries. He was sentenced to thirty-five life terms resulting in twenty-one year's imprisonment.

During the time the massacre happened, the contempt with which he spoke to the police was incredible. In the local newspapers he is supposed to have said something like — "Well, it is only work for you. You will go home to a nice hot meal. Look at me", showing them his manacles and expecting sympathy.

Controversies regards the aetiology are now current. Certain sources say the government had indirectly benefitted by restricting semi-automatic guns. It was also an eye opener as to how dangerous it was to sell guns without proper verification of identity. Martin had apparently bought guns without any trouble.

Estella Weldon always reminds us of fitting the punishment to the crime. Supposing Martin was an unusual case of Asperger's or an undiagnosed form of brain deformity, does Martin's sentence fit the crime? Having a medical and psychiatric background, nowadays one would have sent him for different tests with paediatric specialists initially who may have done intensive investigations including MRI, PET and SPECT neuroreceptor, synaptic concentration in the living human brain. (Reference: Catherina Mela has given papers at Research Conferences in Athens.) Parents also needed ongoing support. Everything revolves around society. As Hanna Segal writes "Silence is the Real Crime". Martin Bryant's mother is now openly wanting his case re-opened which she feels would be a satisfying step for her and Martin, regardless of the result. When he was first questioned, he had said "Not Guilty". It is said that later he was encouraged to change his mind and he gave the statement of being Guilty.

One cannot guess the future, although certain persons living locally also believe Martin is not guilty.

There are cases where analysis is done for treatment with suitable mentally-handicapped youths. A good example is by Joan Symington in the article *"The Analysis of a Mentally Handicapped Youth"* (The International Review of Psycho-Analysis, Psychoanalysis of Children, Vol. 15, 1988, Part 2, p. 243-250, Pub: Bailliere Tindail for The Institute of Psycho-Analysis London).

In addition, Hanna Segal's article *'Silence is the Real Crime'* (1987) would be useful for parents, especially those who feel that the public will feel contemptuous towards them if all details were openly discussed. Research oriented clinicians also could help with isolation of the aetiology, such as exploring neurological origin.

Breivik's single-handed massacre of seventy-seven innocent victims

Brief references from Aage Borchgrevink (Translated by Guy Puzey)

The life of Anders Behring Breivik appears to have been dedicated to The Norwegian Massacre in order to prove the fact that he wanted to save Norway and certain other countries from being taken over and annihilated by aggressive Muslims who were the followers of Osama bin Laden.

The consequence of unacceptable, life-long humiliation towards himself by others and the absence of constructive boundaries to help the victims to escape safely from Utøya, were important predisposing and precipitating factors that provoked Anders Behring Breivik into committing this atrocious crime.

A bomb exploded in the city of Oslo, Norway, at 3.15 pm on the 22nd July 2011. There was fire on both sides of the street in Norway and a smell of sulphur, like rotten eggs when the bomb exploded.

Sometime later, the scene then moved to Utøya, which hosts a very relaxing yearly event enjoyed by numerous holiday makers.

A young single white man, Anders Behring Breivik, dressed in a police uniform, suddenly started shooting seventy-seven people at Utøya in Norway and injuring a further hundred. Breivik was considered to be criminally sane and sentenced to preventive detention for twenty-one years.

For many years Anders Behring Breivik used to frequent a place known as the 'Palace Grill' situated in the West End of Oslo. In early 2012 he walked across to a refined TV star and introduced himself to him. It felt uncomfortable for both. There was something strange about Breivik. He is described having a kind of flat, stiff and expressionless face, except for an 'artificial smile'. It is important to note that Martin Bryant, from Tasmania, who was also imprisoned for murder had a similar artificial smile. Brevik's eyes stared and he blinked a lot. He appeared to be sedated. He managed to tell the TV star at a well-known hotel in Norway, that in one year's time he would be three times as famous as him. Breivik then started lecturing about Muslims and immigration policies, as well as crusades of the Knights Templar. The TV star signalled the bouncer and Breivik was pushed out of the door. This was a common occurrence among those who frequented the Palace Grill. Nobody took much notice.

Earlier, on the 20th October 2010, Breivik had come to the bar alone, treated a woman to a beer and started talking with her. He explained that Knights Templar were what his book was about. He said he was inspired by Literature. "My book is going to be big" he said, "It's a masterpiece." (Crusaders had not been a common topic of conversation in Norway in the last 900 years.) Nevertheless, Breivik considered himself as a crusader.

He was obsessed with his desire of being seen and remembered, but had no gifts or talents. He would describe how a twenty-two year old monk from Kyoto's Temple of the Golden Pavilion had burnt down the Temple and admitted to the crime. He too, like Breivik, had boasted to a prostitute that he might be in the newspapers soon. He was seen as a stubborn recluse. He was sent to prison in a psychiatric facility where he died a few years later. He considered himself to be the sovereign of the inner world. Fire was a way of freeing him from earthly beauty by destroying it. The burning of the temple was to overcome feelings of powerlessness which had ended in self-contempt. Breivik identified with the monk who said he would punish his teachers and schoolmates who tormented him regularly. Breivik also said that celebrities become famous by killing another celebrity, for example Mark David Chapman after killing John Lennon in 1980.

Ted Kaczynski, 'the Unabomber' motivated by revenge had

sent bombs to other academics by mail. He saw himself as some-one special and more important than others, which suggested a narcissistic personality.

Anders Behring Breivik's childhood is described as *belonging to a fatherless civilisation*. His father, Jens Breivik, divorced his wife, Wenche, when he was about one year old. His father, Jen, then married Tove in 1983, after having met her twenty years earlier in London. When Breivik was four years old, Jens Breivik heard that his son, Anders Behring Breivik, was unhappy and he went to court to obtain custody. Unfortunately, this failed. However, Anders was given permission to visit his father and stepmother. One day Tove decided to take Breivik to the beach, as he seemed to be looking sad. She asked him how he was. He then smiled and said "You're really nice Tove". He would follow his step-mother Tove, rather than his father Jens.

Anders Behring Breivik was very sensitive as a boy and cried even if they drove over a mouse! He was sweet and well-man-nered when there were guests. He looked up to his father, but stuck close to his stepmother. His father, Jens Breivik, was trained in business and economics. Wenche saw her ex-husband as a mon-ster, her devil incarnate. He too thought his wife was mad and impossible to talk with. Child Welfare dropped the case. The boy remained a battlefield between them. Jens saw little of his son over the next few years, even when in Oslo, but tried to sup-port his ex-wife financially. His mother took sides with his big sister and *often attacked Anders too*, as he was an extension of the despised Jens, his father. It falls to reason that Breivik missed his father greatly as he was often unavailable. Unfortunately, Tove and Jens divorced soon after, but Tove continued to see Breivik.

One night when Tove and Anders Behring Breivik were together, Breivik heard some noises under his bed and discovered that a stray cat had had a litter of kittens there. He begged Tove to keep just one of the little kittens. Tove refused as it would be too much for her. Breivik was very disappointed. Tove then hired a mo-ped for him, but asked him to use it only with her permission. He disobeyed her and she became cross. She realised that she had been too strict and asked for his forgiveness. They parted on good terms with Breivik buying Tove a gift of a picture of the nude Greek goddess Aphrodite. However, even at the time of parting he remembered the kitten which he thought he could have taken with him. My own views are that a pet could possibly have been a great idea. It may have been a turning point in his life, similar to the Birdman of Alcatraz who was a genius and wrote books on canaries after he nursed a tiny fallen baby sparrow.

Anders Behring Breivik lacked empathy, as well as imagination and spontaneity with joy and pleasure. A psychologist felt he had alexithymia. He was described as a divergent child, with attachment disorders. Peter Fonagy (1996) links empathy to attachment. He believes self-image develops through attachment. Fonagy calls this ability 'mentalisation'. When the mother is observed as a separate identity, the child tries to anticipate what the mother thinks and feels. The *child mentalises*. However poor mentalisation ability can lead to misunderstanding social situations.

It was decided that Anders Behring Breivik's diagnosis had many contradictions. It was decided that he was not autistic. It was his mother who could not predict boundaries and limits for her son. The children were often left home alone. There is a possibility that separation/individuation from mother had not occurred satisfactorily. Rage, remorse and unstable, non-predictive behaviour in children can encourage aggressive or violent parental behaviour. This may sound like Don Quixote charging at what he thought was a giant and was grounded by the sails of a windmill. A mental health worker described Breivik as being narcissistic 'floating over waters like an inflated Zeppelin and lying on the ground like the smoking wreckage of the Hindenberg, during the war'.

At another incident at the 'Palace Grill' in Norway, Breivik shouted to a woman "I'm going to kill you!" She had been dancing around him in the dark courtyard waving her shawl and her dress. All this was typical of Oslo social life. He usually clung to famous men, but it was women he threatened to kill, calling them traitors and whores. It was a matter of him finding his own niche. He described the 9/11 attack of Osama bin Laden and Mohammed Atta being broadcast around the world. It was then that Breivik thought Europeans and Americans alike suddenly saw Islam in a new light.

Anders Behring Breivik's mother felt provoked by him. The sister did not present the same kind of challenge as her brother.

It was recommended that child welfare keep an eye on his sister's development too. An example of fear being annihilated are statements like "Don't leave me, or I will hate you", in those with borderline or emotionally unstable personalities. It can be that Breivik had a genetic predisposition to mental instability on his mother's side, as well as attachment related disorders in having been present in previous generations. Parental rejection is linked with aggression. A rejected child stores anger and hatred that can burst at any moment.

An example was a patient of mine who had a tendency towards violence and could not bear to say goodbye to me when I was leaving on my holidays. She said, "If you go to the door, I will throw this heavy paper weight at you and kill you". I smiled and replied, "Then, you will never have Dr Rustomjee, again". She laughed and said, "You always have an answer". She was always very close to me and I was certain she would never hurt me. I had given her plenty of notice of my leave times and introduced her to the person who would look after her in my absence. There were no more violent threats.

Morg the Graffiti Bomber

Three fourteen year old's in dark clothing had snuck away from home near midnight with fresh spray cans, to spray animations on wooden fences. Anders Behring Breivik created Morg the graffiti Bomber. Morg was seen to be a weirdo according to other taggers. A friend and Morg painted writings on walls. This was a cartoonish era in which Breivik was involved with creating Morg. The company Marvel Comics had been in business since 1939 and were known for producing Super Heroes like Spiderman, Captain America etc. One of them is Morg, known as the executioner. His double-edged axe was an executioner's axe with which he used to behead his own people mercilessly. This is how Morg fitted into real life stories. His illustrations depicted a swollen red torso with muscles like inflated balloons. His double-headed axe hangs in front of his crotch like a colossal phallus. He had some characteristics of Cane, the brother killer. Morg could also be bought online as a plastic action figure. Anders Behring Breivik would cultivate a number of avatars over the years, but Morg was his first. By then, he had changed schools. The headmaster was feared, but not respected. A number of pupils came from outside Norway mainly Pakistan. One solution was to start a gang just for Norwegians. Most gangs became violent and criminal. However, integration was successful in Oslo. Breivik's friend Rafik had come from a different primary school and was one of Breivik's neighbours. They were inseparable according to other pupils. However, his friend was a Pakistani. It was as if the caterpillar had turned into a black butterfly. Later Rafik's relatives were involved with another gang and this led to them separating.

Morning on Utøya

Utøya features caves and beaches, fields and woodland. Couples could easily disappear in thickets or caves on the western side.

Utøya was politically supported by many parties. The youth was more capable than the political or trade movement. The participants on Utøya were represented by the whole country and also came from all over the world. The summer camp was usually very popular. It is about fixing things that are falling apart.

Occidentalism reflects Anti-Westernism

Oswald Spengler from German culture wrote about the downfall of the evening land of the West. Oswald Spengler, the young Afghan Jihadist, allegedly said "Americans love Pepsi Cola, we love death". They hate the mechanical Western reason without depth or soul parting not only with God, but with time honoured institutions, such as family and nation. Osama bin Laden is supposed to have stated this in 2002 that "The values of the western civilisation under the leadership of America have been destroyed and the symbolic towers that speak of human rights and humanity have been destroyed and gone up in smoke".

Anders Behring Breivik and Avatar Syndrome

Anders Behring Breivik wrote that "The avatars in the world of witchcraft have five attributes, strength, intellect, stamina, spirit and agility. In the world of witchcraft one can play alone. However, it takes time to play from one level to the next".

The Anti-Jihadist Avatar

The Justiciar Knight came into being in the years 2006 and 2011. On July 22nd 2011 he planned his book launch. He then dressed as a Justiciar Knight and as a Juggernaut with armoured weapons and spikes.

Anders kept trying to control his fear of dying. He realised that being paranoid will make matters worse. Also, he was frightened of spiders. He felt he was a member of the 'living dead'. He imagined himself in numerous different positions, e.g. being right or left wing, Orthodox, Catholic or Protestant, as well as Islam. He also stated his dislike for Oslo for numerous reasons, namely that the European Court of Human Rights which he believed was racial and political. He worried about feminisation of society. He feared castration evidently, and hence preferred a patriarchal society. He felt that his mother was his Achilles heel.

He finally reached Utøya and started his murderous rampage. One and a half hours later he was captured and kept in police custody. He admitted to his killings. He pleaded 'not guilty' in a closed door hearing on July 25th. However, he was given the maximum sentence of twenty-years, which can be extended.

CHAPTER 2:

Birdman: Murderous Rage

Robert Stroud: The Birdman of Alcatraz

An authentic autobiography of Robert Stroud, known as the Birdman of Alcatraz, is probably still a mystery in many aspects. Jolene Babyak (1994), daughter of Arthur Dollison who worked in the Bureau of Prisons, as well as being an associate warden, was transferred to Alcatraz in 1953 when Jolene was aged seven. They then moved to the prison island as part of a civilian community of two hundred people. Stroud was aged forty-five at that time. Parts of Stroud's life became clearer, more recently, about three decades after he died. Since then Alcatraz has become a tourist attraction and a national park. Jolene Babyak has written a detailed historical account in her book 'Birdman: The Many Faces of Robert Stroud' (1994).

In this chapter, following most of the historic details, will be my personal psychoanalytic viewpoints regarding his life and the punishments he survived.

Background

The movie, with Burt Lancaster playing the role of Robert F Stroud, is a compelling classic production which was nominated for an Oscar. Stroud had been a convict for fifty-three years and has always been the most famous prisoner in America. He has always been linked with the prison on Alcatraz, an island from which prisoners who tried to escape by swimming, died before reaching the mainland.

Birth and Infancy

Stroud did admit at one stage that he was a child born of incest. According to his mother, his father had wanted an abortion, but mother categorically refused. This led to severe physical violence by father to his wife during her pregnancy by punching her abdomen, to force a miscarriage, before she was six months pregnant. His mother touched the hearts of all to whom she described her husband's aggression. Robert Stroud was aware that his father wanted him to be aborted until he was six months in utero. Hence Stroud felt he was an unwanted child. Initially his mother became his protector until he got married, without her permission. She then turned her back on him and destroyed his chances of freedom from prison.

Stroud had collected more enemies among men who knew him and more admirers among those who didn't. Stroud himself also blamed both parents for provoking each other leading to constant physical and verbal attacks. Surprisingly he did say that once when he discussed these issues with his father, they both agreed that parricide would have been more appropriate. Jolene Babyak points out that "prison administrators had also behaved like his father" and wanted him dead too. This is similar perhaps to the "chosen trauma", described by Vamik Volkan (2003). Jolene was aghast when she observed the far greater number of bullet holes outside Stroud's cell (about twenty) were obviously aimed by the guards to kill him, even when he was much older and tried his best to have reconciliation during this period of rebellion by other convicts who had initiated a mutiny in 1946 towards the prison staff. Jolene writes, "Stroud was cantankerous and bitter, but there weren't reasons enough to warrant such a deadly response". She adds that, "not all bitterness from behind prison walls was raged by convicts".

Apparently, Stroud in his youth was a pimp and had become furious when a certain prostitute had not been given her negotiated share of the money. In a fury of impulsive rage, he murdered the man. He then immediately went to the police and said "I shot a man". During other similar occasions he also confessed to his own wrong doings.

The Hollywood production shows an initial episode when Stroud is in a poorly ventilated train car and smashes the window for air. He had seen another convict covered with sweat and breathing laboriously. He had genuinely felt very sympathetic for that convict. Most of the other convicts rose up and cheered his actions. This sets the tone for the whole movie.

Stroud never lied. He was a homosexual even until he was 70 years old, he shaved his body completely. Whenever he was discovered as seducing a younger convict, he took the active role of every forbidden act, saying that it was himself that had initiated the episode.

Stroud's Birth

Stroud admitted at some stage that he was a child born of incest. According to his mother his father had wanted an abortion, but mother categorically refused. This led to severe physical violence by his father to his mother during her pregnancy, by punching her abdomen to force a miscarriage before she was six months pregnant. Hence Stroud felt an unwanted child and his mother took the role of being his protector for many years. While in prison he came across a female visitor who was very loving towards him and intended to help him in many ways. He then got married without his mother's prior permission. Mother turned her back on him and did not visit him after that. Prior to that she had pleaded for his death sentence to be reduced with President Woodrow's wife, to exempt him from a death penalty. Stroud was delighted but this was short lived as his mother walked out on him as soon as he got married without her permission. Prior to that she had never blamed him.

Once in a fit of anger at a relative not being allowed to visit him as he had come on the wrong visiting day, Stroud got entangled with an armed warden and killed him. He said he had empathy for the wife of the warden, but not for the warden himself. This was done in front of other guards and criminals, including killing a guard in front of other guards and criminals, when he was informed that a family member had been refused access as the person had arrived on a day when visitors were not allowed. Boundaries were not respected by Stroud until the day he was refused access to an empty wooden box inside which he could have looked after the birds for whom he was caring. It was a prison guard who taught him to speak respectfully, if he asked for a favour. Stroud thanked the guard genuinely. It is pathetic, that a genius like the Birdman Robert Stroud was admired by a large majority of learned ornithologists and others, only after he had reached adulthood. He wrote on ornithology, treating sick canaries back to health, how prisoners needed to be rehabilitated, so that they would be able to learn new skills and become employable.

Summary

His mother treated his double murders with denial, as if Stroud had not done anything wrong. Stroud himself later in life, blamed both his parents.

There were congenital abnormalities in one of his sisters. Stroud was fond of her and sent her money regularly out of his earnings, when he was working.

In 1961 when Stroud was about seventy years old, he went

to court with the motion to dismiss his 1918 indictment. When asked about his scientific accomplishments as an ornithologist he said his research and cures of septic fever and avian diphtheria were now all out of date. This was probably his first example of Self Contempt, as if what he had done didn't matter anymore now that antibiotics were used. The courtroom, which had been full of ladies wearing stuffed bird hats who had come to cheer him, were devastated and did not come back after lunch.

Some months later, he asked his wife to agree to a divorce, as there was no possibility for them to enjoy life together, now that he was bound to remain in prison. After he got married, his mother walked out on him, discouraging authorities to declare him fit to leave prison and be a free man. The US Parole Board in 1962 described him as just a homicidal homosexual. Different prison officers saw him with a different viewpoint.

Stroud was known to have 'atrocious' table manners. Apparently, a former officer Bill Rogers once said they were "Just about like a boar pig". He ate raw meat with his fingers, shovelling it into his mouth. "His mouth would hang open and his lips would droop." Stroud kept complaining about nephritis, gout, hyperthyroidism, pellagra, etc. Most symptoms were bizarre and confusing. Stroud often battled himself into a corner to justify his victimisation. He complained to Washington that the dentist refused to make him a denture. When queried, it was explained that the dentist couldn't fit the denture until Stroud had a tooth removed — which he had refused. This was a ruse he often employed. He felt he knew more than they did. He shaved his entire body at least weekly over twelve years. His demoralisation increased as did his depressed state. He attempted suicide at Alcatraz in 1952. With his usual egotism, Dr Meltzer wrote "He intended to cut his femoral arteries", so as to let all his blood out and die.

Most of the public were unaware that for most of his solitary confinement Stroud was actually in the prison at Leavenworth, Kansas and not at Alcatraz.

At that moment Stroud was considered by them as a hero, with courage and good intentions for all convicts. The second killing which the prisoners witnessed was of the prison guard, who arrogantly and routinely followed prison rules, and stopped him seeing a family member without having any 'Moral Remorse'.

Nevertheless, there is clearly a very kind side to Stroud. On one of his walks in the prison courtyard he comes across a sparrow which has fallen off a branch of a tree and is trying to protect itself from the stormy weather. Stroud takes the sparrow to his cell and puts him in a warm stocking and feeds him freshly killed insects and bugs off the ground. Other convicts feel encouraged by what Stroud has done in the nurturing of the sparrow so that the bird could now even fly without problems. Guards who were outside his cell also felt a lot of admiration as well as empathy for Stroud. Other inmates followed his example and encouraged their visitors to bring them canaries. Robert Stroud got more birds, mainly canaries and looked after them lovingly with the help of light empty wooden boxes which helped to isolate the birds and discover incurable bird diseases. He was acknowledged as a genius who taught himself bird haematology, histology, anatomy, as well as pathology, more than any other ornithologist at the time.

In 1959, Stroud was transferred to the Medical Centre for prisoners in Springfield, Missouri, for medical reasons. In 1962 his publicity was handed over to Hollywood. Thomas Gaddis, a writer and Stanley Fulman, a lawyer, "They were selling the movie, the book and the man" (p. 8). During court hearings he would never present himself favourably. Burt Lancaster who played the part of Stroud, in contrast, displayed genuine grief that, of the fifty-two years of his life which Stroud had spent in prisons, forty-three were in solitary confinement. His lawyer, Fulman, was also amazed by witnessing Stroud obviously sabotaging himself. During this period, Thomas Gaddis, a writer, had been involved in writing a book on Robert for ten years. Sadly, he was not given access to Stroud in person.

It was often referred to as common knowledge that Stroud was a homosexual and had a great time with every podgy young boy he saw, so was a pederast. Officials suppressed his 2,000 word manual on prison history because it contained descriptions of sex between male convicts. The most endearing photograph of him was taken when he appears as a kind, wise, smiling and caring man with no evidence of demoralisation.

The Bird Man later in life

CHAPTER 3:

Crime and Punishment

FYODOR DOSTOEVSKY: DESCRIBES RASKOLNIKOV'S "SACRIFICIAL LOVE" FROM MOTHER AND FATHER, AND SUPPORT FROM SOFYA SEMYONOVNA

Dostoevsky is described by Sigmund Freud in 1961 in his chapter on Dostoevsky and Parricide (Vol. XXI, pp. 177-194) as one of the greatest creative artists, a moralist, a sinner and a neurotic. Freud considers Dostoevsky's place in literature as being second only to Shakespeare. Freud particularly marvels his work on the 'Brothers Karamazo'. The episode of the 'Grand Inquisitor' is considered by Freud to be one of the peaks of literature in the world. Dostoevsky describes a moralist as a man who has 'gone through the depths of sin' and only then is able to reach the highest summit of morality. This chapter we are considering is by Richard J. Rosenthal in *"Do I dare disturb the Universe"*, a memorial to Wilfred R. Bion (1981, Ed. J.S. Grotstein, pp. 167-180). Rosenthal analyses the hero Raskolnikov's Transgression and the Confusion between Destructiveness and Creativity from the book *'Crime and Punishment'*. A story of three murders is transformed very elegantly into literature, where the origins of rage, arising from hate towards his parents is unravelled. Rahv (1962) suggests that Raskolnikov takes us on a journey, in order to unravel his motivations for all his murders. He travels from 'pride to humility, hate to love', as well as living from guilt laden isolation to mixing with selected friends.

Raskolnikov remembered an agonising nightmare he had

during his childhood, when aged seven. He was strolling one evening with his father on a feast day. He remembered seeing an old grey mare who was being forced to pull a cartload of drunk men. The mare was whipped mercilessly. Finally, the mare falls down, whereupon her owner continues to beat her. The owner shouts "She is my property" to people who realise that the mare is old and limited. The mare puts all her energy in getting up and pulling the cartful of drunk patrons. Naturally, the burden is too much. She falls down again and is now beaten to death by her owner who had lost face. His father arrives at the scene and Raskolnikov cries to his father "Pappa, Pappa what are they doing to this horse". "Come along says his father; they are all drunk and playing pranks, the fools. Come along and don't look." Raskolnikov in the dream puts his arms round the mare's neck and lovingly kisses the mare's eyes. He becomes tearful again when she dies. He motions in a frenzied manner with clenched fists at the tavern owner, Mikolka. His father takes Raskolnikov away. He wishes his father would have taken some action, but sadly father guides him away from the scene. Raskolnikov now loses all faith in his father and in certain people except for a few friends whom he had trusted.

Raskolnikov tries to take a deep breath and awakes from his nightmare. He says "Thank God it was only a dream. He felt as if his whole body was broken and his soul dark and troubled. "God", he exclaimed. "Can it be that I will really take an axe and hit her on the head and smash her skull?" He was "Trembling like a leaf", as he said it. "Lord", he pleaded "Show me the way". I renounce this cursed .... dream of mine. Later on, when he recalled the dream, it seemed as if it was 9.00pm.

Raskolnikov's anger is now directed to a certain pawn broker, Alyona Ivanovna, who used to charge him excessively for him to retrieve certain articles which he had originally pawned to her. These were previously given to him by his father. He feels murderously enraged towards her. A further unforeseen calamity occurs. The pawnbroker's step-sister, Lizaveta, suddenly comes home early and witnesses the murderous act. He now feels trapped and has no alternative, but to destroy all incriminating evidence by killing the pawnbroker's step-sister. He now feels worse than before. He feels compelled to share these feelings with his best friend.

The decision to confess his murders arises from his growing trust in a female named Sonya (a daughter of a friend, Marmeladov), who had previously been used by men for their sexual pleasures. Sonya was very kind to everyone who met her. It was she who advised Raskolnikov to go to the police. She promised to stand by him. Sonya's true love for him and her own truthful nature, along with her wish to accompany him to Siberia for the term of his imprisonment, was the turning point in his life to regain his own true morality. Sonya was the sister of a close friend of his. Prior to that, he had accepted the so-called 'sacrificial love from his mother and sister"' which disgusted him. The money his mother sent him periodically would be given away to the first beggar he saw. By doing so he did not feel indebted to his mother. However, he avidly read her letters which explained her recent developments.

It is of importance to know, at a neurological level, that Raskolnikov had epileptic episodes in childhood, where he lost consciousness for periods of time. This was never medically explained.

Sonya was very different. She did not cover up the truth of his murders. She helped him to take responsibility for his actions. She remained loving towards him, regardless of when he would be ready and willing to openly confess to the murders of the pawnbroker, the pawnbroker's step-sister with the unborn pregnancy of a male, in her womb. Rosenthal describes "The confession being the central point of the testing of Raskolnikov's rebirth".

Raskolnikov had previously adopted a belief in his own falsely believed 'Superior Morality'. He had written in his notebook about dividing people into either being 'Extraordinary', meaning far above the average of being an Ordinary person. He had categorised extraordinary persons as having the right to do extraordinary things. These thoughts were in his mind, before he pawned anything to Alyona Ivanovna, the pawn broker. However, when he went to her place, all that he saw in her, were her deep piercing eyes and the Contempt from her about his own father's wristwatch, which he had brought to her pawnshop. He felt unhinged. She treated both him and the watch as being worth very little.

As he had run out of money, mostly as a result of excessive alcoholism, he had decided to pawn some other belongings of his family which he had been given. He felt intimidated by the pawnbroker's 'piercing eyes' and her greed at giving him very little money for pawned articles. Moreover, if he had not paid, in the allocated time, the price to be paid by him was increased by her. It made him loathe her as if she was a 'louse' — a parasite. He develops considerable contempt and hatred towards her and keeps thinking that he would be doing a service to kill the pawnbroker, as the world would be better off without her. He was avoiding his own responsibility by projecting his own hatred and contempt on her. He was untrue to himself at this stage.

Then, the thought comes to his mind to kill her, without anyone noticing that he had murdered her. He had lived with an illusion that he had superior morality, compared with others like the pawnbroker. He hated her power over him financially and felt he had no alternative but to murder her. He realised that as there was still some doubt in his mind, he should ask a close friend of his for help. He was aware that his friend had the capacity to reason difficult issues. He then realised that he would be in debt to his friend. He changed his mind and made the final decision to murder the pawn broker for not returning his belongings to him, unless the payment was made to her with her terms agreed upon. His superego, like that of all others, made him to feel like a murderer and brought reality back to him. This led to him feeling extremely miserable. He decided he had no other way of living, with such overwhelmingly hateful and contemptuous thoughts leading to murderous feelings towards Alyona Ivanovna. There was no alternative open to him, but to murder her. He had overheard her step-sister Lizaveta would be late coming back to this apartment, so it was a good opportunity for him to fulfil his desire. He had also borrowed an axe from his apartment and hidden it under his clothes, when he went to kill the pawn broker.

Tragically, the pawnbroker's step-sister, Lizavetta, comes home early and he feels forced to kill her too. Her abdomen now shows signs of pregnancy, which does not deter Raskolnikov. Similar to the dying grey mare in his previous dream, he recognises her kind eyes, but feels he now has no alternative. He feels very sick and realises that he cannot live without sharing his burden. He confides in his best friend without much benefit. He then becomes totally wrecked and very ill.

His mother and sister now arrive to see him. His mother was still living with very high expectations of him studying at St. Petersburg. She would send him money and a letter regularly. The money had been saved by her fr4rom his father's pension. She also expected her daughter, who would be financially well endowed, to also help her brother by marrying a person she did not love sufficiently to be a lifelong partner.

This had been the start of Raskolnikov's hate towards his mother. He thought of the money being given to him, as what he termed 'Sacrificial Love'. He continued to need to be considered as being a superior individual with high morals. Nevertheless, he also realised that committing murders had not solved anything. He now no longer felt he could lead a happy life with high morals. He hence forced himself to visit Sonya, whom he now admired greatly. She was always honest and truthful. She advised him to go to the police station and give himself up and even volunteered to accompany him. She was totally devoted to him and accompanied him every step of the way. She also went to Siberia where he was sent as a prisoner. Both had difficulty adjusting to Raskolnikov accepting that he was not an extraordinary person, but one, who could admit and volunteer the truth about his crime, as well as accept his punishment. Raskolnikov also confessed to his mother. She too was able to accept his actions and reasons for his murders.

After an initial period of difficulty in understanding and accepting Sonya, he never accepted her wisdom. He was sent to prison and was relieved to see the prisoners looked up to Sonya87 as their 'good little mother'. Raskolnikov felt very relieved on all counts. He and Sonya were happy with their final decision.

I will end this chapter with Keats' words:

"Beauty is truth, truth beauty — that is all
Ye know on earth, and all ye need to know"
J. Keats, *'Ode on a Grecian Urn'*.

CHAPTER 4:

Similarities and Differences in
Various Reasons for Murder

ADDITIONAL VIEWPOINT ON MARTIN BRYANT, ANDERS BREIVIK, ROBERT STROUD AND RASKOLNIKOV IN THE NOVEL "CRIME AND PUNISHMENT"

This is an additional viewpoint of four cases of murder. Three cases are of Martin Bryant, Anders Behring Breivik and the Birdman. The last case is the very famous novel Crime and Punishment written by Dostoevsky. The main character is Raskolnikov.

The Birdman of Alcatraz

His relationship with his mother is symbiotic. Father had wanted him to be aborted, but mother protected him from all dangers. She supported him and loved him dearly.

He became close to a prostitute who helped him to recover after a serious chest infection. However, he introduced her to a pimp for a sum of money. The pimp gave the woman ten dollars less. This made Stroud, The Birdman, furious and he shot the pimp at point blank range. He then went to the police station and reported the event immediately, presuming the murder would be considered to be justified. That was not the case and Stroud was imprisoned for sixteen years.

He idealised his mother and stabbed an inmate at Leavenworth Prison, who teased him about having her photo in his cell. This wound was not lethal. Some weeks later he once more intentionally killed a prison guard who had refused his close relative to see him on a day, which was barred for all visitors. Stroud was now sentenced to death.

This shows Stroud's problem was being insightless. He had poor verbal abilities to work through problems without resorting to killing. Most importantly, he needed to obey all boundaries laid by the law leading to criminal offences. This seems as if Stroud believed that his omnipotence would save him from criminal punishment.

His mother spoke with President Woodrow's wife and his sentence was reduced to life imprisonment. Stroud was overjoyed that his mother had saved his life once more.

His mother had always been very possessive and may well have treated him as if it was acceptable for him to behave in an omnipotent and grandiose manner.

He then proposed to a female with whom he intended to open a business. The proposal was made first and mother informed later. She found this unbearable and walked out of his life forever, with a massive narcissistic self-injury. They never spoke to each other again. Both had unforgivable, non-reparative defence mechanisms which prevented them from making up with each other. Those like him lead a life of solitude without friends.

Relationship with his father remained very poor. Robert was fond of one of his sisters to whom he gave money regularly.

Relationships in General

Mother had advised him that if you sleep with a woman, you need to protect her. This may have led him to kill the pimp and then tell the police without any feelings of guilt. The woman however did not protect him at all during the hearing of the case. This reveals his innate loss of reality. Obviously, he had taken it for granted that the woman would fight for his cause and leading to a lenient punishment.

Relationship with Father

Father agreed that Robert should have killed him (patricide) years ago. He too did not respect human life, even his own. Father and mother provoked each other all the time they were together. Father lived with a woman opposite their home for some time, even after his parents were separated!

Change in Personality

He looked after a baby sparrow and taught the bird to fly. He was an intellectual genius and looked after all canaries which many prisoners bought. He wrote two books on diseases of birds, before antibiotics came on the scene.

A guard who supervised prisoners taught him gratitude before giving him the empty box for caging his birds. Stroud then changed a lot of his mannerisms for the better. He kept improving and was able to help the lives of many prisoners when the prisoners tried to take over the prison. The officers then started shooting prisoners. By now, Stroud had become wise and became the mediator between the prisoners and the guards, as well as officials of the prison. This improved his relationship with all the inmates and guards. However, he remained unhappy that only limited rehabilitation was offered to all prisoners.

In later life Stroud suffered from dental and physical problems. Although, he finally died an uneventful death, he was able to walk on grass in a Rehabilitation Home and will always be remembered for his researches into treatment of sick birds. A movie starring Burt Lancaster was made of his story.

Crime and Punishment by Fyodor Dostoevsky

Raskolnikov goes to study in St Petersburg, but drops out. He does not seem to miss his studies after that.

We, the reader, cannot understand his desire to live where he is.

He throws his mother's hard-earned money away to beggars. He does not want to be indebted to his mother. He is also indebted to his landlady, from whom he rents his room. He has not paid her for many weeks. He avoids her. He feels that she is aggressive and may tell him to vacate, so builds his days for leaving the house, so that she is not at home and would ask him for rent. However, he is indebted to her as he is living on her mercy as the rent is invariably overdue. However, she does not ask him to vacate the house.

As soon as he leaves the house, he feels great and free of burdens. He can do what he likes now as he has only a few friends. Finally, he decides he needs money, so he goes to a Pawnbroker, who is very particular regarding the time he has to return the money or less there is extra for him to pay. He thinks she is better off dead, as after he pawned once, he has no money to get the article, namely his father's wristwatch back from her. As he values his freedom, the only option he feels is to murder her. His transference to her and his own mother appears similar. Both give money and love making, he feels it is a sacrifice they are making. So, it is felt to him as 'sacrificial love', only. Mother is hoping her daughter will marry a rich man, so that she does not need to work hard to send him whatever he needs. He thinks the world is better off without people like the pawnbroker. He considers her to be a louse!

In unconscious Self Contempt, he cannot accept that it is he, who is at the mercy of both women. So, he endures his ambivalence and considers himself in a grandiose manner to have Superior Morals to most of society. The daughter of the pawnbroker appears pregnant and he likes her, as she does not crave for money, unlike her mother. He plans the murder at a time, the daughter has not returned home. She unfortunately arrives earlier than expected, so feels trapped and has to murder her too.

He then gets fever, feels very weak, guilty of his sins and loses the will to improve his lifestyle.

His rationalisation is also an unconscious repeating of his father's attitude which he remembers from a childhood dream where his young son, Raskolnikov, kisses the eyes of an old grey mare who is killed with merciless whipping by her owner, when she cannot run fast enough to carry too heavy a load of people free of charge. His father remains aloof in the dream similar to all other watchers at this place. No-one stops the mare's owner from killing the mare! They all seem relieved that the mare is now dead and not forced to run with a load she cannot carry. The dream seems to have left a mark on Raskolnikov and his sympathies are with the dead mare. One may wonder if he identifies with the weak mare who has no more will to live. Certainly, it is expected of him to study and he cannot do so at present. His health weakens. His mother and sister arrive to meet him.

He realises he needs help and confides in Sonya, the sister of a friend of his. They both feel attracted to each other. Sonya too, used to work as a prostitute, but not anymore. She is clear in her thinking and advises him to confess the murders. Raskolnikov is himself very stressed and very weak. He realises she is saying the truth, especially when she promises to come with him to Siberia where prisoners are kept. He thinks about confessing his misdeeds to the police and even tells his mother and sister. They accept his wishes, and do not look down at him. He goes ahead with his plan, makes his confession and is sent to prison in Siberia. He feels jealous when the other prisoners look up to Sonya, as a godmother. He gets over his initial concern about it. Sonya and he feel much better about not living in guilt together.

Martin Bryant from Tasmania, Australia

In April 1996, Martin Bryant aged twenty-eight was imprisoned for having committed a massacre at Port Arthur in Tasmania.

As Martin's mother is currently trying to re-open his sentence for Life Imprisonment, it is premature to discuss recent developments any further at present. Even now very little is known of his relationship with his father who committed suicide shortly before the massacre at Port Arthur in Tasmania. Dr Cunningham Dax, a well-known and highly respected Consultant Psychiatrist, was consulted by Martin Bryant's father, mother and Martin about receiving a Disability Pension. He praised both parents for the work they were putting in already. He hypothesised that it would be very difficult for Martin after his parents had died. The main verbatim details given in the news at the time of the shooting was Martin's conversation with the police as they took him to the police station. Apparently, Martin spoke to them as follows, from my own memory of what was circulated to the public.

He said to the police:

"Well it is only work for you!"

"Look at my hands!" (Showing them the manacles)

"You will go home and have a nice cooked meal to eat. I don't know what I will eat."

It is not possible to come to any conclusion about the above three sentences. I have not treated people with an IQ of sixty-six. Also, I do not work with criminals. There is mild contempt only with asking for sympathy as I hear it. I would have expected at least some Omnipotence still existing after the massacre. The constant dialogue of Anders Behring Breivik about becoming world-famous, combined with years of work which he had prepared and distributed, fits in with his premeditated massacre of innocent lives.

Hence, I cannot say, whether or not, Martin Bryant, who has single-handedly massacred thirty-five people, would be concerned in comparing himself with a policeman and asking for his sympathy, without referring to the massacre. From everything I had read so far about the massacre, I would expect much more emotion, raised voices, anger, with regards to whatever he did and why, in his own words. In the words of Jacques Lacan 'The unconscious is structured like a language'.

Similarly, in the position of Dr Cunningham Dax, in addition to his kind appreciation of his parent's massive efforts, nowadays, one would refer him to researchers in cerebral dysfunction for specialised Brain disorders. "Many legal defences are examining criminality in relation to brain dysfunction. The frontal lobe is considered as the centre of the mechanism for decision making. Morality is also disrupted by brain damage, drug addiction and brain injury after an accident. People who commit violent crimes have brain disorders. Criminal behaviour like unlawful violence of all kinds arise from particular brain lesions. Thinning of an outer layer of the amygdala is the region of the brain which is the centre of emotion, of empathy, guilt and remorse, which are present in the criminal mind, as well as an 18% of volume reduction in this part of the brain. The Brain and Crime. What is the relationship here?" (Mela, 2015)

Investigations like EEG, MRI, PET and SPECT can conclude that significant frontal lobe dysfunction is associated with loss of control leading to aggression. Different lobes of the brain have different functions. These investigations may not have been available so many years ago. (Mela, 2015)

A point to note is that Martin Bryant did suffer an injury to his neck in the same car accident in which his lady friend died. As there are very few books available on Martin Bryant, it is difficult to study various views which agree or disagree regards the extent of his injury.

Also, I would like to know how his father's very recent suicide had affected him. Sadly, Martin and his parents were not referred to a fully trained psychoanalytically oriented mental health specialist. In the International Journal of Psychoanalysis there are very interesting articles of work with younger children of an even lower IQ treated four times a week, who have been helped greatly with play therapy. Both Anders Behring Breivik and Martin Bryant have more differences than similarities.

Contemptuous indifference with humiliation, precipitating violence

Wayne Rabey, a twenty-year-old geology student, was emotionally attached to a female student. One day when they were studying together, Rabey discovered a letter she had written to a girlfriend. In the letter, she referred to another student in whom she had a sexual interest. She also said that Rabey 'bugged' her in class and that he and another friend were 'nothing'. The following day, Rabey removed a rock sample from the geology lab, allegedly for study purposes. Later that day he met the female student and asked her what she thought of him. When she replied that he was just a friend, Rabey stuck her with the rock and then began choking her. Rabey was later charged with causing bodily harm with intent to wound.

"A psychiatrist testified that the accused had entered into a dissociated state after his conversation with the victim. In this state the accused was capable of performing physical acts, but without being conscious of doing so. A dissociative state is usually caused by a psychological blow."

The above legal example was published in the following website: *Rabey v. The Queen, [1980] 54 C.C.C. (2d) 1 S.C.C.* http://wps.prenhall.com/ca_ph_blair_law_1/6/1550/396810.cw/index.html [last accessed 6th December 2015]

Not only did Rabey lift a rock and struck the girl, but also began to choke her. In my opinion, intensive psychotherapy needs to be mandatory to prevent further episodes. The same would be beneficial for the victim, to explore the reasons for her own contempt to such a high degree. She may well be putting her life in danger if she remains unaware of her own provocativeness.

Contempt provokes disgust. This is regularly seen in cases in law courts between unhappy marriages of different races and religions which have sadly led to violence and death.

PART VI:

TRANSCULTURAL PSYCHOTHERAPY

CHAPTER 1 (a)

Working Between Eastern and Western Cultures[1]

Dr Sabar Rustomjee has worked as a group and individual psychoanalytic psychotherapist in Melbourne for over 25 years. The formative years of her life were spent in India, during which she was greatly influenced by the life and works of Mahatma Gandhi. She then worked in paediatrics in UK. This was followed by working in Australia in Consultation Liaison Psychiatry, conducting groups with patients having First Episode Psychosis, Metastatic Breast Cancer etc. She recently founded the International Organization of Group Analytic Psychotherapy and started a three-year training programme with the support of international group analysis. Email: sabar@iprimus.com.au

Abstract

This article describes differences and similarities in conducting analytic individual and group psychotherapy in a 19 year old single Indian Hindi woman who had recently immigrated to Melbourne. This case is complicated. Transference relationships between therapist and client arising from both eastern and western cultures had to be taken into consideration and required much self-questioning. Not only does the client present in a unique manner, but the entire case material presented is equally unusual. The acceptance of female sexuality in Indian culture expressed lovingly through

---

1   A condensed form of this article was presented at an AGPA conference in a panel discussion, 'Spanning the Globe', chaired by Fern Cramer-Azima in 2001.

dance and music by the client as dancer in her adoration of Hindu gods and goddesses is described. The therapist found herself in an unaccountable state of fear early in the therapy that she was later able to uncover and relate to an early encounter with a potentially unpredictable and violent tribe, the Hijras, who present with a rare form of sexual perversion. The case ends with healthy separation and individuation by the client.

Meeting

'U' was a 19 year old single Indian Hindu young woman who had migrated with her parents and three younger brothers to Australia four years ago. I call her 'U' for unique. In the very first minute that I saw her, despite my being of Indian origin and having lived in India between the ages of 5 and 21, I felt extremely overwhelmed by her presence. I was scared to an extent I had never even dreamt of before. I was puzzled. I did not understand what this feeling was about. I felt irritated and asked myself, "What is happening?" and told myself, "She is only a 19 year old Hindu girl who appears to be pleasant, honest and innocent as far as I can see! The only scary feature I could see was her dress and I asked myself another question, "Why ha she chose to dress in this particular manner?" With this initial explanation, I reassured and contained myself. I realized that my reaction was purely my own transference to her. In fact, she had not as yet even said a single word to me! I slowly gathered my thoughts. I later recalled that she had burst into my consulting room through the entrance door, which I had kept open for her and sat down very hurriedly on a seat that was close to mine. It feels as if someone or something was persecuting her, but I kept this observation to myself for future reference.

She was a very dark complexioned, slender young woman with attractive facial features. She gradually relaxed and smiled awkwardly with a shyness typical of rural Indian women. Her face was painted with delicate decorations mainly around her eyes. She also had traditional floral design of dyed henna on the palms of her hands. These are commonly seen at festive occasions, especially when one is part of a bridal party or a bride oneself. The saddest part was that these decorations were at least a month old, with many faded areas and certain parts totally peeled off. Her hair was long and dull. It had probably not been combed in a few days. It appeared that perhaps up to a month before she had been able to look after her personal hygiene well, but that she was now too depressed to do so. Strangely, despite her lack of care for her appearance, she wore a pair of beautiful, long, pure gold earrings and at least half a dozen gold bangles. In an Indian family, even of moderate means, it is possible to dress attractively as it is customary for relatives to give presents of clothing and jewellery to young women on all festive occasions. As Indians have large extended families, one may get numerous presents every few months.

Her clothes were recently laundered with a log skirt sticking out with heavy starch. Her blouse was long and loose, probably to cover up recent weight loss. Her clothes were a pale green by now very faded and fragmented. Small areas of silver and gold thread hung limply from the cotton fabric.

Most of the time it appeared that she was very brave attempting to conceal an underlying sense of many very severe losses in life. Even though treating depressed and anorectic adolescents was part of my daily work as a psychotherapist none of these explanations helped me to cope with the immobilizing fear she induced in me. Something much more powerful at play that I did not understand at the time, which led me to look for similarities and differences in our backgrounds.

My Story

I was born in Sri Lanka and spent the formative years of my life in India between the ages of 5 to 22 years. My closest Indian friends were Hindus, Muslims, Christians and Zoroastrians. I am a Parsee Zoroastrian. In India I had always experienced considerable respect without any trace of racial discrimination. Parsees are known mainly for their philanthropic activities. I had grown up with limited economic resources and completed my medical studies with the generous help of Zoroastrian scholarships. I felt very sorry for her recognizing her depression and her struggle to put on a brave face to preserve some dignity. In comparison to her, I felt my life had been very overprotected.

I realized my fear of her, represented something about Indian life, which I had long since repressed. I now started to think about the various caste systems in India. All Indians are well aware of the caste system among Hindus which range from the socially elite Brahmins to the 'Untouchables'. Brahmins are easily recognizable by their facial features and other characteristics. The so-called 'Untouchables' are also recognizable, but to me most other Hindu castes blend with each other. The 'Untouchables' are referred to as the 'Dalits' or Harijans'. Many professionals during that era resented the Dalits as a result of Mahatma Gandhi having allocated the Dalits numerous extra privileges. They could enter most professions with a much lower entry score to make up for their underprivileged upbringing. The rest of us on the other hand, had to burn the midnight oil to get the required entry score and had to excel in a number of sports to get a few additional points for entry to our chosen profession. Some Dalits since then, particularly in the major cities, have earned a high intellectual standing and been rightfully appointed to senior positions of responsibility such as in the judiciary system. I considered myself very fortunate to have had an education in one of Mumbai's reputable all girls' private schools during the English Raj.

Returning to the *'here and now'*, I found myself as described earlier, groping around, in totally unfamiliar territory with 'U'. I could not help myself often wishing 'U' had been brought up in a more Westernised background, which would have been more in keeping with my own way of life and thinking.

'U's' story

'U' had been referred to me by her University counsellor as she had missed a large number of days of attendance, was severely depressed, had lost concentration with her studies and suffered significant weight loss. Even though her menstrual cycle was normal and regular, it was feared that she may soon become anorexic.

During routine gathering of her history, she volunteered that she belonged to a caste lower than the Brahmins. She did not reveal what her own caste was and I did not ask her. In fact, I realized quickly that this was an issue of intense humiliation for her. It was sufficient to know that she and her family felt inferior to the Brahmins. Accepting painful, unspoken issues is typical in Asian culture.

'U' volunteered that she was aware that her depressed state was due to the impending break up of a five-year old relationship with an Indian lover from the Brahmin caste. He was now intending to return to India to get married to a Brahmin, women with whom an arranged marriage was to take place shortly. He had not told her about this arrangement at the start of their relationship and so she felt betrayed and devastated and indicated his limited affection for her. It took her some months to acknowledge this fully. I now realized that 'U' seemed to be saying, "Look at me. I am a sad faded person who should have been the bride of a highly respected Brahmin". I saw 'U' weekly for three months, during which she was able to mourn her loss. As her mood improved gradually, she started wearing more attractive clothing. On one occasion, she was dressed like a typical Hindu Goddess while she spoke in what I felt was a distinctly regressed manner. I now realized that I needed to be aware of my own transference to Hindu Gods and Goddesses. Most Indians have statues of Gods and Goddesses in their homes and pray for their blessings to protect them from evil. One interesting fact I learned was that a very popular God named Krishna was also known to have over one hundred wives, all of whom he treated with respect and quality. Indians did not consider this aspect of Krishna to be perverse.

I now started to question my own suitability to be her therapist. I asked myself, "What does analysis expect when the therapist may also at times occupy the position of a certain Hindu God or Goddess in the transference of such a patient?" Could I, as her therapist contain this type of projection while I was dressed in western working clothes and mostly unfamiliar with various Hindu Gods and Goddesses? I had only visited a few Hindu temples, but not to pray. I had been very comfortable singing hymns at school and also praying my own prayers. Nevertheless, it was very pleasing to see that despite my own doubts as to my suitability, 'U' kept on improving.

'U' was certainly a person one could not overlook. As her mood improved, she started to look stunning. She very rarely repeated the same outfit twice and appeared well groomed. Later in therapy, she told me that her father was always furious with for dressing up the way she did with so much gold jewellery, but that she took no notice of him. She simply liked what she wore and so she wore it. Her mother supported her and according to 'U', "She does not mind how I dress". 'U' now obviously also appeared to enjoy her sexuality. At the beginning of her therapy when she was very fragile, I had considered it unwise to try and explore her presentation or affect deeply but some months later that changed. 'U' came in smiling and wearing anklets with tiny bells that jingled. It now suddenly dawned on me that in fact 'U' was dressing up like an Indian dancer going on stage for a performance! We were now finally able to discuss this more openly. Her face beamed and shone with relief. At long last, I had been able to identify where her passion and secret wish in life had always been. Maybe it was then that she realized that, unlike any god or goddess with super-natural powers, I was human after all as it had taken me so long to come to this conclusion. Then she told me that her father had not wanted her to be a dancer, but that her mother did not mind. She also said that her brothers also like to dance. Her ambition had always been to pursue training in traditional classical Indian dancing one day.

Sexuality in Indian Culture

In order to understand sexuality in the Indian culture one needs to have an idea of Indian erotic art. Classical Indian dancing espe-cially was an expression of devotion to a particular god, with the dancer identifying herself as his Goddess, devotee and lover, giving her all through dancing and music.[2]

While discussing her passion for classical dancing, without any prompting 'U' was now able to confide that she had been sexu-ally molested several times in life. The first time was when she was in grade one and less than six years old. "The man was the son of a family friend", she said. The second incident was with "a

---

2   Lannoy, R (p 63-67) Temple eroticism may not make sense to those who have not visited temples in India nor seen how the total of the imagery is in accordance with a religious affirmation of life. The Western world has condi-tioned one's ideas on society, religion and sexuality to assume a distinctively moralistic approach. Hence, we judge erotic art as morally good or morally bad. Nevertheless, we need to make a conscious effort to understand that in India more than a thousand years ago, there was religion in which the erotic art was accepted in all its forms and was regarded as a valid means of attaining religious salvation. Orthodox Indian dancing was one of the expressions of sexuality and considered in high esteem. The dances often had themes of sacrifice to the gods and goddesses.

very good family friend". The third was by "a relative" when she was in grade six. There were others too. In most of these cases, one of her brothers was in the same room and, at times, asleep on the same bed. The final sexual encounter she had was with her present lover. She said she loved him and so believed, "It is supposed to happen when two people love each other" .. This was especially as he said he loved her too. It is important to note that she still held those who had molested her previously with a degree of awe and respect.

It is my practice to always ask the meaning, in their own culture, of the names of the people, that clients describe. When 'U' described her father, she described him as an alcoholic. When I asked her what her father's Christian name meant, she said in a very respectful, soft tone of voice, "It is God's name". Similarly, the majority of all those who had also molested her also had 'God's name'. Only her lover's name was different, as was her own! Her own name was that of a river. Her father apparently also had a history of having problems with the police for regular drink driving. Nevertheless, she respected him greatly.

This explained why she still held I awe those who had sexually molested her and even respected them at an unconscious level. She may well have been equating them with an Indian God, perhaps Krishna who had many wives.

The Group and the Individual
At this time, it became clear to me that she could now benefit greatly from combined group and individual psychotherapy. As she intended staying in Australia, we discussed how she could gain from understanding the Australian, way of life too. She continued in once weekly individual and started once weekly group psychotherapy, approximately four months after starting with individual therapy. This was an adolescent group of six members

with mostly women. They admired her, gave her tons of advice and opened out their hearts to her. She obviously enjoyed their generosity, but kept her distance from all of them. During therapy among other issues, she worked at her difficulties in separation and individuation from her parents and her lover. This was especially so as the lover was also a family friend and moreover, had God's name. Besides, he had tutored her brother and herself in English and other subjects at University level.

The group helped her to get in touch with her rage towards him. Soon afterwards her ex-lover's wife came to Australia. He tried to hold on to his wife as well as on to 'U'. By then 'U' had worked hard and succeeded at letting go of him. When 'U' had her next birthday, he gave 'U' a number of expensive presents although he was already married to his wife. She was now no longer confused and was well aware of how he had abused her trust. She kept his gifts unopened in a distant part of their house, which no one used. She felt this was a great achievement for her. She also was able to enjoy her own birthday party and invited a number of friends and relatives. She said she even managed to sneak an Australian boy into the party whom she liked greatly. As he was going overseas shortly, the relationship though short-lived, gave her a great deal of self-confidence. The group helped her tremendously, although she still could not reciprocate in the same way. Cultural differences as well as her limited English were probably two important reasons.

At this time, she described a dream where all her relatives including her grandmother forced her to marry within an arranged marriage to another relative who was intellectually very clever. The venue of the dream shifted from home to a picnic with a wedding scene. She saw herself as a bride in the dream saying, "No, no, no!" and screaming. She then sees an old well and realizes that the only alternative is to jump into the well, rather than agree to an arranged marriage but she succeeds in running away with everyone chasing behind her. One could interpret the dream in many ways. She herself said that she was now able to think independently about certain Indian customs like arranged marriages with which she had been brought up. She now wanted a marriage based on love. This dream had no gods or goddesses. It had a clear element of sexual human desire and intimacy. It was also associated with shame at betraying her caste/tribe. There was the final theme of self-sacrifice by wishing to drown herself in a well or say persecuted with people chasing her.

(The Third Gender) — a Hijra
© Mike Garten.com.http://mikegarten.com

As 'U' described her feelings in this dream, I too started to resonate with my original fear of her, when she rushed into my consulting rooms on her first session. It seemed as if at that time she had wanted me to protect her from the persecuting forces outside.

At long last, I could now also finally get in touch with the repressed persecuting fear in my life. I remembered being part of a bridal party of a relative being driven to the wedding pavilion. Suddenly, a tribe of Indian Hijras surrounded our car. Hijras are a totally separate tribe, 8% of whom in Mumbai are said to have undergone a procedure of removal of their penis, scrotum and testes by a midwife without anaesthesia. Their cries and wails were, said to have been, covered up by the sounds of loud trumpets. Their genitals are mainly masculine at birth, but women with disfigured genitals also join the tribe. Some children were even kidnapped with the express purpose of making them Hijras. They have been described as 'transgender' or belonging to the 'third gender'. They are impulsive, crude, loud and can be very violent. They demand money on festive occasions, at times going to the extent of displaying their genitals to shock those around, if their demands remain unmet. They are also supposed to have the power to bless or curse persons. They are sometimes hired by the very rich to get their blessings at festive occasions where they dance.

I presume the scene of 'U's' poor hygiene, faded clothes, uncombed hair, incongruent dangling golden jewellery while rushing forcefully into my room, all contributed to my feeling totally disarmed and wondering what would happen next to me. Knowing 'U' well now, I am positive she has nothing in common with any of the Hijra tribe. It was my own fear arising from my own transference. When I worked in casualty departments in public hospitals, it was part of our occupation to treat and see some ghastly, fearful sights. A group of angry Hijras bursting into the casualty ward, was just one such example. During the English Raj, a law (Criminal Tribes Act 1871) was passed against them, hoping to eradicate their existence. They were strictly monitored during that period but after India regained its independence, they were denotified in 1952 yet the stigma still persists.

'U's therapy, lasted approximately two and a half years. During this period, she went through a number of episodes of severe depression. One was precipitated by a change in the contraceptive pill. She realised this herself, but in a masochistic way suffered for number of weeks before asking her GP to return to the original contraceptive medication. At this time, she had problems in relating to other Indian boys at her university. She seemed to be initially over-friendly with them and falling in love in succession with a number of them. Both her individual and group sessions would be dominated by stories of her strong attachments to these boys and how they would almost trick her into believing they cared for her, whereas they seemed to overcome their infatuation for her very quickly after a short period of time and often made a mockery of her niaiveness. This behaviour was accepted by her therapy group in appearing to be quite similar to a person from an Australian culture of the same age. The group which was comprised of young adults of her own age and up, then started reading novels like, "A Suitable Boy" by V Seth, so as to understand her better. The group's reactions helped me as well, as I was aware of feeling critical of her flirting and her need for masochistic suffering.

During her therapy she gained confidence and was instrumental in her ex-lover returning a fairly large sum of money he had borrowed from her family. This was a major achievement for her as it demonstrated that she felt no longer subservient to him. Another of her main achievements was that two years later she started therapy she started Indian dancing classes once again without her father's permission. One brother joined her too. She gradually seemed to improve in many aspects. She started doing part-time work in the evenings and for the first time, had money of her own even though she felt obliged to give it all to the family pool. She would then help herself to money from her mother's purse when felt she needed it. Difficulties in separating from her mother were still ongoing, although to a much lesser extent.

Saying Goodbye

Finally, it seemed to me that she was ready to leave therapy. Her weight was stable and she had started being involved with a more academic and wiser set of friends at University, a significant proportion of whom was Australian. It seemed she had integrated with her social peer group as well as could be expected at that time. She then suddenly regressed and became involved with an Indian lecturer. She held him in awe especially because he had a separate office of his own at the campus and of course he had the 'name of god'. He seemed to be somebody who always talked about his previous girlfriends. He boasted he had these girls totally under his control during the time of his relationship with them claiming to know their past, their future and their very thoughts. This naturally frightened her as well as attracted her to his powers. It was also in keeping with her Indian cultural upbringing where it is acceptable to feel totally devoted to one's husband and willing to sacrifice everything if need be. Even with the help of the group this attachment to the senior lecturer did not appear to change.

In my own counter-transference to her I was not concerned about her safety anymore. I felt she was quite capable of ceasing the relationship if and when she wished to do so. It was at this time that she brought in the picture of an Indian goddess, 'Dukh Devi' (Goddess of sufferings). She described the picture as follows, "It was as if by miracle my dance teacher gave me her picture. I always wanted it all my life". It is almost as if her dance teacher knew how important such a picture would be for her and produced it. She may have felt that Ms 'U' needed such a Goddess who would understand and be able to share her sufferings forever.

It was at this time that I felt either I could have persisted with the therapy and tried to help her to alleviate her need for ongoing suffering or else I could set her free into the big wide world and allow her to regain her place within her own Indian culture, with her own family and her friends. She seemed close to her group of friends who were mainly from university and less attached to the therapy group and individual therapy. She was also increasingly absent from both her individual and group sessions.

After considerable deliberation, I decided that by setting her free I would also be helping her to develop further her need for separation/individuation and also attempt to cope by herself with her masochistic tendencies. She was still entering into unsuitable relationships followed by unnecessary excessive suffering. I was aware that if she had been an Australian, I may not have discharged her at this stage. Perhaps my experience with Indians helped me to realise the importance of letting her go now, so as to enable her to grow up by herself. I also knew 'U' would return to see me if she really got into difficulties. She still remained very close to her mother.

Fortunately, 'U's' life did turn out to have a good ending. Some months later, the same physician to whom she had initially been referred for her loss of weight, wrote to me, saying that she had come for a review and had actually seemed very much happier than when he had previously seen her. Her weight gain had been stabilised and she was enjoying her Indian classical dancing tremendously. She obviously had great talent in this area. He said she had continued to blossom with her university work as well and now no longer needed time off due to ill health.

A couple of months later she came to see me with a box of chocolates. She confirmed her current happier frame of mind. She told me she was still single, had withstood her parent's attempts to engage her in an arranged marriage and had broken off the unhealthy relationship with the lecturer. With great pride she told me she had bought the chocolates from her own money and not by dipping into her mother's purse. I believe this case history reveals how a sensitive handling of a person from a different culture can be instrumental in a positive outcome.

References

Dehejia, Vidya (1999), *The Great Goddesses. Female Divinity in South Asian Art* (copyright Smithsonian Institute) Munich, London and New York: Arthur M Sackler Gallery in association with Mapin Publishing Pt Ltd, Ahmedabad, India and Prestel Verlag.

CHAPTER 1 (b):

Difficulties in a Naïve Young Indian Female in Adjusting to a Western Culture in Australia

This article describes differences and similarities during conducting individual and group analytic psychotherapy in a nineteen year old single Indian Hindu girl who had recently immigrated to Melbourne with her family. This is a complex case which needs careful unravelling of 'Transference' and 'Counter-transference' thoughts related to feelings emerging between therapist and client towards each other. These may arise from any number of issues. The thoughts and feelings arising may well have a bearing on the personal life and experience of both persons — namely the person who requests analysis (the analysand), as well as the analytically orientated therapist, who accepts the role of the analyst. Both need to be aware during the initial assessment period, as to why the referral for analysis has been made.

Firstly, there is a *precipitating cause,* prior to which there has been *a predisposing, as well as a contributory* issue. There may be some preliminary linking in the mind of the analyst as to the current reason for attending. As it is very early in the treatment, that these thoughts have arisen, they often need to be clarified as time progresses.

However, it is beneficial to all concerned, that the treating therapist or analyst, feels confident regards being able to continue the treatment or is able to give a reasonable explanation why someone else would be more appropriate as a therapist or analyst. To be able to do so, the emotions (as well as the 'vibes' one feels in lay terms) which have arisen on both sides, need to be seriously considered.

Another issue is for the therapist to gradually obtain a clear understanding of the past and present history leading to this current interview. Cultural, racial, intellectual and environmental factors need to be kept in mind. This includes, whether or not both persons have experienced living in the same or in different countries, cultures, their ability to work with persons of different religions, intellectual and financial or other bio-psycho-social factors intertwining with each other. These reactions may start at an unconscious level initially.

An experienced supervisor, who has been trained by having personal analysis in a compatible theoretical background knowledge, is an asset in helping the analyst to truthfully explore the interactions which are occurring. Self-control, with curtailment of impulsive acting-out behaviour, during ongoing treatment, is essential. Both therapist and client do try initially, as best they can, to avoid denial or repression of feelings, as well as concentrating on intrusive thoughts interfering during the here and now of the present. However, it is mainly the efforts of experienced supervisors, who have the additional opportunity to recognise current difficulties arising during therapy. These are major components of treatment within a psychoanalytic framework.

Countertransference of the therapist is a very important component during treatment. A psychodynamic therapist does not focus intensively to the same depth of an analyst, during sessions. The later focuses on interpretation of dreams, free association and parapraxis in greater depth.

Psychiatry in India in the late 1950's and exposed to a Lunatic Asylum

Herewith are contributory features during my very first visit of chronic psychotic inmates.

This occurred during my brief exposure to patients suffering very severe chronic mental illness in Sri Lanka. We were medical students spending a short time of' exposure observing severe, chronic, uncontainable patients. About a dozen of us at a time were escorted to an asylum some miles away from the city. This visit only lasted a couple of hours, while consultant psychiatrists demonstrated the various symptoms certain patients were demonstrating. This was before anti-psychotic medication was available. We then went to a seminar where we were taught greater details.

Interestingly, most of the students were females!

The men had heard from senior students what it was all about and had gone to a nearby cafe, guzzling coconut water and eating their brunch, while waiting for us to join them. We, the curious and adventurous females, were taken by the hospital bus to an enclosure close by. As we entered the place, we all got a nasty shock!

The patients appeared wild and uncontrollable. Their hair was totally matted and unwashed for perhaps a couple of months. Some walked about shouting aggressively, while others were seen in totally catatonic postures.

Those patients who appeared violent were kept behind bars for their own safety. (This was in the late 1950's.) I felt fearful and grossly uncomfortable even seeing these patients, whom I will describe shortly. They would try to reach out physically towards students like myself, screaming relentlessly for most of the accessories we were wearing. It felt as if they were trying to tear off all our clothes and accessories. We were instructed to keep on walking forwards, without showing any emotions, passing by their advances and keeping our personal fears under total control. Thankfully, while we walked down the corridors, we had full police and/or guards protecting us on both sides. Hence, we really had no fear of being harmed. The main discomfort was their loud pleading screams begging us to come close to them. It felt like the 'nameless dread'. The inmates kept their eyes focussed on us all the time.

This was all only in mainly one large locked ward with plenty of ventilation. Senior fully trained psychiatrists were allocated for these patients, once again with full protection of police and guards. If not for having endured this experience, I may not have been able to treat my present anorexic patient as calmly. We were expected to attend for a week, but we too, like the men, stayed absent from the 'wild uncontrollable' ward and mainly attended the seminars only. There was no attendance sheet or questions and answers to submit. No-one complained and no-one felt traumatised at the time. However, the memory lingers on. I was used to the matted hair and the screaming. Since when I lived in India, from 1946-1958, we had one middle aged neighbour living next door who was identical regards matted hair, but wore clean clothes. One person stayed at home to look after her and give tablets, while the rest had jobs in the city. She was quite harmless and never ran away or reached out for other's belongings. She mainly muttered to herself.

A Naïve Patient "U" (for Unique) presenting with symptoms of Anorexia Nervosa

Treated with Individual Therapy combined with Adolescent Group Psychotherapy.

This particular patient was referred to me by a university counsellor for treatment of Anorexia Nervosa of over four months duration. Fortunately, the patient's menstrual cycle was still regular. The counsellor was a friend of mine and knew my work. Moreover, she knew that I was brought up in India between the ages of five and twenty-one. Also, I have considerable regard, as well as knowledge, for many racial and cultural aspects of Indians.

As a female, analytically orientated therapist, who had fortunately also been brought up in India for most of her youth, I could also intuitively make accurate important decisions, for example regards when it is appropriate to intervene and when to wait silently. Finally, an Indian therapist also needs to be confident regarding when the time is appropriate for discharge due to readiness for the patient to cease therapy.

Most Indian children are surrounded by relatives, who encourage dependency and are very reluctant for adolescents and even adults to leave the family home. Four beds in a bedroom are the norm, due to space limitation, as well as separation/individuation problems.

Awareness and understanding of one's own Countertransference

I truly believe this is the most important key that opened numerous doors of how I felt at the first sight of my patient. I could not identify with her in any way. She seemed so different from what I had unconsciously conceived her to be. I felt somewhat scared of her, on her first visit. I realised it was her unusual strange appearance, combined with how she had dressed herself. I did not feel any prejudice towards her. I started thinking through reasons for the *incohesion* (Hopper) and how we both could overcome them. One needs to be able to discern the truth, without turning a blind eye. One needs to know one's enemy without escalating anger or starting on a destructive pathway. Finally, one needs to make sufficient attempts to look at all sides of the origins of destruction and curbing calamities arising. In summary, one needs to remain aware that by turning a blind eye to one's own transference, it is not possible to help another man, woman or child.

I thought clearly about my feeling that I was either hers or someone else's worthless object. I realised this was probably projective identification. I asked myself, over and over again, as to when and where had I felt that scene before.

Here was my final counter-transference realisation:

It had nothing to do with my new anorexic patient. It had to do with my own memory of the women locked up in cages in the lunatic asylum in India, with poor hygiene, matted hair, dishevelled clothes, along with loud screaming, trying to frighten all of us observers, who were mainly female medical students. As we were well surrounded by police protection and guards, we had felt very safe and secure. This memory came back to me now fifteen years later. Moreover, I had no one to protect me in my consulting room, as my secretary had left early that day.

I smiled and welcomed my patient. I will refer to her as 'U' for 'Unique'.

U's (Unique) Strange Entrance and Acting — In of her desire

'U' had come in barefoot and running into my consulting room without even ringing the doorbell. Then, she looked all around carefully and interestingly at each part of the room. I signalled a comfortable chair, opposite to where I was seated. She seemed oblivious of my existence at first and then rushed to sit on the couch, just next to where I was seated. She pushed away a pillow from the couch and changed the seating arrangement to suit her. I introduced myself: and waited for her response. She handed me the letter from her counsellor. I now turned my head to be able to see her. I had never seen an outpatient at my consulting rooms like her. I felt a chill down my spine. I had only seen females like her at the Lunatic Asylum. Her hair was long and matted. It had not been washed or combed for a few weeks. She was dressed in an ankle length, faded green, highly starched thick cotton unironed petticoat which had dropped to her lower abdomen, due to the gross recent loss of weight. Similarly, she had worn a loose, totally creased blouse and had a faded dupatta scarf draped around her shoulders. She smiled weakly with embarrassment. Her shyness was typical of a young rural Indian young female in her late teens. She had thick make-up with delicate typically Indian decorations around her eyes and forehead. She also had dyed the palms of her hands and the soles of her feet with henna. All her decorations were almost faded by now. Her outfit had been embroidered all over with gold and silver thread. She had worn four expensive pure gold necklaces, attractive dangling golden earrings and a number of gold 2bangles on each hand. Had her outfit been newer, her hands recently decorated, nails manicured and her hair groomed and designed appropriately, she would have been dressed suitably for an Indian wedding party, if not the bride herself! Apparently, her mother supported her regarding the clothes and expensive jewellery she wore regularly. Her father would be upset with her, but she had full support from her mother, so did not take heed of his views. Prior to her weight loss, she certainly would have been a very beautiful female. She now smiled weakly at me, but said nothing. I waited patiently.

It seemed perhaps, that this was her decision to put something she wished to say, into action, rather than describe it in words. As I did not wish to force her to disclose anything, she was not yet ready, I encouraged her to talk whenever she felt ready to do so. She started to talk after a few minutes. During routine gathering of details of her history, she reluctantly volunteered that she belonged to a caste lower than the Brahmins. There are four main castes in India with Brahmins deemed to be of the highest order. Her family looked up to those with intellectual achievements greatly.

She did not reveal to me what her own caste was and I did not find the need to embarrass her any further. I had quickly realised that this was an issue of humiliation for her. It was more than sufficient to know that she and her family felt inferior to the Brahmins. She volunteered that she was aware that her depressed state was due to the impending break up of a five year old intimate relationship with a young Indian lover from the Brahmin caste. He was now intending to return to India to get married to a Brahmin female with whom his family had arranged a marriage many years ago. This was now decided to take place shortly. He had not told her about this arrangement at the start of their relationship and hence she felt very betrayed and devastated, as she had hoped they would marry in the near future. He lived close to them and most of the time after work, he came to her home. He had apparently encouraged her to believe that nothing would change between them, even after his marriage. She certainly did not want to be second to his wife and hence had realised that their relationship needed to end soon. She had low self-esteem and did not consider herself to be ready for marriage.

She was an extremely dark complexioned, very thin young female, with attractive facial features. It is important to note that for most Indians, the fairer the female the more attractive she is seen to be. Moreover, a slim female is considered unattractive and unhealthy. I wondered why she had needed to make a dramatic entrance and sit down exactly next to me. I introduced myself and waited for her response. She looked at me quickly and handed me the letter given by her counsellor. I now was able to look at her and felt a chill down my spine. I had never seen anyone like her as an outpatient. Her hair was long and totally matted, as if it had not been washed or combed for a few weeks or even a month. Ms U was dressed in faded green, highly starched, very thick cotton, unironed petticoat which was now almost near her lower abdomen, due to recent loss of weight. Similarly, there was a creased blouse, and a faded tom dupatta (scarf) around her shoulders, all of Indian origin. She smiled weakly in awkward embarrassment with shyness very typical of a rural Indian female. She had considerable facial make-up with typical delicate Indian decorations around her eyes and on her forehead as well as having traditional floral designs of henna dyed on the palms of her hands and soles of her feet. All these had now faded. Also, her nails showed traces of old nail polish. It seemed that recently she had not been able to attend to these aspects of self-grooming as well as she had done before. On closer view of her outfit it was freshly laundered, but had evidently been well worn. It was embroidered all over with gold and silver thread. She wore silver anklets and had very attractive dangling pure gold earrings and with a number of golden bangles on each arm as well as three or four pure gold necklaces. From both an Australian, as well as from an Indian cultural point of view, she would have been considered to be rather unusually dressed for an initial interview with a psychotherapist. Had her outfit been newer and her hands recently decorated and manicured, she would have been considered to have been quite suitably dressed for an Indian wedding as a guest, if not a bride. My initial impression was that 'U' may have been covering up a depressed interior. As the session proceeded, I realised I was correct with regard to her depressed mood. Later in therapy she told me that her father was always furious with her for dressing up the way she did with so much gold jewellery, but she took no notice of him. She simply liked it and so she wore it. Her mother supported her and did not mind how she dressed. She obviously appeared to enjoy her sexuality and enjoyed what she wore. I considered it very unwise to try and explore her presentation during this fragile, initial phase of her therapy.

She was certainly a person one could not overlook. Her outfits were always well laundered and her colour schemes were always matching with very bright typically Indian colours. She very rarely repeated her clothing. In an Indian family of moderate means, it is possible to dress attractively, as it is customary for relatives to give presents of attractive clothing to young females. As Indians have large extended families one may get numerous presents on a birthday and at religious festivals — such as Divali etc.

After my initial astonishment at her attire, I paid no more attention to it. However, as her mood gradually improved, her dresses became even more attractive. Some months later, it suddenly dawned on me that in fact 'U' was dressing up like an Indian dancer going on stage for a performance. Even at her first visit, she had rearranged my consulting room as a room suitable for a dancer! When we were finally able to discuss her desires more openly, her face beamed and shone with relief that at last I had been able to identify what she loved and represented and what her secret wish in life had always been. She told me her father had not wanted her to be a dancer, but that her mother did not mind and moreover her brother too liked dancing. Her ambition was one day to pursue training in traditional classical Indian dancing. I initially thought that this may be so as it would then enable her to enjoy her femininity which she told me had so far been a source of great pain, shame and dissatisfaction in her life.

In describing her sexual history 'U', was able to confide that she had been sexually molested several times. The first time she was molested she was in grade one and less than six years old. The man was "the son of a family friend" she said. The second incident she said was with "a very good family friend". The third she said was by "a relative, an uncle" and the fourth by "grandma's brother's son" when she was in grade five. In most of these cases, her younger brother was in the same room and at times on the same bed sleeping. The fifth sexual encounter she had was with her lover. She said she loved him and so she believed "I is supposed to happen when two people love each other". This was especially as he said he loved her too. It is important to note that she still held those who had molested her previously with awe and respect.

It is my practice to always ask what meaning there is of the names which clients describe especially related to their own culture. When 'U' described her father, she described him to be an alcoholic. When I asked her what her father's Christian name meant, she said, in a very respectful tone of voice "It is God's name". Similarly, the majority of those who had also molested her had "God's name". Only one had the name of a river. Her own name was that of a garland of flowers, she said. Her father apparently also had a history of having had an affair with a family friend's daughter. Nevertheless, she said that she respected him as well, although she did not allow him to control her.

This explained why she held those who had sexually molested her with awe and respect. At an unconscious level, she may well have been equating them with an Indian God, perhaps Lord Krishna who had many sexual partners and yet this was not considered perverse. He respected all of them.

I asked her what she thought about my name 'Sabar'. She replied that she knew it meant 'patience' and that it applied to everyone, not only to Gods or Goddesses. I agreed with her. I started her in once weekly individual psychotherapy, but it became obvious that her symptoms of anorexia remained static, although she was also under the care of an eminent physician. I then realised the importance of adding group psychotherapy, as she obviously needed additional peer group experience. She now started combined group and individual therapy. Among other issues, she now worked at her difficulties in separation and individuation from her parents and her lover. This was especially important as the lover was also a family friend and moreover had 'God's name. Besides, he had taught her brother and herself English and other subjects they learned at University.

Soon after her ex-lover's wife came to Australia, 'U' had her twenty-first birthday. At that time, he gave 'U' a number of expensive presents, although he was already married to his wife and they were living in Melbourne a few streets away. By then she was aware with the help of psychotherapy of how he had abused her trust. She was much less confused and much more in touch with her feelings of rage. She refused his presents and just kept them unopened in a part of the house, as she did not feel able to return them. She felt this was a great achievement for her. She also was able to enjoy her own twenty-first birthday party and invited a number of friends and relatives and even managed to sneak an Australian boy into the party, whom she liked greatly. As he was going overseas shortly, the relationship, though short-lived, gave her a great deal of self-confidence. The group helped her tremendously at this stage. She gained great maturity.

At this time, she described a dream where all her relatives, including her grandmother, wanted her to marry within an arranged marriage, to another relative, who was intellectually very clever. The venue of the dream then shifted from home to a picnic with a wedding scene. She saw herself as a bride in the dream saying "no, no, no" and screaming. She then sees an old well and realizes the only alternative is to jump into the well, rather than agree to an arranged marriage. However, she then runs away with everyone chasing behind her. It seemed to her as if she was now able to think independently about certain Indian customs like arranged marriage regarding which she had been brought up. Instead she now wanted a marriage based on love. Her dream seemed to also have an element of sexual desire being associated with shame and resulting, if not by death, then by feelings of persecution.

Through her therapy, which lasted a total of approximately two and a half years, she went through a number of periods of severe depression. One was precipitated by a change in the contraceptive pill. She realised this herself, but in a masochistic way suffered for a number of weeks before asking her GP to return to the original contraceptive medication.

At this time, she had problems in relating to other Indian boys at her university. She seemed to be initially over-friendly with them and falling in love in succession with a number of them. Both her individual and group sessions would be dominated by stories of her strong attachments to these boys and how they would almost trick her into believing they cared for her, whereas they seemed to overcome their infatuation for her very quickly after a short period of time and often made a mockery of her naivety. This behaviour was accepted by the group as appearing to be quite similar to a person from an Australian culture of the same age. Nevertheless, the group which was comprised of young adults of her own age, started reading novels like 'A Suitable Boy' by Vikram Seth, so as to understand her better. She soon became a very well-integrated member of the group. The group's reactions helped me as well as I was aware of feeling critical regards her flirting.

During her therapy as she gained confidence, she also was instrumental in her exlover returning a fairly large sum of money he had borrowed from their family. This was a major achievement for her as she felt no longer subservient to him. Another of her main achievements was that two years after she started therapy, she started Indian dancing classes once again, without her father's permission. Her brother joined her too. She gradually seemed to improve in many aspects. She started doing part-time work in the evenings and hence, for the first time, had some money of her own. However, she felt obliged to give it all to the family pool and would then help herself to money from her mother's purse if she needed it. Individuation/Separation difficulties from mother were still ongoing. She would inform her mother of this when she felt in a mood to do so. As we have mentioned before, difficulties in individuation are very common in the Indian culture. It is similar in Japanese culture too. It is referred to in Japan as 'Amai' (Takao Doi).

There was also one occasion when her father attempted to molest a younger girlfriend of hers. At this time 'U' became a pillar of strength for both the younger girlfriend, as well as the rest of the family whilst she took her father to task for his attempt. Her father became severely depressed. She was instrumental in helping both him and their family during this crisis.

Finally, it seemed to me that that she was ready to leave therapy. Her weight was stable and she had started being involved with a more academic and wiser set of friends at University, a significant proportion of whom were Australian. It seemed she had integrated with her social peer group as well as could be expected at that time.

However, she then suddenly regressed and became involved with an Indian Senior Lecturer. She held him in awe, especially because he had a separate office of his own at the campus and, of course, he had the 'name of God'! He seemed to be somebody who always talked about his previous girlfriends. He boasted he had these girls totally under his control during the time of his relationship with them. He claimed to know their past, their future and their very thoughts. This naturally frightened her as well as attracting her to his powers. Moreover, it was also in keeping with her Indian cultural upbringing where it is acceptable to feel totally devoted to one's husband and be willing to sacrifice everything if need be. Even with the help of the group this attachment to the senior lecturer did not appear to change.

Nevertheless, in my counter-transference to her, I was not concerned about her safety anymore. I felt she was quite capable of ceasing the relationship if and when she wished to do so. *This was very different from how I would have felt about an Australian female of her age.*

It was at this time that she brought in the picture of an Indian goddess, 'Dukh Devi' (Goddess of Suffering). She described the picture as follows. "It was as if by miracle my dance teacher gave me her picture. I always wanted it all my life". It is almost as if her dance teacher knew of the importance of such a picture for her of a Goddess and produced it. She may have felt that Ms X needed such a Goddess who would understand and be able to share her sufferings. I wondered if now, I was no longer her Goddess of Suffering. It felt a great relief for me.

It was at this time that I felt either I could have persisted with the therapy and tried to help her to alleviate her needs for ongoing suffering or else I could set her free into the big wide world and allow her to regain her place within her own Indian culture, with her own family and her friends. She now seemed to be close to her group of Australian friends who were mainly from university and less attached to the therapy group or to her individual therapy. She also had a number of increasing absenteeism's from both her individual and group sessions.

After considerable deliberation, I decided that by setting her free I would also be helping her to develop her need for separation/individuation and also attempt to cope by herself with her masochistic tendencies. She was still entering into unsuitable relationships followed by suffering. I was aware that if it had been an Australian patient, I may not have discharged her at this stage. Perhaps my experience with Indians helped me to realise the importance of letting her go now, so as to enable her to grow up by herself. I also knew 'U' would return to see me if she really got into difficulties. She still remained very close to her mother. I felt, I now needed to make the first move towards offering her a healthy and more independent life.

Fortunately, 'U's' life did turn out to have a good ending. Some months later following her termination, the same physician to whom I had referred her initially for her loss of weight wrote to me that she had come for a review and had actually seemed very much happier than when he had previously seen her. Her weight gain had been stabilized and she was enjoying her Indian classical dancing tremendously. She obviously had great talent in this area. He said she had continued to blossom with her university work and was now no longer needing time off due to ill health.

A couple of months later she came to see me with a box of chocolates! She confirmed her current happier frame of mind. She told me she was still single, had withstood her parents' attempts to engage her in an arranged marriage and had broken off the unhealthy relationship with the senior lecturer. Moreover, with great pride she told me, she had bought the chocolates from her own money and not by dipping into her mother's purse!

I believe this case history reveals how a sensitive handling of a different, but very familiar, culture can be instrumental in a positive outcome. My exploration of her Transference and my Counter-transference, were crucial in helping me regards treatment and her readiness to cease Combined Individual and Group Therapy.

CHAPTER 2:

A Unique Technique of Counselling Contempt
A case study by Pittu Laungani

Introduction

The purpose of this chapter is to highlight the centrality of Unbearable Shame and its tragic consequences when left untreated. The differences in outcomes between bearable and unbearable Shame, as well as between Shame and Contempt are clarified.

The feeling of Shame is a universal experience which is encountered frequently, in varying degrees and in numerous situations in our everyday lives. It needs to be recognised that every shame producing event both challenges as well as threatens the core sense of integrity in ourselves. Shame is the most personal and private of all feelings. Shame can either be bearable or extreme.

Bearable shame can be described as an emotion which enables the recipient to be able to put it under scrutiny and gain benefit through learning from the experience. It can be normalised as being a part of everyday living. It can then be felt to be no more than a temporary embarrassment which is dismissed and soon forgotten by thinking through events that led to it. One can even learn through the experience.

On the other hand, **Unbearable shame** arises when one feels an emotionally overwhelming humiliation, accompanied by the conviction that one's credibility, honour and very sense of self-worth has been totally destroyed forever (*Shame lurks unseen,*

Mollon, P., 2002, p. xii). Due to its serious consequences, the therapist needs to be vigilant, as it can lead to lethal consequences when left untreated. Moreover, it could keep on re-emerging with lifelong recurrences.

Working with Unbearable Shame

Helen Block Lewis (1971) discovered a very high frequency of unexplored and untreated shame markers when looking through transcripts of a large number of cases who had not achieved therapeutic success. It seemed obvious during her research with Witkin et al (1954) that the topic of shame had not been openly discussed by these therapists at the time. Some years later when shame was able to be discussed more openly, there was much better understanding of the dynamics associated with the events that had occurred then.

Donald Nathanson (1987, p. 1), in '*The Many Faces of Shame*', states that "Shame guards the boundaries of the self" and implores therapists to explore the "centrality of shame", during therapy. Of the same opinion have been Alexander (1938), Lewis (1992), Wurmser (1997) and others.

James Gilligan (2000, p. 48) who wrote about Shame, "Without a minimal amount of self-esteem, the self-collapses and the soul dies". When we cannot protect ourselves ... something gets killed within us, our souls are murdered.

The Experience of Shame

Shame is about losing one's honour. Cassio in Shakespeare's Othello says, "Oh! I have lost my reputation — lost the immortal part of myself and what remains is the bestial" (Shakespeare, 1564-1616, Othello II.3.250). In this context, loss of honour is compared to soul murder. Hence, it is no wonder that we as human beings, trying our utmost to avoid a confrontation with

Shame. Instead we put up numerous resistances, often the commonly used defence mechanisms of the ego. Some of these include Denial of Shame, Repression of Shame, Rationalisation of Shame and Disavowal of Shame which means turning a blind eye and making light of certain shameful incidents, which would have been considered much more seriously in another person. Disavowal with not directing full responsibility to the person in power is often seen with regards to well-known public figures where even the press, for whatever reason, prefers to remain quiet.

Today's society, especially in western cultures, finds it more acceptable to initially link stresses with terms, such as being *"demoralised"* (Clarke, D. M., & Kissane, D. W., 2002), which may lead to depression. This may then be treated openly with antidepressants. It is more acceptable to discuss the origins of demoralisation. The ventilation of feelings with a trustworthy friend or colleague may help greatly too. During the acute period of carrying a burden of undisclosed shame and suffering produces tremendous emotional pain. One may also often lose one's courage to defend oneself. At such a time, it may feel it is far easier to adopt a passive victim role, rather than be the one who fights aggressively to regain one's reputation. This needs supportive intervention.

Dr Pittu Laungani, a brilliant counsellor

Dr Pittu Laungani, a brilliant counsellor who had achieved a Lifetime Award in Multicultural Psychology from the University of Toronto, worked with a young Indian female who had a history of rape. He worked empathically, in a very appropriate, caring manner. He gave her sufficient space to think, converse with him and overcome her shame. He even spent his own time to study her Sikh religious text, "Adi Granth" from which they discussed suitable parts. The treatment was very successful and ended appropriately. He received a wedding invitation from her family sometime later!

Pittu Laungani describes the necessity for clinicians to be experienced in multicultural counselling as *"Indian society not unlike other eastern societies is a family-based and community-orientated society"*.

My Relationship with Pittu Laungani

I have been privileged to meet Pittu Laungani for many years prior to his death. Pittu had the exceptional capacity to blend with people from various cultures. It would have never occurred to analytic psychotherapist to read the bible of an Indian Sikh lady, so as to help her to break the barriers between herself and her therapist. Similarly, Pittu had a mind of his own and when he was suffering intensely with incurable illness, he and his wife picked up the courage to confront the doctor and say to him that it seemed that the doctor was behaving as if there's no more hope for Pittu. The doctor must have felt enraged. He turned his back and went out and changed all the medications. This started Pittu on the road to recovery!

Pittu clarifies differences between Eastern and Western cultures very clearly. In individualism he states that the reference is on personal responsibility, self-reliance and self-achievement. This contrast with communalism which emphasises a collective responsibility, which includes the needs of the family. In addition, social behaviours tend to be cast and religion related.

Similarly, cognitivism emphasises rationality and logic. This can be compared to emotionalism in western society which emphasises on feelings, emotions and intuition.

Freewill emphasises the freedom of choice when compared to the western world, whereas easterners believe in limited freedom of choice with restrictions imposed by one's cast and family orientation. The western world believes where there's a will there is a way, whereas the easterners believe their success and failures are related to one's *Karma*. It was a great honour for Pittu to have received a lifetime achievement award in Multicultural Psychology by the Ontario Institute of Adult Education and Counselling, University of Toronto.

Hindu spirituality in life, death and bereavement

Pittu Laungani gives us a first-hand knowledge and insight combined with detailed clinical descriptions of cultural, religious and spiritual aspects of death and bereavement practices around the world. Culture is described as being a "pattern of values passed from generation to generation". This includes knowledge, customs, beliefs and laws.

The Incorrect Diagnosis of Death In a Hawker

Pittu starts by sharing a very vivid personal experience of the death of a much-loved Hindu hawker who was on his daily rounds with prepared delicious savouries. The death ceremony was very well attended as Kali was extremely popular with a pleasant manner.

The funeral pyre was constructed by Brahmin priests and set alight. Suddenly a piercing scream was heard from Kali who had been incorrectly diagnosed as being dead. He was resurrected and carried to his home amidst great joy.. Pittu describes the Hindu religion law of Karma and Buddhist pathway to Nirvana. Each one of us, in our own cultures and religions, will see this event in our own way.

The tragedy was that the average person who had much love for Kali and looked forward to seeing him daily, now suddenly became afraid of his spirit. They may have wondered whether or not the same frightening incident would reoccur. It is advisable to compare our own value systems and our fears when such a frightening experience occurs right in front of our very own eyes. Freud may have named it as an uncanny experience.

Guilt

As there are numerous points of view about Guilt as well, I personally apply the understanding of the origins of Guilt from Melanie Klein's seminal paper "*Love Guilt and Reparation*" (1937) in which she states that, "love and gratitude arise spontaneously in the baby in response to the love and care of the mother". However, "The power of love is there in the baby, as well as destructive impulses". Guilt can arise in young babies and children from the perfectly normal phantasy of destroying the mother, when the mother appears to frustrate the child by not complying with immediate gratification. The guilt can then be resolved through reparative measures between both mother and child.

Guilt followed by remorse in Asian Mythology: Ajase Complex by Heisaku Kosawa

Guilt in Asian mythology is described below, very clearly. It describes how guilt arising from a cold and calculated attempt by Queen Idaike to murder her own son at birth, was able to be resolved through love, reparation and forgiveness. As can be seen, although the guilt caused great pain and suffering, it was not soul destroying for either. This is known as the *Ajase Complex* originally written by Heisaku Kosawa, a Japanese psychoanalyst, in 1953. It describes how Queen Idaike organises the murder of a hermit, followed by an attempted murder of her own son Ajase, both of which were finally resolved through remorse and sacrifice. She seeks and follows the advice of Lord Buddha and devotes herself totally to the care of her son who had discovered her past crimes and then fallen ill. Ajase, with his mother's remorse, love and dedication, recovers and forgives her. Following his father's death, he becomes "an enlightened sovereign". In this case reparation of his mother following guilt, contributed to a successful outcome.

Queen Idaike's initial attempt to harm her son can be seen as the action of a 'Pale Criminal'. This is proven by her reparation.

The Indian myth of Ganesha has a similar theme, but here it is his father, who after cutting off his son's head, feels intense guilt and remorse and replaces it with the head of an elephant. Ganesha is now a revered figure in Hindu homes and considered to bring good luck. So, once again we see a successful outcome following remorse after guilt.

Criminals from a Sense of Guilt

In telling me about their early youth, particularly before puberty, people who have afterwards often become very respectable have informed me of forbidden actions which they committed at the time — such as thefts, frauds, and even arson. I was in the habit of dismissing these statements with the comment that we are familiar with the weakness of moral inhibitions at that period of life, and I made no attempt to find a place for them in any more significant context. But eventually I was led to make a more thorough study of such incidents by some glaring and more accessible cases in which the misdeeds were committed while the patients were actually under my treatment, and were no longer so youthful. Analytic work then brought the surprising discovery that such deeds were done principally because they were forbidden, and because their execution was accompanied by mental relief for their doctor. He was suffering from an oppressive feeling of guilt, which he did not know the origin, and after he had committed a misdeed this oppression mitigated. His sense of guilt was at least attached to something.

Paradoxical as it may sound, I must maintain that the sense of guilt was present before the misdeed, that it did not arise from it, but conversely — the misdeed arose from the sense of guilt. The pre-existence of the guilty feeling had of course been demonstrated by a whole set of other manifestations and effects.

But scientific work is not satisfied with the establishment of a curious fact. There are two further questions to answer: what is the origin of this obscure sense of guilt before the deed, and is it probable that this kind of causation plays any considerable part in human crime?

An examination of the first question held out the promise of bringing us information about the source of mankind's sense of guilt in general. This invariable outcome of analytic work was to show that this obscure sense of guilt derived from the Oedipus complex and was a reaction to the two great criminal intentions of killing the father and having sexual relations with the mother. In comparison with these two, the crimes committed in order to fix the sense of guilt to something came as a relief to sufferers. We must remember in this connection that parricide and incest with the mother are two great human crimes, the only one which, as such, are pursued and abhorred in primitive communities. And we must remember, too, how close other investigations has brought us to the hypothesis that the conscience of mankind, which now appears as an inherited mental force, was acquired in connection with the Oedipus complex.

In order to answer the second question we must go beyond the scope of psycho-analytic work. With children it is easy to observe that they are 'naughty' on purpose to provoke punishment, and are quiet and contented after they have been punished. Later analytic investigation can often put us on the track of the guilty feeling that induced them to seek punishment. Among adult criminals we must no doubt accept those who commit crimes without any sense of guilt, who have either developed no moral inhibitions or who, in their conflict with society, consider themselves justified in their action. However as regards the majority of criminals, i.e. those for whom punitive measures are really designed, such a motivation for crime might very well be taken into consideration. It may throw light on some obscure points in the psychology of the criminal, and furnish punishment with a new psychological basis.

A friend has since called my attention to the fact that the 'criminal sense of guilt' was known to Nietzche too. The pre-existence of the feeling of guilt, the utilization of a deed in order to rationalize this feeling, glimmer before us in Zarathustra's sayings 'On The Pale Criminal'. Let us leave it to the future research to decide how many criminals are reckoned among these 'pale' ones.

[In the editions before 1924,'obscure sayings', -- a hint at the idea of a sense of guilt being a motive for misdeeds is already to be found in the case history of 'Little Hans' (1909*b*), Standard Ed.,10, 442, as well as in that of the 'Wolf Man' (1918*b*), Standard Ed., 17, 28, which, though published later than the present paper, was in fact mostly written in the year before it. In this latter passage the complicating factor of masochism is introduced. Thanks to 'Little Hans' being supervised (via his father), by Sigmund Freud. He became a famous orchestra conductor, and always introduced himself as 'Little Hans'.

Guilt in 'Pale Criminal'

Sigmund Freud (1914-1916), in helping us to understand the psychology of guilt, discusses the possibility of there already existing in the Pale Criminal a sense of guilt long before the crime was committed. The Prophet Zarathustra had written this to the notice of all, so as to make people aware of the intensity of guilt leading to a criminal offence based on masochistic self-punishment. Society needs to respond with attunement rather than abandon with shame.

Friedrich Nietzsche

Friedrich Wilhelm Nietzsche (1844-1900) believed that far more important than having the courage of one's convictions, one should have the courage to attack one's convictions. He lived his life by this policy and influenced numerous thinkers and writers who came after him.

Nietzsche was born the son of a Lutheran minister, in 1844. He was given a very pious upbringing. However, with the death of his father when he was five years of age, the family lost their status and wealth at one stroke. His father Karl Ludwig died of 'Softening of the brain', which caused insanity, and early death. The exact cause of the softening of the brain was never proven.

After his father's death the family moved to a small town where they were respected and lived happily. Friedrich was a frail child and missed a lot of schooling, due to severe headaches. He developed a love of music, which helped him to separate him from his companions and other childhood pursuits. Due to his overpowering sister Elizabeth he developed a negative mind set about women. He enjoyed the company of intellectual men such as Richard Wagner, the great composer and musician.

Nietzsche served in the Prussian army as a medical orderly. There are stories of him being stricken with dysentery and diphtheria, which may have led him to develop syphilis. He suffered physical collapse after he was released from the army, which plagued him for the rest of his life.

Nietzsche excelled academically and won a scholarship to the University of Bonn where his studies were mainly in Theology. Due to his prolific writing of articles on classical literature, he was offered a chair in Classical Philosophy at the University of Basle,

Switzerland. From about 1869 he excelled in teaching, though he had frequent bouts of illness. During this he wrote extensively.

Nietzsche's life changed dramatically when he fell in love with a young attractive female Russian aristocrat, Lou Salome. Their relationship ended badly for Nietzsche, and was crushed by his sister Elizabeth's influence. This left Nietzsche severely depressed. This period was followed by recovery which led to him writing 'Thus Spake Zarathustra', his most profound work.

After 'Thus Spake Zarathustra' he wrote feverishly producing eight major works, but this was the end of his writing as he had a severe mental breakdown in Italy. He never recovered from his insanity, living the rest of his life first in an asylum, then with his mother, and finally with his younger sister Elizabeth until his death in August, 1900.

The Solitude of Unbearable Shame
Sabar Rustomjee – 12/04/2007

General Considerations about Unbearable Shame

The feelings of Shame is a universal experience which is encountered frequently, in varying degrees and in numerous situations in our everyday lives. It needs to be recognised that every shame producing event both challenges as well as threatens the core sense of integrity in ourselves. Shame is the most personal and private of all feelings. As very appropriately described by Paul Mollon (2002) *'Shame lurks unseen'*.

Bearable Shame can be described as an emotion which enables the recipient either to be able to put it under scrutiny and gain benefit through learning from the experience or be able to normalise it as being a part of everyday living and not feel more than a temporary embarrassment which is dismissed and soon forgotten.

On the other hand, Unbearable Shame arises when one feels emotionally overwhelming humiliation, accompanied by the conviction that one's credibility, honour and very sense of self-worth has been actually destroyed forever. As the emotion of shame is not easily visible, it draws little attention as long as the shame producing event remains hidden to the outside world.

Following an episode of childhood humiliation when during play, an 'unruly' donkey unseated him and his face was scratched all over by thorns, Nelson Mandela says, "I had lost face among my friends. Even though it was a donkey that had unseated me, I learned that to humiliate another person is to make him suffer an unnecessarily cruel fate. Even as a boy I defeated my opponents without dishonouring them". Later on, he also poses the question, "Is there such a thing as a person being justifiably shamed?"

Working with Unbearable Shame

Shame can be acute or chronic, with lifelong recurrences in the shamed person {Helen Block Lewis (1971)} discovered a very high frequency of unexplored and untreated shame makers, when looking through a large number of transcripts discussed by these therapists at the time. Some years later when shame was able to be discussed more openly, there was much better understanding of the dynamics associated with the events that had occurred then. Unfortunately, by this time these patients had returned with new complaints 0f even greater intensity Donald Nathanson (1987) in "Many faces of Shame", states that "Shame guards the boundaries of the self" and implores therapists to explore the "centrality of shame", during therapy. Of the same opinion have been Alexander (1938), Lewis (1992), Wurmser (1997), and others.

In the cases described in this article, this very issue is kept well in the forefront of our discussions.

Dr. Pittu Launghani, in his work with unbearable shame, has pointed out all of the above very painstakingly. His knowledge and experience in this field of cross-cultural research in this matter, as well as his personal life experiences and competence in Indian cultural and religious issues has provided us with the opportunity of studying his wrings and exploring our own horizons in this field.

The Experience of Shame

Shame is about losing one's honour. Cassio in Shakespeare's Othello says, "Oh I have lost my reputation — lost the immortal part of myself and what remains is bestial" (Shakespeare, 1564-1616. Othello II.3.250). In this context loss of honour is compared to soul murder. Hence it is no wonder that we as human beings try our utmost to avoid a confrontation with Shame. Instead we put up numerous resistances, often the commonly used defence mechanisms of the ego. Some of these include Denial of Shame, Repression of Shame, Rationalisation of Shame and Disavowal of Shame which means turning a blind eye, and making light o shameful incidents which would have been considered more seriously in another citizen. Disavowal is often seen with well-known public figures where the press, for whatever reason prefers to remain quiet.

Although, the various origins of Shame can be clearly seen in individuals, families, nations and even globally in society, e.g. after the September 11th terrorism attack, *the experience of feeling shame as a distinct emotion was not openly acknowledged either in the US or by the allied nations at the time*

More over during the acute period of carrying a burden of shame and suffering under tremendous emotional pain, one often loses one's courage to defend oneself. At such a time, it may feel it is far easier, to adopt a passive victim role, rather than be the one who fights aggressively to regain one's reputation. This can then lead to *living for years in the solitude of unbearable shame.*

society especially in western cultures, finds it more acceptable to bypass acknowledging the emotion of shame and instead to link it only with terms such as being ' depressed ', which can then be treated with antidepressants, or as being 'burnt out ' 'demoralised ' or harassed in the work place, for which legal action can be taken etc. Although these terms may be very accurate, what is taken away from the descriptive chain is *the emotion of unbearable shame which is an integral part of the* Today's *above.*

Hanna Segal, an English psychoanalyst, presented a paper at the inaugural meeting of 'International Psychoanalysts against Nuclear Weapons' in 1985 titled 'Silence is the Real Crime', where it is shown how nations,' muddle into war' whilst feelings of helplessness and terror increase one another in a vicious circle leading to omnipotently believing that war will provide the perfect solution to the present and to all similar future conflicts.

Two Case Histories of Sexual Abuse described by Dr. Pittu Laungani

The cases describe the Art and Technique of Multicultural Counselling and Psychotherapy. The first case describes in minute detail **Dr. Laungani's style of "Counselling in Action" (2003).**

Case 1. Is a case of sexual abuse in an Asian family, where 3 children between the ages of 13 and 15 who are all abused by the same uncle — the husband of an aunt, for a period of over 10 years. The most severely affected was a young female aged 15 years who was the oldest.

Dr. Laungani's contact with the case came from a certain police station, where a police sergeant arranged for two Asian gentlemen (who were brothers as well as being fathers of the children) to come to give a history, with Dr. Laungani agreeing to be in the position of both an interpreter of the Punjabi language, as well as an expert on cultural issues.

Noteworthy points in the technique used by Dr Laungani:

1. It is important to note that in all cases described, Dr Laungani, always reassures the reader that all possible recognisable features have been painstakenly removed by him so as to ensure confidentiality.

2. He also highlights the fact that he isolates the allocated task at hand, and never oversteps the boundary of what he believes he has been the area he has been asked to work upon.

3. Only when he is assigned to another related task, e.g. a change from being a cultural or linguistic expert, to being asked to be a counsellor, does he then assess the new role before accepting its obligations, consequences, etc.

4. During his counselling, with his tremendous experience, he then clarifies, separately the emotional reactions of all the different persons involved, in their interactions towards himself and others, through their observed manner and expressed emotions. He refrains from using the 'transference' or 'countertransference', but describes vividly and with clarity the emotions, involved on all sides as well as his own feelings at pertinent moments in time.

   - Examples of this are:
      a) How he is approached by the referring agency. In this case there is considerable respect given to him by the police sergeant, through Dr Laugani's previous contact with Scotland Yard, Hence the whole work starts on a very positive note with the involvement of trust.
      b) The attitude and emotions of the two "gentlemen"

(as graciously described by Dr. Laungani) who are brothers as well as being fathers of the molested children when they were brought by the police to try to get a clear understanding of the relevant details of the sexual molestation. He describes how the two brothers 'waved' their hands in a dismissive way, away from Dr Laungani (as if his presence was distracting them) at the time of their introduction. The brothers implied that nothing constructive could emerge from this interview, which was felt to be an unnecessary ordeal, and the issue of child molestations was a family matter only which they the brothers would decide as to what the outcome would be.

It is quite possible that an inexperienced counsellor, and one who was not 'culture centred' may well have become personally offended by all of the above. Yet we see Dr. Laungani's observation of the pouring of sweat on the brothers faces, depicting their rage, despair and helplessness He is able to openly own his own admiration of both brothers feelings of intense awareness of how all family members including their niece/daughter would be affected by such a public revelation by the media, as well as accepting the detrimental effects it would have to their family business. This is a very good example of the importance of a culture centred approach.

Laungani's strength in sharing with all of us, his own emotional reactions as he heard the story unfold is admirable. He writes "It was as if some malevolent demons had wrenched my soul apart". Therein lay the strength of Pittu Laungani — his ability to be so honest and so clear about his deepest feelings. These words reminded me, not only of those whom I have already described above regards to bearable shame, but also James Gilligan's words, "Without a minimal amount of self-esteem, the self-collapses and the soul dies. Thus, we cannot protect ourselves ... something gets killed within our souls are murdered" (2000).

We now move to examine the positive features of the case, with assessment by Dr Laungani which led to success.

1. The father of Jaswant, the 15 year old, began to develop deep trust in Dr Laungani. This must have had an impact on Jaswant's trusting of the counselling process too.

2. Dr Laungani did not put any demands on Jaswant e.g. regards the frequency or infrequency of attendance. At one time there was a 5 week gap — when her grandmother died!

3. There was no expectation of Jaswant being obliged to reveal anything she did not wish to do.

4. Hence Jaswant was allowed to become aware that she was in total control — very unlike the uncle who molested her for his sole pleasure.

5. When her grandfather developed a sudden heart attack, she was able to weep during the session, which reveals her regaining trust in a male, knowing Dr Laungani would be compassionate and not hurt her in any way.

6. Despite Dr Laungani's initial concerns that progress was slow, he began in the 6th session to realise that in addition to her grandmother, he had been her only life-line. He realised the importance of her trust in him.

7. He also started reading some hymns from her Sikh religious text 'Adi Granth'. This provided a common ground for discussion between them, and she may well have appreciated the effort he put in, in every way to help her regain trust in respectable and responsible men.

8. When the decision was made to cease therapy, she was able to be tearful, acknowledging the loss she would feel with the closure of sessions.

9. For Dr Laungani, the happy ending was when 7 or 8 years later he received an invitation for her father for Jaswant's wedding.

Guilt

As there are numerous points of view about Guilt as well, I personally apply the understanding of the origins of Guilt from Melanie Klein's seminal paper 'Love Guilt and Reparation' (1937) Ll1 in which she

describes how, ' love and gratitude arise spontaneously in the baby in response to the love and care of the mother'. She says, 'The power of Love is there in the baby as well as destructive impulses.' Guilt can

arise in young babies and children from the perfectly normal phantasy of destroying the mother, when the mother appears to frustrate the child by not complying to all the child/infant's demand for immediate gratification. At the moment of such frustration, the child may be seen to have a so-called 'massive tantrum' as mistakenly termed by society quite often. Klein explains how, ' In the baby's mind the conflicts between love and hate arise, and the fears of losing the loved one become active.' The child may well then fear that he or she has in fact destroyed the mother, which will give rise to 'guilt and distress, which enter as a new element into the emotion of Love'. However, 'side by side is the proffered urge to make sacrifices, so as to put right, loved people who in phantasy have been harmed or destroyed.'

The guilt then is resolved by reparation between the two. The mother hearing her baby's distress may use a more soothing and comforting voice and hold and contain the baby. The baby realises that in fact the mother herself, and mother's love for the baby has withstood the test of survival, there is tremendous relief. The baby/child acknowledges some time later, between sobs of self-consolation that no damage has been done to both himself/ herself or to the mother.

Guilt Followed by Reparation and Forgiveness in Asian Mythology

I am by no means saying the all, guilt can be repaired, but that where there is only guilt without shame, reparation can follow guilt through sacrifice and mutual forgiveness. There are two examples in Asian

mythology, one of the Ajase Complex and the other of Ganesha, both of which have a story of extreme guilt followed by reparation.

The Ajase Complex originally described by Heisaku Kosawa a Japanese psychoanalyst in 1953, describes sacrifices made by Queen Idaike which eventually led to resolution. Queen Idaike initially desires to have a child so that her marriage becomes more secure and her husband does not leave her in favour of a more fertile or younger wife. She cannot wait 3 years to conceive as advised by a soothsayer and hence murders a hermit who was going to be re-incarnated as her son. She then feels guilty and fears retribution from her unborn son (the hermit re-incarnated) whom she conceives. She then plans to kill Ajase her son, as soon as he is born for fear of his revenge. Fortunately, however, her son Ajase survives.

Mother and son develop a good relationship until prince Ajase discovers her past arranged murder of the hermit and her actions for his own death. Disillusioned by the mother he had idealised, out of sheer rage, he intends to kill her. Instead probably due to his own unresolved emotional conflicts, he is unable to commit the act and instead becomes very ill and is covered all over his body by foul smelling sores. The queen his mother becomes devastated and consults Buddha who advises her to now devote herself fully to the care of her son. She thus repairs her misdeeds of the past, Ajase recovers and forgives her as well. Following his father's death Ajase becomes 'an enlightened sovereign'.

Kosawa has written a paper titled 'Two Types of Guilt', one being a comparison of paranoid and depressive guilt and the movement from a punitive to a reparative guilt (Okonogi, K. 1978 L12l, t979121).

An example of Love, Guilt and Reparation in a young female aged 17, who presented with a serious eating disorder and later became the victim of rape. She also suffered from a short term episode of bipolar depressive illness. The family were from a Western Culture.

In this case reparation following guilt contributed to a successful outcome.

The issue I wish to highlight in this case is that there was considerable love as well as considerable guilt in the interactions between mother and daughter. Mother related to her daughter in a very possessive manner, staring at every movement her daughter made. At their first interview she actually turned her daughter's chair so as to face herself and make it difficult for the daughter to even look at me! In due course mother confided that she felt helplessness and guilt at not being able to help her own daughter. Similarly, the daughter felt guilty at not being able to fulfil mother's dreams/expectations of her. Father initially, kept out of mother/daughter interactions, almost as if he did not exist, until their daughter developed a sudden episode of bipolar depressive illness a few months after starting therapy. Father then visited her daily in hospital, and came to become a respected family member. It was only then that father and daughter, began to have meaningful discussions and developed an openly caring relationship. Improvement of the eating disorder along with reparation of guilt between mother and daughter leading to daughter's recovery occurred after a period of approximately 3 years.

The patient I am describing was the only long-awaited daughter who came from a family where her father who was a rather simple man, was totally devoted to her, but unable to verbalise it, possibly for fear of incurring wife's displeasure. He was intimidated by his wife and it seemed that he never dared to discuss anything important with her either. He seemed to live in the shadow of both his wife and daughter.

Mother outwardly presented as being very intelligent and strong, and was a well-known public figure, but in fact was very dependent on a couple of her friends who also appeared to have no insight at all as far as child rearing or realising the importance of the role of the father for a child. They had 2 sons both of whom had addiction to marijuana.

The parents hardly ever went out anywhere without taking their daughter with them. Mostly it seemed they both stayed impatiently at home each day, waiting for a certain almost ritualistic behaviour pattern to start.

Their daughter, my patient had a fixed routine. She would come down the staircase totally dressed up, loudly demand money from the mother, and succeed in obtaining it with little protest. She would then walk to the local 'milk bar' in high heels (pretending to be all grown up), buy the junk food (chocolates and chips), return home, go straight to her bedroom, unwrap the covering paper with as much noise as possible, devour the food in just a few minutes, and then start vomiting very loudly. As if by clockwork, the family would become electrified. Mother would race up the stairs, clean up all the vomit, spray perfume around the room, start talking baby talk to her daughter, give her a warm bath and comb her daughter's beautiful long black hair. Then both mother and daughter would snuggle into daughter's bed for an hour or so, both feeling quite content with each other and with themselves. There was absolutely no trace of any shame. The guilt at not being the idealised mother or the idealised daughter was soon repressed. Crucial issues in regards their daughter's eating disorder, her progressive weight loss, sadness at her having no friends call to see her following her having left school 3 years ago, a decision made at the time unilaterally by mother no reason given to the school, and surprisingly apparently the school did not question the same either .All this seemed extremely frustrating to myself. My patient said she had difficulty in concentration at school, but I did not think it would have warranted her leaving school at the age of 14 without any psychological testing done etc.! The above history was obtained in dribs and drabs from my patient over a period of about 3months. After the initial interview mother had shown no interest in meeting with myself.

Then one day her mother suddenly rang me to say, ' My daughter vomited a lot today, so I am cancelling your session and taking her for a picnic to cheer her up.' I then felt it was now appropriate for myself to enforce some guidelines for ongoing therapy. Unlike her husband I was not willing to stay in mother's shadow and neither did I feel intimidated by her. I had been well aware from the beginning that at some stage mother would attempt to sabotage the therapy, just as she had done with her daughter's schooling, her daughter's eating habits encouraging her by giving her money daily and then rewarding her as soon as she vomited by snuggling into bed with her etc., sabotaging school friends and even her daughter's by my patient. However, very firmly I told her I disagreed with her decision, and unless her daughter came for the session that day, relationship with her father. I did not mention any of the above as it was privileged information, given I felt I could not help her daughter any more. This took her by total surprise as nobody had so blatantly been so blunt with her. Mother then very quickly accepted my authority and said she would bring her daughter as soon as possible. We had a joint session that day with mother and I reassured her that her daughter was progressing satisfactorily at present and we all needed to be patient during times of difficulty. I also tried to discuss the importance of setting boundaries for her daughter especially when she regularly went out late at night with some very young obviously irresponsible young neighbours and arrived home in the early hours of the morning! Mother made no comment. About a month later my patient arrived for her session looking shocked and flustered but no worse, and said she thought she had been raped when she went out the previous night and had got drunk. Very innocently and surprisingly she told me, 'I thought my mother would have saved me. She always does.'

She also described how guilty she felt that she got herself into constant difficulties in life. but then it felt worth the pain as soon as her mother forgave her. She then felt loved and worthwhile when mother, once again 'made it all better'. Unlike other cases of rape. where the victim and the family feel devastated, here the incident was taken both by the mother and my patient in a rather trivialised manner. Once again it was obvious that when my patient got herself into difficulties, mother also felt worthwhile and loved that her daughter needed her and only her. All this was carefully discussed with both parents and daughter. I mentioned months. After the initial interview mother had shown no interest in meeting with myself.

Then one day her mother suddenly rang me to say, 'My daughter vomited a lot today, so I am cancelling your session and taking her for a picnic to cheer her up.' I then felt it was now appropriate for myself to enforce some guidelines for ongoing therapy. Unlike her husband I was not willing to stay in mother's shadow and neither did I feel intimidated by her. I had been well aware from the beginning that at some stage mother would attempt to sabotage the therapy, just as she had done with her daughter's schooling, her daughter's eating habits encouraging her by giving her money daily and then rewarding her as soon as she vomited by snuggling into bed with her etc., sabotaging school friends and even her daughter's relationship with her father. I did not mention any of the above as it was privileged information given by my patient. However, very firmly I told her I disagreed with her decision, and unless her daughter came for the session that day, I felt I could not help her daughter any more. This took her by total surprise as nobody had so blatantly been so blunt with her. Mother then very quickly accepted my authority and said she would bring her daughter as soon as possible. We had a joint session that day with mother and I reassured her that her daughter was progressing satisfactorily at present and we all needed to be patient during times of difficulty. I also tried to discuss the importance of setting boundaries for her daughter especially when she regularly went out late at night with some very young obviously irresponsible young neighbours and arrived home in the early hours of the morning! Mother made no comment. About a month later my patient arrived for her session looking shocked and flustered but no worse, and said she thought she had been raped when she went out the previous night and had got drunk. Very innocently and surprisingly she told me, 'I thought my mother would have saved me. She always does.'

She also described how guilty she felt that she got herself into constant difficulties in life. but then it felt worth the pain as soon as her mother forgave her. She then felt loved and worthwhile when mother, once again 'made it all better.'

Unlike other cases of rape. where the victim and the family feel devastated, here the incident was taken both by the mother and my patient in a rather trivialised manner. Once again it was obvious that when my patient got herself into difficulties, mother also felt worthwhile and loved that her daughter needed her and only her. All this was carefully discussed with both parents and daughter. I mentioned previously about my patient's short relapse into what appeared to be a bipolar illness which only lasted a couple of weeks- She denied taking any drugs.

She attended regularly now, and we were able to discuss her difficulties in separation/individuation from mother, becoming her own self and having her own identity rather than seeing mother as a saviour for life, developing a close bond with father etc. Her eating disorder ceased. She eventually married a suitable young man when she was in her mid-twenties. They had children and were able to insist on clear boundaries between her mother and their children.

The family had needed to identify and own their current, disowned aggression. The hostile dependant/ambivalent insecure relationship between daughter and mother, was now replaced by a more secure and stable one.

Nobody in the family seemed to have feelings of unbearable shame at any stage which may in retrospect have been an important prognostic factor in the recovery.

The Art and Technique of Helping Minds to Meet in an Analytic Framework

Clinical Applications

A suicidal client nearing the end of her therapy, said one day that, when she first came to see me, she was certain I would have an expressionless face and never show or even entertain the slightest emotion! She said that is what had been taught to her in senior school by one of her teachers of how psychiatrists worked. It was only when she witnessed my feelings of genuine sadness about something she was relating, that she started to trust me and believed that her wellbeing really mattered to me. Until then she thought I was helping her because, as she said "You are good at your job and you do not want to fail".

She trusted none of her friends or family, so it was naturally not easy for her to trust me as a total stranger. It was very helpful to her to bring out her negative transference towards myself so that we could discuss these openly although we were nearing the termination of her therapy.

Similarly, once a young schizophrenic client, whom I had treated for a year or so, confided in me a plan she had in driving herself and her young child, aged 7, to the top of a certain mountain close by, very early in the morning the next day (when her child was still groggy from sleep) and for her to then jump down the cliff with her child. I could not stop myself and tears spontaneously streamed down my face. I sobbed as I visualised the scene, especially her innocent little son betrayed by his sick mother whom he loved so dearly (similar to how her own mother had betrayed her trust. Her mother had destroyed their family home, at a time of severe depression). Having known of her risk of suicide, I had already spoken with her religious priest who had agreed to drive to my rooms at very short notice and take her for hospital admission. So, I simply held her hand and told her how important it was for her to be admitted voluntarily in a psychiatric hospital (I did not even need to tell her about the priest or face her with the reality that I could call the police to take her to hospital as an involuntary patient against her will, if need be.

She stared at my tearful face in disbelief for a few minutes and then angrily said, "Oh, alright then, if it really means that much to you, I will go to hospital". Both these clients in their own way needed to know that I had genuine emotions before they were ready to trust me fully. Clients like her intuitively realise that if I was willing to stand by them when they were most vulnerable and was not likely to turn my back on them during these previous moments. Needless to say, it is only when spontaneous feelings from the hear are revealed, that these feelings will be recognised and accepted as genuine.

Group Interventions in Patients with Epilepsy

I was invited to represent the IAGP members to discuss psychosocial care of patients with epilepsy. This study endeavours to evaluate the effectiveness of psychoeducational group interventions and medication in psychosocial care of patients with epilepsy, which was currently being practised at the R. Madhavan Nayar Centre for Epilepsy care, Sree Chitra Tirunal Institute for Medical Science and Technology (SCTIMST), Thiruvanathapuram, Kerala, India

1) My main aim was to introduce an analytic framework in the origins of Epilepsy. It was also to highlight the effectiveness of group intervention, when the seizures are controlled with medication or remained intractable.

2) To assess the quality of life of patients who were attending an Intervention Program.

3) In an analytic orientation, a family history and possible psychosocial traumas which may be responsible in precipitating epileptic seizures, which need to be explored.

4) The current study consisted of two epileptic scales used by the Malayalam version of Quality of Life in Epilepsy Scale (QOLIE — 31) developed by Cramer. A (1998).

Conclusion

The conclusion of this study in Thiruvanathapuram showed psychiatric education was found to be more effective in dealing with psychosocial problems of patients with epilepsy.

Common symptoms in Epileptic, Psychiatric, Drug Abuse, common neurological and emotional signs were evident. Personal as well as Group Analytic therapy produced improvement in the following areas. Results were as follows.

1) Over protective parents of epileptic patients   -- 8/10 (80 %)
2) Living with Shame of the Disease   -- 6/10 (60 %)
3) Problems with Marriage   -- 4/10 (40 %)

The other 5 patients were not married.

4) Feelings related with social aspect that "nobody will marry you, if they know you have Epilepsy "was presented by all the patients". (100 %)

The above study appears to complement the presence of an analytic framework to precipitate an epileptic attack. Hence in my opinion, Professor Sigmund Freud would be correct in his conclusion in discussion with Fyodor Dostovesky (who was his patient) regarding the problem felt by Raskolnikov towards his own father. The latter was evident in the nightmares Raskolnikov developed after the incident, where his own father refused to save the life of the old grey mare, who was beaten to death by the tavern owner, when she could not pull the cart full of drunk patrons, from the tavern.

Freud suggested that this may have eventually led to Raskolnikov killing the pawnbroker and her pregnant step-sister. The above is an example of Transference of murderous feelings towards the pawnbroker which were belonging to his own father. This was despite the fact that his father did leave to Raskolnikov a silver wristwatch at the time of his death. This had been pawned to the pawnbroker as a pledge to get cash for food for himself while he was in Petersburg. Here Freud believed that Guilt was the more powerful feeling to overcome self-dignity.

CHAPTER 3:

An Important Transcultural way of Reverence in Hinduism

Ganesha "Lord of all Kings" Contempt and Reparation with his Father

Swarmi Parthasarathy known as "Swarmi" and as A. Parthasarathy was born in 1927, Chennai, India. He carefully studied and translated the Vedas offering subtle philosophical themes into a principle of reality. He has multiple degrees in literature, science and law.

'Vedanta' is derived from two words 'veda' meaning knowledge and 'anta' implying eternal principles of life and living. It provides self-realisation. Swarmi has written 9 books including three best sellers. They include the 'Bhagavad Gita' and 'The Symbolism of God and Rituals'. He is considered to be a leading corporate guru for international institutions, world presidents and business schools. He teaches clarity of thinking which is needed to reduce stress in everyday life, increase productivity at work, maintain harmony in relationships and master the technique of living honourably.

The Name Ganesha

'Ganah' in Sanskrit means 'multitude' and 'Isa' means Lord. Ganesha hence means 'Lord of all beings'. Ganesha is the first son of Lord Siva who represents reality.

He is also known as 'Ganapathi' or 'Anana' meaning elephant

faced. Being the Lord of all obstacles, he can remove obstacles and overcome challenges.

In Hindu mythological literature he is described as having a human form with an elephant's head. One tusk in his head is broken and he has a large stomach. One leg is folded in. A rat dutifully sits at his feet asking for sanction to eat food which is spread out near him.

Ganesha seeks for eternal truth. The large ears and elephant's head on a human body is meant to represent supreme wisdom.

Gross intellect distinguishes opposites, namely day and night, black and white, joy and sorrow. Ganesha has fully developed both his gross and subtle intellects.

The trunk of the elephant can also perform both gross and subtle activities. It can uproot a tree, as well as pick up a needle from the ground. Ganesha's intellect penetrates both the material and spiritual worlds. This is a state which a man of perfection aspires to achieve. He should not be swayed by agreeable and disagreeable circumstances. A man of perfection has transcended the opposites in the world. Once man has mastered the influence of these pairs, he becomes a 'Ganesha'. He can then experience and undergo heat, cold, war, peace, birth or death. These facts are studied by Swarmi.

One can control one's own desires by the destruction of 'Vasanas' (a rich food item). This is done by offering roasted rice which loses its capacity to germinate and dilate the stomach. Ganesha's one leg on the ground indicates one personality dealing with the world, the other leg indicates supreme reality which allows to be rooted in the Atman (soul) within himself. At the feet of the Lord is spread material wealth, power, prosperity and food. He always has these at his command, although he is indifferent towards them. Next to the food is the tiny rat looking towards Ganesha. The rat does not touch the food, but waits for his master's sanction. The rat represents desire.

Ganesha has four arms. One holds an axe and symbolises the destruction of desire. The second hand pulls the seeker out of his worldly entanglements and offers its bliss discovered from within his own self. The third hand holds a rice bowl that gives satisfaction and contentment. The fourth hand holds a Lotus which draws attention that each one can aspire to obtain supreme state of Reality. The beauty of a delicate lotus is a flower to be admired.

Ganesha occupies a place of distinction reaching the supreme goal of reaching the maximum which life, strength and courage offer oneself. The Bhagvad Gita believes that it is alright to die for a cause. However, it is not at all the correct action to kill another for the pleasure it gives oneself! Here I would like to add that it is not praiseworthy to scorn, humiliate and destroy another, with contempt, just so as to give oneself a feeling of worthless superiority.

Although Mahatma Gandhi never encouraged his wife to give up eating meat, of any type, she did so, of her own volition. Vegetarian food canteens are equipped separately from non-vegetarian ones. Vegetarians believe they are more well balanced in their diet and are healthier and less aggressive than their counterparts. (I am not aware of research studies in this area.)

Contempt and Reparation in the life of Ganesha and his Father

Lord Siva realises his mistake by giving orders to cut off his son's head unknowingly. He had not known his son's existence. He repairs his own action by producing a more versatile alternative in the form of Ganesha.

Ganesha and his father both teach restraint in fulfilling all their desires and to wait until these are offered to them. An example is that of the rat at Ganesha's feet waiting to be offered the food.

The Anti-Group

When a child has a fantasy of destruction, it is important for the child to be aware of external reality that exists outside the inner self. This provides a learning experience of great significance. Foulkes always believed in trusting the group, which emphasises "the positive aspects of the group". The regressive and destructive aspects are clarified by Bion and Klein. The anti-group by Morris Nitsun (1996) believes that certain anti-groups can be resolved, but in others it may have the capacity to destroy the foundation of the group.

Ganpati

Among the various gods and goddesses, the Hindu culture reveres the elephant faced deity, known as Ganesha or Vinayaka. India celebrates one day per year in a festival known as Ganpati.

Ganesha means the supreme one who now needs no leader himself. In analytical terms he behaves like an omnipotent deity, who has overcome all obstacles and challenges. He can keep on doing so for all time. The majority of Indian businesses and households keep a statue of Ganpati near their front door to bring them good luck and prosperity.

The origin of Ganesha starts with him being the first son of his father Lord Siva who represents reality.

The Origin of Ganesha

His mother Parvati was often left all alone in her palatial house when Lord Siva went to conquer neighbouring aggression of districts that wanted to overcome the land belonging to Lord Siva. She longed to have a male child and being a Goddess was finally able to do so without the help of any man. She named him Ganesha. He was very dearly loved by his mother and allocated to the task of protecting her. One day his father Lord Siva returned triumphant from a battle and returned to his wife's room. However, Ganesha would not let him in, as he did not know who he was. Siva was furious and told one of his huntsmen to take the boy away and kill him. Parvati heard the noise, came out and was covered with tears and severe grief. She begged Siva to reverse his decision, which he did. He now ordered the Huntsman who had already cut off Ganesha's head, to replace it, with the first animals' head he came across. The Indians pride themselves on how they were the first to have a successful organ transplant.

Mythology Attributed to Ganesha

He carries a noose, demonstrating the importance of slowing down and examining the other person's intentions. In addition, he has a sharp gold object which can cause fatality to a stranger if he or she is forcing the way inside the house to harm his mother, Parvati. When he realises there is no danger this is a blessing from Ganesha to enter the house.

An example of a myth; Ganesha was riding a mouse and sadly fell to the ground. The full moon in the sky laughed at him, contemptuously. Ganesha broke off one of his tusks and threw it at the moon. This is why the moon is never perfectly round in shape. Ganesha reigns over the divine and demonic. He honours both humanity and spirituality. He shows the way to sincere divinity. In one sense Ganesha stands at the threshold of the old and the new complex modern age in which we live. He provides a bridge connecting the truth to what is untrue; he brings together beings in harmony.

Ganesha believes the root cause of suffering is that of narcissism, which is our sense of wanting to be unique, special and separate from all others. The narcissistic people love themselves. However, we need to share our uniqueness with each other, our family and our community and with God. It is only then that we are closer to freeing ourselves from a self-absorbed personal desire from becoming a self-absorbed person who is unable to enjoy the company of others. (James H. Bae, "Ganesh" pp. 38-39)

CHAPTER 4:

Indigenous Australian Culture

Sigmund Freud's explanation of Totem and Taboo

The Horror of Incest

Australian aborigines are regarded as a distinct race, showing neither physical nor linguistic relationship with their nearest neighbours, the Melanesians, Polynesians and Malayan people. They do not build houses or permanent shelters and do not cultivate the soil. They live on the flesh of animals, they hunt and live on roots they dig. Kings or Chiefs are unknown among them. Communal affairs are decided by a council of elders. It is doubtful they have a religion. Tribes living in the interior are more primitive than those living near the coast. Yet we find that they set before themselves with the most scrupulous care and painful severity, the aim of avoiding incestuous sexual relationships.

What is a Totem?

It is an animal or more rarely, a plant, or natural phenomenon (like rain or water) which stands in a particular relation with the clan. The totem is:

1. The common ancestor; and
2. Their guardian spirit and helper, which sends them oracles;
3. Spares its own children. Clansmen are under a sacred obligation not to kill or destroy their totem, avoid eating its flesh or deriving benefit in any other way.

The Totemic character is inherent in all individuals of a given class. From time to time, festivals are celebrated at which clansmen represent or imitate the motions and attributes of their Totem through ceremonial dances.

The Totem is not attached to one particular place. The clansmen are distributed in different localities and live peacefully side by side with members of other totem clans.

Wherever there is a Totem, there is a law against persons of the same totem having sexual relations with one another and consequently against marrying. This 'exogamy' is an institution related to totemism.

The punishment of violation is 'avenged in the most energetic fashion by the whole clan'. In Australia, it is punishable by death. Totems are not changed by marriage. When a man of a Kangaroo totem marries a woman of an Emu clan, all children belong to the Emu clan. Their son cannot have intercourse with his mother or sisters who are Emus like himself! It also prevents intercourse with everyone else belonging to his clan. The part played by the Totem is taken very seriously. There are similarities in Melanesia, New Hebrides and New Caledonia.

Taboo and Emotional Ambivalence condensed from Sigmund Freud's Totem and Taboo (1913)

Wundt 1906 describes taboo as the oldest *human unwritten code of laws*. Taboo is older than Gods, dates and probably before religion.

Taboo is a Polynesian word. On the one hand it means 'sacred', 'consecrated'. On the other hand, it also means 'uncanny', 'dangerous' and 'forbidden'.

Taboos are not based on 'divine ordinance'. Unlike Totems they do not fall into any system. Taboo prohibitions have no grounds and are of unknown origin. They are accepted without question by those who are dominated by them.

The direct aim of taboos is:

1. Protection of important persons — chiefs, priests against things that harm;
2. Safeguarding of the weak — women, children and common people from the powerful *mana* of chiefs and priests;
3. Dangers of coming into contact with corpses by eating certain foods;
4. Guarding the chief acts of life — birth, initiation, marriage, sexual functions, etc., against interference;
5. Securing human beings against the wrath or power of gods and spirits.

The violated Taboo brings about its own vengeance

Prohibitions imposed by taboos are mainly directed against liberty of enjoyment and freedom of movement and communication. They may also be aimed towards abstinence and renunciations. At times they also appear to be concerned with trivial details and purely ceremonial.

A taboo is the 'objectified fear of the demonic powers'. This fear can also at times be split into two forms:

a) veneration; and

b) horror

There is an ambivalent attitude towards tabooed objects, i.e. the desire/compulsion to touch a prohibited object and violate a taboo, as well as the opposite such as a veneration of the taboo. The latter is difficult to attain, as peace of mind is obtained only by renouncing all temptations. Hence in summary due to the ambivalence regards taboos, there is a great temptation to transgress the prohibition and take the risk of breaking the taboo. This then leads to ongoing neurotic guilt.

The above is seen in obsessional neuroses. In such an example there is both, namely a wish and a counterwish.

Treatment of Enemies through killing leads initially to:

a) Uninhibited and ruthless cruelty, this is followed by a wish to ..
b) Appease the slain enemy
c) Restrictions on the slayer
d) Acts of expiation and purification
e) Ceremonial observations

The need for the ceremony is to asking forgiveness through sacrificial acts combined with dancing for forgiveness. The request is to be friends with the enemy and also with the sinner who has been killed. The slain is implored to love the new hosts, since it has now become one of them. There nevertheless remains a fear of the spirit of the slain enemy towards his original clan.

Taboo upon Rulers

Rulers need to be governed by two principles

- Ruler must be guarded from his enemies
- Ruler must also be guarded against magical powers

These taboos show the severity of the punitive 'Superego' (as referred to by today's Freudians). Taboos, the evil magical powers, are directed only for punishment. There is no bartering to allow for less punitiveness by the Superego. Death is mostly the only punishment. One of the ways it is achieved is by 'pointing the bone'. According to the English language she felt that *Contempt filled with Death wishes was being inflicted towards her and the members of her clan.*

A Visible Example

During a ward round in a certain hospital in Melbourne, we were shown an emaciated young aboriginal female. According to her, a bone had been pointed at her and her entire clan. She was too weak to eat, drink or even speak! Certain members of her clan had already died.

From Totem and Taboo to Aboriginal Dreamtime Stories: Biame, Rainbow Serpent; Namarrgon, the Lightening Man

Aborigines believe that certain spirits gave birth to humanity. **Biame** a Great Spirit started Creation. However, the world needed the Sun Goddesses' light and warmth. The world slowly became Creative, with birds and animals. Then the morning star came out. (Reed, 1993, pp. 19-65)

Dreamtime started as Australia had previously been devoid of life. Man and woman were now created and gave rise to babies. There was peace and harmony.

One interesting Dreamtime story is the *Rainbow Serpent* whose name was Goorialla. He had lost his tribe and now was frantically searching for them. Finally, he finds his tribe and shows them beautiful gear to wear and dance. Everyone seems happy for a short period of time. Then a big storm came. Everyone found shelter except two Bil-bil brothers. Even their grandmother could not offer them any shelter. Finally, they went to The Rainbow Serpent who was exhausted, half asleep, and opened his mouth wide and swallowed both the brothers.

Next day this tragedy was discovered and everyone searched for the boys without success. Finally, it occurred to them that they must be in the Rainbow Serpent's stomach. So, they cut open the stomach and rescued the brothers. Goorialla became furious. The mountains shook behind him. The Bil-boy brothers became bright lorikeet parrots and flew away.

Goorialla was disappointed, but forgave his clan. He turned himself into a star and went into the sky. His eye now became the eye of a shooting star. At night everyone sees him watching over them.

Questions we could consider regarding the Rainbow Serpent Was he treated as a human without power by his own clan or an ancestral spirit with power who had the capacity to punish? Nevertheless, his clan had unbearable rage without realizing that the Rainbow Snake could easily destroy all of them if he was not respected as an ancestral spirit.

1. He certainly had feelings of loss — Wanted to connect with his tribe as he missed being with them.

2. He even watched over them by becoming an everlasting star in the sky after his rage subsided. This demonstrates the kindness that was in him.

3. Similar to any ancestral spirit, he did not want to be taken for granted by the Bil-boys. Maybe he was also cross with the Grandmother who would not look after her grandsons.

4. One then could ask why if others in their clan made humpies to protect themselves from the storm, why didn't the boys do the same?

5. Why had nobody disciplined the boys to respect the Rainbow Serpent's wishes?

6. Not wanting to be forced by being woken up by the boys — was it a God-like or human behaviour? If the RAINBOW SERPENT was considered GOD-LIKE why were his wishes not respected by the boys?

7. Why are the people not punished for cutting the Rainbow Serpent to free the boys, if in fact the RS had God-like powers? Also, why is there no remorse either from the 2 boys, or the people?

8. The Rainbow Serpent's final work of watching over the people by becoming a star, can it be part of his remorse? Or was it simply a part of his original kind behaviour?

Namarrgon the Lightning Man

Namarrgon, commonly known as the 'lightning man', is responsible for the violent electrical storms which occur on the Arnhem plateau. Namarrgon and his family came from the sea and travelled Australia. He uses stone axes that are mounted on his head, elbows and knees to split the dark clouds and strike the ground, creating lightning and thunder. He also has a band wrapped around his body with axes to shake the earth and the heavens.

He has a family. His wife, is mother to the grasshoppers and his children are bright orange and blue. They come out early every year in the storm or wet season to look for their father.

Life started among the Aborigines in the North of Australia from the Djang'kawu sisters. They brought out the morning star and the moon as a husband. Together they produced all other stars. Biame now acknowledged that creation had begun and the world was full of beauty. It needed a created life, without evil shadows. The caressing warmth of the Sun Goddess then appeared. The world now became full of light, birds and animals and the lakes which overflowed. Man, and finally woman, were then created by Biame.

In 2006, the total population of Australian Aborigines and Torres Straight Islanders were 517,000.

Gradually adventurous movies like '*The Rabbit Proof Fence*', '*Ten Canoes*' and many others, have by now clearly demonstrated the differences between Australian and Aboriginal lifestyles. This brought Australians education of Aboriginal life closer to each other.

Aborigines have suffered tremendously over the years in the hope that their needs would be understood. At a congress I attended in Central Australia, about four years ago the speakers revealed similarities and differences between current Aboriginal and Australian Culture. One can hope equality will keep on occurring without racial prejudice.

Culture specific violence centred around greed, intense jealousy and payback behaviour and grievance displays

This chapter explores the difficulties that both Aborigines and non-aborigines experience in their relationships mainly when primitive states of mind in both remain inflexible. Culture specific conflicts with violence, centred around intense jealousy, payback behaviour and Grievance Displays are partially described below. The ways responsible groups of Aborigines and elders address these is also described.

'Post-colonial' aboriginal settlement life continues to present many challenges in terms of maintaining social order and harmony between disparate groups of Aboriginal people. This is often seen in remote settlements which have a number of language groups, clans and families or when a group has been relocated to another group's country. Protocols and agreements for use of country, access to resources and authority to make decisions continue to provide the basis for group dynamics and power relations in remote settlements. This is described by Jenny Walker and referring to Peter Ryan 2005.

Aboriginal dispute resolution strategies take the form of avoidance, strategic relocation, exile or formalization of conflict and dispute procedures. One example of the latter can involve a supervised witnessed and regulated fight with public anger and/or grievance display. Arbitration or resolution may follow.

The accent is on the community remaining in harmony, rather than helping the emotionally injured individual. The individual's needs are attended to only if the community is not disrupted.

An example of **Grievance display** is that of an old man of considerable cultural status who became very upset and angry with some members of his family. He got his peers, went to a centrally located shop with a guaranteed audience. He removed his shirt and mounted a display of shouting and spear rattling for about half an hour. During that time, no-one interrupted him or tried to stop him. No-one made eye contact with him, or tried to leave. When he was finished, he put his shirt back on and left, apparently satisfied that he had made his point and that he had been heard. Everyone's normal activities resumed without any comment being made.

Jealousing is a fluid concept with a wide range of feelings. It is like many aspects of Aboriginal law it is difficult to translate into non-Aboriginal modes of interaction and cultural domain.

The examples given by an Australian anthropologist Jenny Walker (Work in Progress, Aug 2010) as part of her thesis regards Aboriginal Law:

1. An aboriginal man who had a need to show his emotional pain in public by displaying and throwing dangerous weapons in a frightening manner. People around made no reproach, showed respect, but avoided eye contact. Their tolerance displayed acceptance of his grief and feelings of being traumatised.

2. Another male burnt his new car because he wanted to stop there being territorial warfare — different parties putting a claim on his precious car and destroying each other.

3. Petrol sniffing controlled by local Aborigines and elders in a safe manner.

4. Elders of two parties intervening to avoid 'delousing' becoming out of hand with violence, when jealousy between two women was affecting the baby conceived by one of them and the baby's father. The father was not given any access to his own child. Here the 'much loved baby' was an expression/symbol of the connectedness of the two families and the convergence of family interests. **Relatedness is a primary cultural imperative for aboriginal people and**

relations are a primary resource. The family of one of the females who was jealous, was given an ultimatum by her own family, to stop being violent to the mother of the baby or else there would be unpleasant repercussions for her in her own family. It could result in her losing the support of her family so that she would be marginalized and lead a '**social death**'. Naturally their daughter stopped the violence and both families became more integrated with the baby as their common loved object.

Jealous for country

'With the best of intentions', the local Land Council made a list of whom they considered to be the legitimate traditional owners of the country on which the settlement is built. This considered people who were not on the list to be of lower status and not entitled to anything. This was despite the fact that some had been in the settlement for generations. Two families (two warring groups) may have been descended from the same grandparents and the family fight becomes intractable. Violent assaults were commonly fuelled by alcohol.

An example is given of an ex-night patroller who had moved away from the settlement and confronted a determined 'drunk and armed grog runner' outside the settlement. The night patroller used his cultural status and negotiating skills leading to the grog runner putting down his weapon and not entering the settlement. Nevertheless, he was reported to the police and subsequently arrested. This incident enhanced the night patroller's status and gave him the reputation of being a hard man who was extremely effective. He was protecting the social fabric of the settlement by responding in a concrete and immediate manner to threats of violence to the fragile social fabric of the settlement.

Senior aborigines worked with night patrols in their capacity as senior law men. This role was seen as being analogous to that of a lawyer. Reconciliations were made the 'aboriginal way' which enabled resolution. The authenticity of cultural law in the use of the Land Council List authenticated Aboriginal Law. However, there remained a confusion caused by switching by cultural law and Non-Aboriginal Law. It will probably need ongoing management by cultural insiders — for example by local Patrollers from both sides of the dispute. Then the police and courts may be able to achieve a manageable stability between the warring parties.

Aboriginal people may find themselves in a situation where they are held responsible for an accidental injury or death or a person's self-harming behaviour.

Payback

Payback is one of the high-profile aspects of Aboriginal Law. It is also more problematic for non-Aboriginal law and culture to deal with. Cultural Law, payback included, has more complexity and depth than assumption of 'right to inflict physical punishment' (Ref: Professor Harry Blagg — Zero Tolerance or Community Justice? The role of the Aboriginal Domain in Reducing Family Violence). This was described in a paper presented by Harry Blagg in a conference in Mackay 2007 titled *'Breaking the Chains — Reclaiming our Future'*.

There are many payback stories described by experienced Australian anthropologists and mental health workers. The purpose is to redress the balance, thereby healing the rift caused by the offending party or parties' actions. The redress needs to be delivered as soon as possible and supervised by the appropriate people so that the metaphoric wound to the social fabric and family structures does not fester. Unfortunately, for the family of the offender, culpability under Aboriginal Cultural Law is not confined to the person who committed the offence as it is under non-Aboriginal Law. It is commonly seen that settlement patrol cars are called in to supervise aggrievances, especially in the late evening and at night and sought them out along with elders of the family.

The Patrol cars often save the person's life by their prompt action without exposing themselves to possible blame and subsequent payback.

Details of settlement are helped by experienced mental health workers in the field. Details can only be given at a later date depending on each situation.

CHAPTER 5 (a):

The Life of Albert Namatjira

Albert Namatjira (28 July 1902 — 8 August 1959), born Elea Namatjira, was a Western Arrernte-speaking Aboriginal artist from the MacDonnell Ranges in Central Australia. He became a household name in Australia as he was considered to be Australia's most outstanding artist of the time. Namatjira was the first Northern Territory Aboriginal person to be freed from restrictions that made Aborigines wards of the State. In 1957, he became the first Aboriginal person to be granted Australian citizenship. Namatjira was also awarded the Queen's Coronation Medal in 1953 and was honoured with an Australian postage stamp in 1968. His birth name was Elea, but once baptised, his name was changed to Albert (as an English version). He married his wife Rubina at the age of 18. He painted Australian countryside brilliantly with the most unusual and delicate paintwork.

The height of success for Albert Namatjira as a painter has been well acknowledged for the last 40 plus years. His first exhibition was held in Melbourne in 1938.

Nevertheless, Albert was always delighted to visit the Australian outback. Namatjira had a setback when he was in prison for supplying alcohol to an Aboriginal. However, his sentence was reduced to only two months in view of his health and humanitarian work. He died in Alice Springs in 1959 as a result of weakness of the heart and pneumonia.

CHAPTER 5 (b):

The Life of Cathy Freeman

Sporting Career of Cathy Freeman

From her book *'Cathy. Her own Story with Scott Gullin'* (2003)

The memorable words in her life are:

"I'm just a little black girl who can run fast and here I am sitting in the Olympic Stadium with one hundred and twelve thousand people screaming my name.

How the hell did I get here?"

Aged fourteen, she said to her vocational guidance officer, "Yeah, I want to win a gold medal at the Olympic Games".

Running made her feel happy. She started coming to age earlier than many others. She grew up without restraints, enjoying running barefoot everywhere. She also stayed with her coloured friends in Mackay. Here she noticed the differences between the lives of the whites and the blacks and initially thought that everyone white was always rich. However, she didn't pity herself in the slightest. She had her mind focused on running and never wavered in her dream to win gold.

She came from a sporting family. Her father Norman was a legend in the field of Rugby. He sadly became an angry alcoholic when he realized his wife changed her religious belief to becoming a Bahai and then married a white man named Bruce of the same faith. All these changes between her parents initially upset her considerably. However, she was able to always remember how close she was to her own father and would go riding with him during her Christmas vacations. She was nine years old when her parents remarried. She resented her mother's change of affection to Bruce, but coped with it.

Gradually she realized her father had made a huge sacrifice, by letting go of his wife amicably. She also gradually appreciated the ongoing help and support she received from her stepfather with regards to achieving her dream of being an Olympic gold medallist. He would regularly take her for training twelve laps on a sawdust track. This was 400 meters long. She trained barefoot three times weekly!

Her mother is described as a very emotionally strong lady, who was by her side whenever possible. Cathy was never arrogant or proud and remained grateful and aware of the hard work put in by so many adults and sponsors as they recognized her outstanding ability to outclass all others and win consistently.

She did not wear rose coloured glasses either and recognized very clearly the instances of blatant racism she experienced. It broadened her horizons about other people being jealous of her too. There were incidents when her stepfather came to her aid, at a railway station and also at school. Cathy was given a certificate, while the second and third positions were given medals!!

Cathy had an older sister Anne-Marie, who was quadriplegic and wanted their mother all to herself when they visited her. There was a memorable occasion in Cathy's life when she did not feel like going for training. Her mother helped her to compare her own fortunate life to the life-long disability and handicaps her bigger sister had to bear the rest of her life.

Cathy was quick to realise her own talents which she had since her birth. She never considered missing training sessions. She could now say to herself, "Oh God! I'm so glad I'm not like Anne-Marie". She went through a period of wanting to win every time and dedicate it to Anne-Marie.

Cathy's focus was always on her own success and racism did not overshadow her dreams of a lifetime. Moreover, her stepfather Bruce was a great protector. After that period, Bruce realised she was far above his capacity to coach her and she was placed in a boarding school of high repute. Just as before, she overcame her hurdles. She kept excelling despite many problems. She then changed direction and felt she had to win for herself, her disabled sister and for her own father who had died. She felt her dead relatives were now looking after her too.

After a complex relationship with her trainer Nic, who became her mentor and then a lover finally breaking up very sadly, she recovered from her traumas. She then married Alexander who was much older than her too.

She finally describes her final steps to victory at the Olympics. She was now very popular internationally and very proud to be an Aborigine and an Australian. She set a standard of overcoming the racial barrier, as well as getting the fastest of times, even breaking her own record at times. As Australians we are all proud of her hard work and dedication to athletics.

Cathy Freeman brought great admiration from around the world for being the first Australian Aborigine to carry the Australian Flag, as well as winning the 400 meters Gold Medal at 2000 Sydney Olympics. She also won a Silver Medal in the 1996 Atlanta Olympics. She set a standard for overcoming the racial barrier and even breaking her own record. All Australians are very proud of her dedication to athletics. Another example is how Cathy overcame contempt of racism with great dignity.

PART VII

ISSUES REGARDING
COMPLIANCE

CHAPTER 1:

Transforming Impossible Demands
into Constructive Desires

Non-compliance is a vast multi-dimensional issue which is grossly understated. It indicates *violation of rulers, frames and boundaries* which may or may not go unnoticed in daily life, depending cn its intensity. Frame modification of high intensity gives the frame breaker 'unconscious illusions of omnipotence and immortality'. Denying this rule ultimately implies denying the basic *existential golden rule, that **life is framed by death***. Denial of ill health is hence extremely harmful to the wellbeing of all persons.

There is a universal need for crime and punishment when life is based on concepts of *immortality, denial of reality, grandiosity and 'keeping up illusionary appearances'*. These features are often observed in patients with narcissistic, omnipotent, and/or border-line traits. The roots of these thoughts are based in contempt of those who never deviate. The solution to face reality, with courage, appears both in John Keats' wise words of having 'negative capability' which implies having the 'capacity to endure ambiguity, doubt and mystery, without irritably reaching out for fact and reason'.

Rudyard Kipling, the importance of facing reality

Rudyard Kipling's 1910 poem 'If' also leads us to the same destination, by travelling on his path leading to:

> *"If you can dream — and not make dreams your master;*
> *If you can think — and not make thoughts your aim;*

If you can meet with Triumph and Disaster
And treat those two imposters just the same;"
Source: *A Choice of Kipling's Works* (1943)

Kipling implies the importance of facing reality and veering away from a wishful fantasy land. Children too need to make an authentic entry into previously unfamiliar pastures. In order to do so, they need to be clear, articulate and thoughtful about what they offer. Numerous impulsive examples can be seen in Alice's encounters in Wonderland during her dialogues with the March Hare and the Hatter:

"Then you shall say what you mean", the March Hare went on.

"I do", Alice hastily replied, "at least — at least I mean what I say — that's the same thing you know".

"Not the same thing a bit" the Hatter corrects her, "Why you might just as well say that, I see what I eat, is the same thing as, I eat what I see!"

Nevertheless, even in her dream Alice keeps up her curiosity of the unknown, during many examples, and does not flinch even when the Queen orders "Cut off her head!"

Starting from a very early age in life, here is another example of how impulsively non-compliance presents itself; here is an example where parents and carers need to be experienced in the capacity for 'holding and containing' especially when the child suffers a congenital biological disorder.

Here is Example one, where harm comes to no-one and healthy training, along with empathy, can be learned from early childhood.

Noncompliance in a child with Autistic Spectrum Disorder who is transformed into accepting reality

A little autistic Indian girl, aged four, whom we can refer to as 'Asha', started playing a game with another Indian school friend 'Usha' in the playground where there were chairs placed around in a circle. Asha for no apparent reason suddenly lifted a chair and flung it in the playground where it could easily have hurt another child who was innocently walking by. Here we see the following interplay. Asha 'acts out' due to her inability to verbalise the notion, "I'm sick of playing this game, I want to throw the game away!" She has no idea this could hurt anyone else. She is fearless and defiant. I saw this happening and without a word take both Asha and Usha into a toy room to play with some other toys. Asha looks at me enquiringly, wondering why I am not scolding her or hitting her, maybe as her parents have done out of desperation. Nothing further is discussed about the event. The next day, Asha says to me "I will never throw a chair again". I praise her and tell her she's a good girl to say this. True to her word, during my presence, she never repeated this behaviour. We had reached a common ground of respecting each other's will and power, as well as recognising and accepting the strengths and limitations of each other.

Examples of Interplay between Desire, Will and Power (Ernest Jones)

Mankind's belief in freewill seems to be stronger in proportion to the unimportance of the decision. "Everyone is convinced he/she is free to choose whether to stand or to sit at a given moment, to cross his right leg over his left or vice versa", as part of our freewill and determinism. Jones continues to state that, "With vital decisions it seems man at times may feel impelled towards only one choice", e.g. the statement of Martin Luther King Jr. "Here is my stand. I cannot do it any other way". Also, when we ask someone why a certain choice was made, the answer may be "I couldn't help it — I just did it". Just as a lover would say when trying to explain why he fell in love, thereby emphasising that there was no question of any other possible alternative.

Society smiles at lovers whilst shaking their heads, i.e. some being happy and others silently thinking "the poor fool, throwing away all freedom of choice". On the other hand, society respects political leaders and reformists who are totally dedicated to their cause. *Certain politicians, like Gandhi, are worshipped even if the penalty for non-compliance means death.*

The fight for free choice or freewill arises from one's own fierce objections to being subjugated and felt to be crushed by another or of one being coerced against one's own freewill with one's liberty being snatched away and all personal freedom destroyed. Hence, it is no wonder perhaps that in some countries, there is too little emphasis in law to enable as much freedom as possible to be given. Why then are certain forms of non-compromise more acceptable than others?

I will quote Gandhi, who openly stated, "They may torture my body, break my bones, even kill me, then they will have my dead body, not my obedience" and that "There are eternal principles which admit of no compromise and one must be prepared to lay down one's life in the practise of them". I myself agree with his views that faith, as a function of the heart, needs to be reinforced by reason in order to survive, especially as blind faith may not withstand the test of reality. Hence, one may divide non-compliance into two groups, viz. those where powers of reasoning are possible, but the patient makes a conscious decision to become non-compliant. This is observed clearly on occasions when medical staff insist/demand that in order to remain alive, it is essential that all simple pleasures in life be given up, one may encounter patients who then resort to giving up all initiative to remain alive. For such patients, it amounts to soul murder, along with feelings of annihilation and fragmentation of one's capacity to even think clearly. In the face of such annihilation anxiety, it can at least be understood, if not accepted, that a degree of compromised non-compliance may be considered as being the only essential alternative in life.

Pittu Laungani had a life-threatening illness of polymyositis. When he realised that the medical treatment he was getting was not helpful and, in fact, making him feel worse, he confronted his consultant one day and told him so very clearly. The consultant walked away without a word, but changed his whole medical regime. Low and behold, Pittu kept improving visibly, finally leading to his discharge from hospital. He had to however carry an oxygen cylinder with him at times when he could not breathe deeply. He led a very constructive life, writing prolifically and got a well-deserved life time meritorious award for his work from Canada.

In summary:
- Non-compliance is accompanied in a quarter of the cases with staff problems.
- Depression is correlated with poor outcome for patients.
- Low frustration tolerance and gains from the sick role contribute to non-compliance in 50% of cases.
- Non-compliance can be part of a suicidal behaviour in addition to concealed death wishes on the part of the relatives and caretakers.
- Non-compliance indicates violation of rules, frames and boundaries. Denying a rule implies denying the existential rule that life is framed by death. This denial is extremely harmful to the health of the patient.

Omnipotence and Non-compliance, gambling and its disaster

Where omnipotence and non-compliance may both be transitory phenomena during certain phases in life. Omnipotence, as a primitive survival mechanism has been described as a transitory, but also as an essential and healthy manifestation in ego development of infants and young children (Symington, J. 1985. Int J. Psychoanalysis. 66, 481).

The example of Omnipotence, as described by Romain Rolland, very sensitively in his description of 'Jean-Christophe' arguing with the clouds in the sky. He describes Christophe as a young child, looking up at the sky and commanding the clouds go in one direction and becoming very angry with them for disobeying his command. Finally, when he was faced with the realisation that the clouds were not going to change their direction, he then changes his own command for them to now 'go' in the opposite direction to which he had originally commanded them. They continue as before, but they are now seen by him to obey his last command and he is delighted with them as he is now able to feel that his belief in his own omnipotence is restored. This is a good example whereas children grow older and psychologically healthier, omnipotence is gradually abandoned and the reality principle is able to be accepted without the person sustaining a major narcissistic injury.

Here are certain situations in adult life when the reality principle feels too harsh to bear and the individual turns to the pleasure principle in a semi-permanent manner. Gambling is one such arena where the thrill of the pleasure experienced by the gambler is openly acknowledged, e.g. Dostoevsky who confesses "The main point is the game itself, the thrill — on my oath it is not the money". Most professional punters claim they follow their systems closely, working 12-14 hours a day and never giving into wild betting. They never admit that professional gambling can eventually also prove to be a financial disaster. Instead, they write articles full of denial, grandiosity and omnipotence like "Yes, you can win", "Double your luck", "Pick 'em easy", etc. Their advice however, on reading the articles is to put aside personal whims, likes and dislikes and become duped into accepting the harsh discipline necessary for punting success. Hence, whilst following the pleasure principle themselves, they advocate into theoretically believing they are in strict adherence to the reality principle. In addition, they don't have to rely on anyone or sell their soul in any way. Perhaps this actually helps them to continue their illusory omnipotent lifestyle. This demonstrates triumph as an illusion of a manic defence.

While considering Omnipotence of the Self, it is often fear of the fantasy the Omnipotence of the other which leads to fear of the obliteration of the self.

Aspects of Grandiosity

Once a severely diabetic patient refused to wear socks or slippers in the ward. It had been painstakingly explained to her, that in a case of extreme diabetes, ulcers are very difficult to heal and may need amputation in extreme cases. The patient turned around and haughtily replied "I have not been pricked by a nail yet!" She continued to walk barefooted until she learned the outcome the sad way. Although she did not need amputation, she developed many other diabetic complications.

Noncompliance in Narcissistic Personality Disorder

These additional features are observed in Narcissistic Personalities:

- Excessive Self-Centredness
- Pervasive pattern of Grandiosity
- Omnipotent sense of Self-Importance
- Grandiose sense of self and accomplishments
- Lack of Empathy
- Intense Envy
- Fragile Self-Esteem

- Responds to criticism with Shame-Rage cycle
- Exhibits cool indifference to others
- Friendships are formed, only if person can benefit from them
- Partners are treated as objects, who can bolster the narcissistic person's Self-Esteem

CHAPTER 2:

Noncompliance in a Study in Consultation-Liaison Psychiatry in Renal Medicine Inpatient Unit

Sabar Rustomjee, Graeme Smith (ANZ Journal of Psychiatry)

Reference Consultation-Liaison Psychiatry to Renal Medicine: Work with an Inpatient Unit

SABAR RUSTOMJEE, GRAEME SMITH

(ANZ Journal of Psychiatry, 1996, Vol 30. 229-237.)

Clinical data from Micro-Cares and collaboration with case notes revealed:

Two hundred and ninety nine patient referrals were made to Liaison Psychiatry Service in a three year period, between 1990 and 1992.

Non-compliance was one of the three most frequently cited reasons for referral by the Nephrology team to the C-L Psychiatry Service.

Non-compliance is a common, but potentially treatable, cause of failed dialysis and transplant rejection.

- It indicates violation of rules, frames and boundaries.
- Frame breakers get 'unconscious illusions of omnipotence and immortality'.
- It denies the existential rule that life is framed by death.
- Alcohol and Drug abuse are important factors in Noncompliance.

In 38 noncompliant patients, where the consultant/consultee agreed, the diagnoses were as follows:

It was accompanied in:

42.1%	with Personality Problems
47.4%	with V Codes (where the presenting symptom is not directly related to a mood disorder or Bipolar Disorder, but is the principle focus of the presentation and treatment)
34.2%	Mood Disorders
25%	with Staff Problems
23.7%	with Adjustment Disorder
18.4%	with Organic Mental Disorder
1%	no diagnosis

It had 1.9 diagnosis per patient compared with 1.6 diagnosis in other referrals.

Non-compliance is grossly understated. Some studies have shown 50%. It can be obvious with increased weight gain, high K and serum Phosphorus. It is also often unrecorded, due to staff ambivalence with the patient with whom they have a longstanding ambivalent relationship.

Open encouragement can be present as part of suicidal behaviour and death wishes from relatives and carers. "He/she must have some pleasure or otherwise the person is better off dead."

Low frustration tolerance, and gains from sick role, contribute to acting out (24/43 cases Kaplan de Nour).

Non-compliance involves working with concepts of immortality, denial of reality, grandiosity with narcissistic and borderline traits.

	Noncompliance Group Psychiatric Consultation Liaison Unit	In-Patient referrals from Renal Unit
AGE		
15-24 yRs	29%	5.7%
25-44 yrs	36.8%	27.8%
45-64 yrs	21%	41%
> 64 yrs	13%	25.4%
MARITAL STATUS		
Married	53%	67%
Single	29%	16%
Separated/Divorced	18%	15%
SEX		
Male	68%	56%
Female	32%	44%
RACE		
White	79%	87%
Oriental	2.6%	2.8%
Others	18.4%	6.8%
EMPLOYMENT		
Full time	10.2%	16.5%
Part time	10.2%	9.4 %
Disabled	44.9%	26.6%
Unemployed	6.1%	5.9%
Retired/home duties	16.3%	28.6%
Other	8.2%	10.1%
Unknown	4.1%	2.3%

RELIGION

Protestant /Catholic	21%	49%
Other Religions	21%	9.6%
None	29%	18%

CONSULTATION – LIAISON PSYCHIATRY TO RENAL MEDICINE WORK WITH AN INPATIENT UNIT

SABAR RUSTOMJEE, GRAEME SMITH (1996).

The objective was to provide an overview of the work of a liaison psychiatry service to a renal medicine inpatient unit.

The Micro-cares prospective database system was used.

Two hundred and ninety nine inpatient referrals were made over a period of 3 years, from 1990-1992.

The referral rate was 17%.

Demographic data

Females	44.8%
Males	55.2%
Married	66.9%
Single	16.4%
Separated/Divorced/Widowed	15.1%

Reasons for referral by the Renal Unit, for needing psychiatric management were:

Coping Problems	27% (difficulty coping with dialysis)
Depression	20% (nephrologists labelled it mistakenly as anxiety or coping problems)
Noncompliance	11% were 3 most frequent reasons cited.

Routine Pre-dialysis Assessment was requested in 45% of cases. In these cases, dialysis, transplant or death was imminent.

Highest prevalence of diagnosis by Psychiatrist team were:

V Codes	35%
Adjustment disorders	30%
Mood disorders	24%
Organic Mental disorder	23%

High Concordance for referral

Terminal illness
Consultee/Consultant
Suicidal risk
Non-compliance

Low Concordance

Staff problems
Alcohol related problems
Organic Brain Syndrome
Anxiety/fear

In these low concordance figures, the psychiatrists diagnosed a much higher incidence. Organic B.S. was frequently diagnosed by the renal unit as depression or behavioural disturbance. Low incidence of alcohol related problems was due to denial by patients.

Referred patients had a length of stay of 20.5 days, compared with 12.5 days

Psychotropic drugs prescribed in only	25%
Advise to reduce medication	7%
Implementation of medical treatment	28%

Patients are also likely to have Diabetes Mellitus, complications of surgical interventions and circulatory disturbance.

Transferred to psychiatry inpatients	2%
Percentage in professional classes is higher than general medical wards.	23%

Still working   23%

Conclusion — Considerable physical/psychiatric co-morbidity was present.

Conclusion

Integration with a social worker is important as is time spent with the nursing staff for whom renal work, in particular, can be very stressful. Stopping treatment is a common mode of death. As staff had longstanding relationships with the patients, debriefing sessions were vital.

House A (1987) in *'Psychosocial problems of patients in the Renal Unit'* (from Journal Psychosomatic Research; 31, 441-452) concluded that 'psychiatric disorders' can be managed without time-consuming psychiatric care. However, the data presented as above reveals the complexity of psychiatric disturbances. A medical team is absolutely essential. (Smith G C 1995, Journal of Psychosomatic Research, 39: 247-250), unless a psychiatrist is involved, the patients' presentation will be split off from the biological component and dealt without a holistic context. A psychiatrist with a psychodynamic background has the greatest chance of maintaining the holistic approach. (Smith G C *"From Psychosomatic medicine to consultation-liaison psychiatry"*. Medical Journal of Australia 1993)

CHAPTER 3:

Personality Factors in Chronic Haemodialysis causing Noncompliance with Medical Regime

Study of forty-three patients on haemodialysis

A. Kaplan de Nour and J.W. Czaczkes, Department of Psychiatry and Nephrological Services Hadassah University Hospital and Medical School, Jerusalem, Israel (1972).

This is an important study of forty three patients on haemodialysis.

Similar personality factors were studied in this study, but are also similarly identified in other medical cases.

My personal experience of forty years coincides and is concordant with Kaplan de Nour.

In medical treatment, it was considered that these patient's well-being and, in fact, their whole life depended on active participation. Noncompliance in medical wards is still often seen as a patient having a suicidal intention.

The diagram, originally compiled by D. W. Winnicott and modified by myself (see Section I, Chapter two). It shows the steps from a) to d).

a) The survival function of Infantile Omnipotence.

b) Separation and Individuation phase.

c) Able to endure doubt, mystery and ambivalence without ill will.

d) Able to use the object creatively or destructively:

   i. The Creative Use of an object demonstrates the Life Drive

ii. The aggressive and destructive use of the Object is a symptom of the Death Drive.

Compliance and Non-compliance

The medicinal regime is useful and can be found out easily if the patient lies.

Fluid intake is always restricted. Non-compliance is found out by the patient's weight rise.

If there is rise in fruit intake, the blood potassium rises. This is detrimental in kidney failure cases.

Issues irrelevant to compliance are not affected by lowered intelligence.

Nevertheless, reasons for restrictions in end-stage kidney failure need to be explained respectfully.

Understanding leads to better complying with the restrictions. Patients need to have their individuality and not feel totally controlled by the limitations put on them. I usually suggest sucking small ice cubes, covered by their hankies, rather than guzzle water when distressed.

I have used Supportive Expressive Group Therapy for suitable patients with great benefit.

Example of a charming young single man, who in my words was 'very naughty'. His family too did not believe in any restrictions. They would encourage him to eat salty chips!

It was interesting that he was always smiling during the day, but would panic at night and ask for an ambulance to bring him to hospital. No sooner did the ambulance arrive, that he would say he was feeling better, and send the ambulance back. He was not 'acting out' as sometimes, even in hospital, he would get a panic attack!

The first cadaver transplant failed. By that time, I lost contact with him as I was working at another teaching hospital. I went to the original hospital for some work and heard a familiar "Hi Doc!"

Here he was, smoking a cigarette, but was not inside any ward. I was as delighted as he was. It seemed obvious he had a second kidney transplant which had turned out successfully. He rolled up his sleeves and showed me strong and healthy muscles and teasingly asked me "What do you think I am doing nowadays?" I was nonplussed. "I am building fences" he said, and I enjoy it! It was obvious that he was creative and had a very healthy Life Drive. This proved to me that Life Drive can overcome areas of non-compliance. Respect is what he needed and what everyone gave him.

Pathological Factors affecting acceptance or Rejection of Kidney Transplants: Studies by Joseph Steinberg, Norman Levy and Andreas Radvila

Jorge Steinberg, Norman B. Levy and Andreas Radvila

Viederman reported a case of giving up, given-up complex was considered as a psychological reason for a physiological rejection. (p. 189)

Example 1

A spinster aunt, twenty-two years older than her niece, had initially been very close. The relationship ended six years ago, as the niece considered her aunt was overpowering towards her and was not allowing her to grow up.

When an 'opportunity' came for the niece to receive a transplant from her aunt, sadly the niece remained aloof from the aunt, which upset the aunt greatly. It is recorded that the aunt said to her niece "Take my fucking kidney, and I don't want to see you again". (Steinberg, J., Levy N., & Radvila, A., p. 189)

As predicted by the renal team, the kidney was rejected shortly after transplantation.

It is possible the donation of kidneys by family members is a result of guilt about being healthier than the recipient. Mother donors may have guilt about giving birth to a 'defective child'.

Joseph Steinberg is Director and Associate Professor Clinical Psychiatry, State University, New York.

Norman Levy. M.D. Professor of Psychiatry; State University, Brooklyn, New York.

Andreas Radvila M.D. Fellow Psychosomatic Medicine, State University, New York.

PART VIII

HARSH REALITIES IN CULTURE OF CONTAINMENT

CHAPTER 1:

Phantasy by Susan Isaacs

Mrs Susan Isaac's paper "The nature and function of Phantasy"

Susan Isaac discovered that phantasy can be of two types, one of which is purely of an unconscious nature and related to the capacity to hallucinate a memory belonging to early life and childhood. A controversy existed between Ms Anna Freud and Susan Isaac as the former considered a Phantasy only to exist in the first year of life. Susan Isaac had a lot of experience with children aged under four years who had demonstrated to her their unconscious mental processes in a form of a Phantasy.

Mrs Riviere's opinions

Mrs Riviere believed that the Phantasy life is never pure Phantasy, but is a mixture of internal and external reality. Freud agrees with Susan Isaac, in that a person who hallucinates an object is able to do so because he feels that this object is inside himself and he projects it outside where he perceives that its existence as belonging there.

Life and death instincts: Riviere follows Klein's theory and Freud's libido-theory

Mrs Riviere follows Melanie Klein theory. The term Oral sadistic and Anal sadistic terminology were recognised as a primary instinct of destruction by Klein. Klein also believed in attachment of the libido to physiological functions. Riviere (1936) describes the destructive charges of the various organs as follows:

Limbs shall trample, hit and kick;
Lips, fingers and hands shall suck, twist, pinch;
Teeth shall bite, gnaw, mangle and cut;
Mouth shall devour, swallow and 'kill' (annihilate);
Eyes kill by a look, pierce and penetrate;
Breath and mouth hurt by noise depends on the sensitivity
of the child's ears". (p. 514)

In Freud's libido-theory, introjection occupies first place in mental mechanisms of the oral phase and projection (expulsion) in the anal phase of the libido. The original pleasure ego tries to introject into itself everything that is good and to reject from itself everything that is bad (Freud, S., 1925; 369; SE19; 237). Freud's words depict the aim of introjection and projection on the basis of predominance of the life instinct.

Freud (p. 516) says the oral component of the instinct finds satisfaction analytically on the basis of the satiation of desire for nourishment and its object is for the mother's breast. It then detaches itself, becomes independent and at the same time auto-erotic, that is, finds an object in the child's own body (Freud, S., 1923A; 101; SE18; 245).

After the child attaches itself to an object in the outside world, Freud calls the pleasure experienced at the 'breast' the unattainable prototype of every later sexual satisfaction (Freud, S., 1916-17; 264SE20; 314). The internalised breast becomes the core for all further object relations. This gratification is retained forever in the unconscious and not given up in the auto-erotic phase.

According to Klein what happens is the breast is introjected. The sensations experienced when sucking becomes attached to the introjected breast. This forms a core for further object relations. Freud says the basis of the process is called an Identification which is probably the most important kind of relationship with another person. The mechanism of introjection had been embodied in Freud's Mourning and Melancholia in 1917 and before that in *'Beyond the Pleasure Principle'* in 1920.

Narcissism was written in 1914 by Freud and represents an earlier stage than *'The Ego'* and *'The Id'* written by Freud in 1923. Susan Isaac queries this.

In summary, object libidinal experiences precede the auto-erotic phase and the auto-erotic gratification is based on memories. Finally, that Narcissism pre-supposes a more advanced stage of ego development which is responsible for the greater element of regression.

CHAPTER 2:

The Art of Working with Harsh Realities
in a Culture of Containment

Concept of Safe Space: Richard Lovelace "To Althea from Prison", John Milton "On his blindness"

The concept of Safe Space both from an internalised, as well as external, viewpoint is brilliantly described by the 17th century poet, Richard Lovelace, in his memorable poem in 1649.

"To Althea from Prison"
"Stone walls do not a Prison make,
Nor Iron bars a cage;
Minds innocent and quiet take
That for a Hermitage;
If I have freedom in my Love,
And in my soul am free;
Angels alone that soar above,
Enjoy such Liberty."

Once again, the same theme is encountered in the famous lines by the blind poet John Milton who lived in the same era (1608-74), when he questions God's will in the following poem:

"On his Blindness"
"Doth God expect day — labour, light deny'd,
I fondly ask; But patience to prevent
That murmur soon replies, God doth not need

Either man's work, or his own gifts, who best
Bear his milde yoke, they serve him best,
His State is Kingly. Thousands at his bidding speed
And post o'er Land and Ocean without rest:
They also serve who only stand and wait."

So, we need to accept that despite being locked in a prison with stone bars, when one cherishes Love, one can feel free in one's soul. Similarly, even though one can be blind, as Milton says:

"They also serve who only stand and wait."

This is wisdom. There are no conditions that need to be put into place to feel that one is in a Safe Space and can live within a culture of Containment.

Harsh realities of life are encountered by all at different moments in time. Nevertheless, coming to accept these can prove to be more difficult for some than for others. Herewith is an example in which Nelson Mandela works with the harsh realities of life. In 1994 he writes, "As we let our light shine, we consciously give other people the permission to do the same. As we are liberated from our fear, our presence automatically liberates others".

Mahatma Gandhi: "The Law of Love"

Mahatma Gandhi, The Law of Love (1970) advises very strongly against resorting to violence as a means of aiming towards peace. For Gandhi, producing a safe space through containment of non-violence is the product of compassion, forming healthy object relations and empathy for all mankind.

He writes "Non-violence is the Law of our species, as violence is the law of the Brute. If there is a fundamental distinction between man and beast, it is the former's progressive recognition of the Law and its application to his personal life".

He equates Love (or non-violence) with Truth. Non-violence

does not refer to abstention from overt activity, as this does not guarantee freedom from thoughts of violence said Dr Suman Amonkar, a very devoted Gandhian in her plenary address at IAGP's 13th International Congress at Sao Paulo. She quotes Gandhi as saying "It is a sign of spiritual atrophy to support an unjust system, such as a war". (Shanti Sahyog Brochure, India, 2006)

Uncontained and unsafe spaces become evident in wars such as the Vietnam War and the current chaotic situation in Iraq.

War, Violence, Revengeful, Lethal and other Destructive Actions in Group Analytic work

Individual and group psychoanalysts have in their own individual framework considered the place for unbridled violence.

In a group analytic framework, all forms of violence are recognised by Kleinian group analyst Wilfred Bion, through one of his three basic assumptions, namely Basic Assumption Fight/Flight [BAFF], which is a deterrent towards coping with the anxiety of both the known and the unknown. Fight/flight defences avoid the development of a work group where constructive work can occur with all group members without the exclusion/dismissal/premature termination of any one and without the emergence of scapegoating in any group setting.

Other basic assumption resistances hindering work in an attempt to avoid anxiety in groups are described by Bion as Basic Assumption Dependency [BAD] and Basic Assumption Pairing [BAP]. Dependency can be towards the group conductor, whilst pairing could be between any two members and encouraged by the group, as it may be unconsciously seen as an illusion towards producing something of the calibre of the genius/aristocracy. These defences also hinder growth and maturity in members when used predominantly in a saturated, fixed manner and so do not help in overcoming the fear of facing harsh realities in life.

Earl Hopper (2003) points out that Bion did not consider 'The phenomena of perverse pairing and clinging, as well as parasitical dependency, which also are attacks on the work group'. These, he says, 'prevent optimal cohesion and hopeful morale'. Hopper also describes the concept of 'malignant envy', which reflects the Freudian 'death instinct' leading to denigration, which differs from basic assumptions of fight/flight and dependency which reflect idealisation.

Hopper arrives at a fourth basic assumption of Incohesion: Aggregation/Massification (BA I:AM) in his book 'Traumatic Experiences in the Unconscious life of groups'. He also refers to the threats to identity in a large group, as was initially described by Pierre Turquet in 1969, when Turquet suggested a Basic Assumption Oneness phenomenon occurring in large groups (BAO). Here members seek union with a perceived omnipotent force within the group and thereby surrender their individuality. It is implied, by Turquet, that uncontained feelings of aggression and envy would be greatly reduced, if not non-existent, within the context of such oneness developing in large groups.

Obviously, it is the capacity to entertain feelings of love and concern for all mankind, this will be the major deterrent in the realisation of the futility of wars and the starting of work towards achieving peaceful resolution.

Being Mortal

Medical school taught nothing on ageing or frailty or dying. How the process unfolds, how people experience the end of their lives and how it affects those around them seemed beside the point.

Medical school was to learn how to save lives, not how to tend to their demise.

Trained medical students ready or prepared sufficiently to help patients confront the realities of decline and mortality.

Modern scientific capability has profoundly altered the course of human life. People live longer and better than at any other time in history.

Thanks to scientific advances, the process of ageing and dying have been turned into medical experiences handled by health care professionals who, to date, have proved alarmingly unprepared to handle this.

Up until 1945, most deaths occurred in the home. By the 1980's on, 17% did. Advanced ageing and death have shifted to nursing homes and hospitals.

"The necessity of nature's final victory was expected in generations before our own. Doctors were far more willing to recognise the signs of defeat and far less arrogant about denying them". (Sherwin Nuland, '*How We Die*')

Becoming a doctor is bringing the satisfaction of competence; to be technically skilled to be able to solve difficult, intricate problems. To a clinician, nothing is more threatening than being confronted with a patient with a problem you cannot solve.

There is no escaping the tragedy of death. From birth we are all ageing.

Our reluctance to honestly examine the experience of ageing and dying has increased the harm we inflict on people and denied them the basic comforts they most need.

In my grandfather's premodern world, how he wanted to live in his later years was his choice and his family's role was to make it possible. My grandfather lived to 110. Elders are cared for in a multigenerational system.

Both parents and children saw separation as a form of freedom. Children grown up and moving away to make a life for themselves and parents free to sell or rent their properties, instead of handing down. Thereby accumulating wealth for 'retirement'.

International trend that should the elderly have financial means, they have chosen 'intimacy at a distance'. That is, to live alone.

Del Webb disagreed that the elderly wanted to fill their days surrounded and supported by other generations. He proposed that the elderly preferred to spend their later years as 'leisure years' and developed Sun City which promoted active retirement of recreation and dining with others like them. This vision proved incredibly popular and internationally the concept of retirement communities has been embraced.

This was that living has empowered and liberated both the young and the elderly.

One problem remains, however, and that is the independence for every person will inevitably sooner or later become impossible.

Ultimately, we all die, but medicine has pushed the fatal moment of many diseases further outward. Whilst medicine can assist with chronic illnesses to buy back some time and stall the downward descent to death, the patient never returns to the previous baseline, the ultimate course is still downward until there finally becomes a time when there is no recovery possible at all.

The idea that living things shut down instead of wearing down has received substantial support in recent years.

Leonid Gavrilov claims "Human beings fail the way all complex systems fail, randomly and gradually". Human beings function much like machines with complex systems, designed with multiple layers of redundancy, with back-up systems and back-up systems which allows the machine to keep going even as damage accumulates. Until finally, the defect in the complex system is enough to impair the whole machine resulting in the condition called 'frailty'. There are no more back-ups, we are worn down until we cannot be worn down any further.

Medical care can influence whether the decline path is steep or more gradual, allowing longer preservation of the abilities that matter most in life. Most doctors and health professionals do not think about this.

Geriatricians bolster our resilience in old age, our capacity to whether what comes — is limited and unappealing in the medical profession. It requires attention to the body and its alterations. It requires vigilance over nutrition, medications and living situations.

ABOU BEN ADHEM BY LEIGH HUNT

Abou Ben Adhem (may his tribe increase!)
Awoke one night from a deep dream of peace,
And saw, within the moonlight in his room,
Making it rich, and like a lily in bloom,
An angel writing in a book of gold:-
Exceeding peace had made Ben Adhem bold,
And to the presence in the room he said,
"What writest thou?"- The vision raised its head,
And with a look made of all sweet accord,
Answered, "The names of those who love the Lord".
"And is mine one?" said Abou. "Nay, not so,"
Replied the angel. Abou spoke more low,
But cheerily still; and said, "I pray thee, then,
Write me as one that loves his fellow men".

The angel wrote, and vanished. The next night it came again with a great wakening light and showed the names whom love of God had blest and lo! Ben Adhem's name led all the rest.

Creating a Safe Space between Internal and External Conflicts in First Episode Psychosis

Presented at the Fifteenth European Symposium London.
August 2011

Dr Sabar Rustomjee
MBBS, DPM, FRANZCP

A 22 month Experiential Group Project of patients suffering from First Episode Psychosis needed the following:

- 1 year's preparation
- A careful selection of those able to make the journey to a community centre chosen for working in a Supportive, Expressive Psychotherapeutic framework. The group culture needed to reflect empathy, sensitivity, authenticity, trust and non-aggression.

Objectives a young age group of both sexes between 16 and 25 years of age where the psychosis had been the first encounter of a patient in a Psychiatric hospital. This needed to have been less than two years ago.

- Hence chronic patients were eliminated.
- Patients with dual diagnosis were included.
- Reducing the risk of relapse.

Drawings and writings by Patients showing their current values in life and the importance of not burning their bridges.

They summarised this as:

- **Someone to love**
- **Someone to live for**
- **Something to look forward to**

GROUP OBJECTIVES

+ Developing Trust!
+ Reintegration into family & friends; into society!
+ Collect data!
-|-life is interesting when people are social!
-|-To know whats going on with people around you!
-|- To develope more of a life!
-|- To begin goalsetting!
-|- To get stable employment!
-|- Self actualisation

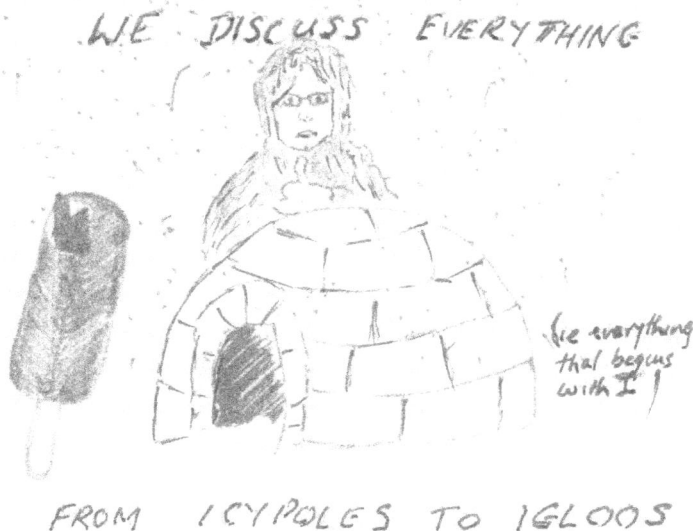

WE DISCUSS EVERYTHING

ie everything
that begins
with I!

FROM ICYPOLES TO IGLOOS

FEAR and
HELPLESSNESS
transformed into

Delusions of
Omnipotence —

Delusions of the
Strength of "The Devil"
and/or
Identification with the
Devil etc.

**IDEAS COMPILED by clients and staff of 1st EPISODE
PSYCHOSIS RECOVERY PROGRAM
GUIDELINES FOR PARENTS AND CARERS**

- NEVER CRITICISE — GIVE SUPPORT AND ALWAYS ENCOURAGE.
- REALISE YOUR CHILD ALREADY IS CARRYING A BIG BURDEN — LIKE ATLAS.
- SO DO NOT PUT EXTRA BURDENS ON THOSE ALREADY SUFFERING FROM 1ST EPISODE PSYCHOSIS.
- PRESENT ONLY INTERESTING ACTIVITIES, EXCEPT FOR VERY NECESSARY ITEMS, E.G. TO HAVE A BATH,

BRUSH TEETH, COMB HAIR, ADEQUATE DIET AND
BASIC CLEANLINESS.

- **DO NOT ENCOURAGE PREMATURE ACTIVITY
WHICH CAN BE FELT AS AN EXTRA BURDEN AT A
TIME WHEN WE ARE SUFFERING FROM EXTREME
APATHY.**

AT TIMES WHEN WE FEEL APATHETIC WE NEED TO TAKE OUR MIND OFF STRESS.

AT THESE TIMES WE MAY NEED TO DAYDREAM.

ADVANTAGES OF DAYDREAMING

TAKES YOUR MIND OFF STRESSFUL THOUGHTS REGARDING
THE PRESENT AND THE FUTURE.

DAYDREAMING CAN PROVIDE US WITH PEACE OF MIND,
WHICH IN TURN PROVIDES INSPIRATION, MOTIVATION AND
BY STRETCHING YOUR IMAGINATION IT HELPS DREAMS TO
COME TRUE. THIS IS BECAUSE WE ARE NOT UNDER PRESSURE
WHEN WE DAYDREAM. WE ARE IN FULL CONTROL. AT THESE
TIMES WE ALSO DO NOT JUDGE OURSELVES CRITICALLY.

FINALLY, IT DOES NOT COST ANYTHING.

WE NEED TO IMPRESS ON OUR PARENTS THAT THE MAIN
THING IS THAT IT IS OKAY TO STAY IN YOUR HOUSE AND
ENGAGE IN SMALL ACTIVITIES FOR A PERIOD OF TIME WHEN
WE FEEL TOO APATHETIC TO DO ANYTHING ELSE.

WHAT HELPS THE MOST

1. LESS BURDEN.
2. LESS EXPECTATION.
3. ENCOURAGING THOUGHTLESS ROUTINES WHICH DO

NOT NEED CONCENTRATION. THIS HELPS US TO FEEL WE ARE NOT BEING BURDENED.

4. LISTEN TO OUR AGENDA AND DO NOT INSIST THAT WE SHOULD FOLLOW YOURS. THIS IS BECAUSE YOU LIVE WITH US, BUT DO NOT KNOW EXACTLY HOW WE FEEL. WE WISH THERE COULD BE A THERMOMETER TO MEASURE APATHY SO YOU WOULD KNOW HOW WE FEEL AND HOW YOU NEED TO REACT TO OUR FEELINGS. UNFORTUNATELY, WHEN WE FEEL DOWN, WE CANNOT PUT INTO WORDS OUR FEELINGS AND SO YOU WOULD NOT KNOW HOW WE ARE.

WE NEED NO PRESSURE ON

"..... COME ON START STUDYING; DO LAWNS; WHY HAVEN'T YOU EMPTIED THE DISHWASHER OR PUT AWAY YOUR CLOTHES?"

WE NEED NO REMINDER ON HOW LONG THINGS TAKE US TO DO.

REGAINING WHAT WE HAVE LOST WILL TAKE A LOT OF TIME. IT WILL HAPPEN QUICKER IF WE HAVE CONTROL OF WHAT WE CAN DO AND WHAT WE CANNOT WITHOUT ANY FEELING OF EMBARRASSMENT.

WE LIKE TO CONTROL OUR FUN ACTIVITIES — SWIMMING, CYCLING ETC. WHEN YOU TELL US TO DO THESE THINGS AND WE ARE NOT READY FOR IT OR THE SPARK OF LIFE HAS NOT COME BACK YET, THEN WE SEE IT AS A CHORE AND AN EXPRESSION OF INADEQUACY.

HOW WE COPE WITH OUR FEELING OF HELPLESSNESS THAT WE HAVE NOT STILL REGAINED WHAT WE USED TO BE.

- WE SAY TO OURSELVES — MAYBE IT WILL COME BACK.
- IT IS JUST A STAGE.
- JUST AN EPISODE.
- I CAN'T DO TOO MUCH ABOUT IT NOW.
- THE BODY CANNOT HOLD TO REMAIN MISERABLE ALL THE TIME. SO, WE WILL REGAIN WHAT WE WERE.
- IN THE MEANTIME, KEEP YOUR FAITH IN US. WHEN WE ARE NOT APATHETIC THEN YOU CAN PUSH US A LITTLE.

MOST OF ALL TRUST US.

DEVELOPMENT OF SCHIZOPHRENIC THOUGHT
By W.R. BION, London

(Read at the 19ᵗʰ International Psycho-Analytical Congress
at Geneva 23-28 July 1955)

In this paper, which must be regarded as a preliminary
announcement, I do three things:-

(i) I discuss the point at which the psychotic personality diverges
from the non-psychotic; (ii) I examine the nature of that divergence; and (iii) I consider the consequences of it. Experience at
the Congress at Geneva showed that the attempt to give clinical illustrations in a paper as compressed as this produced far
more obscurity than illumination. This version is accordingly
restricted to theoretical description.

The conclusions I arrive at were forged in analytic contact with
schizophrenic patients and have been tested by me in practice.
That I arrived at some degree of clarification, I owe mainly to
three pieces of work. As they occupy a key position in this paper,
I shall remind you of them.

First: Freud's description, which I referred to in my paper at
the London Congress of 1953, of the mental apparatus called into
activity by the demands of the reality principle and in particular
of that part of it which is concerned with conscious awareness
of sense impressions. Second: Freud's tentative suggestion, in
Civilization and its Discontents, of the importance of the conflict
between Life and Death instincts. The point was taken up and
developed by Melanie Klein, but Freud seemed to recede from
it. Melanie Klein believes that this conflict persists throughout life, and this view I believe to be of great importance to an

understanding of the schizophrenic. Third: Melanie Klein's description of the phantasised sadistic attacks that the infant makes on the breast during the paranoid-schizoid phase, and her discovery of Projective Identification. Projective Identification is a splitting off by the patient of a part of his personality and a projection of it into the object where it becomes installed, sometimes as a persecutor, leaving the psyche from which it has been split off correspondingly impoverished.

Schizophrenic disturbance springs from an interaction between (i) the environment; and (ii) the personality. In this paper I ignore the environment and focus attention on four essential features of schizophrenic personality. First is a preponderance of destructive impulses so great that even the impulses to love are suffused by them and turned to sadism. Second is a hatred of reality which, as Freud pointed out, is extended to all aspects of the psyche that make for awareness of it. I add hatred of internal reality and all that makes for awareness of it. Third, derived from these two, is an unremitting dread of imminent annihilation. Fourth is a precipitate and premature formation of object relations, foremost amongst which is the transference, whose thinness is in marked contrast to the tenacity with which it is maintained. The prematurity, thinness, and tenacity are pathognomic and are alike derived from dread of annihilation by the death instincts. The schizophrenic is preoccupied with the conflict, never finally resolved, between destructiveness on the one hand and sadism on the other.

TRANSFERENCE

The relationship with the analyst is premature, precipitate, and intensely dependent. When the patient broadens it under pressure of his life or death instincts two concurrent streams of phenomena become manifest: First projective identification, with the analyst as object, becomes overactive with the resulting painful confusional states such as Rosenfeld has described. Second, the mental and other activities by which the dominant impulse, be it life instincts or death instincts, strives to express itself, are at once subjected to mutilation by the temporarily subordinated impulse. Driven by the wish to escape the confusional states and harassed by the mutilations, the patient strives to restore the restricted relationship; the transference is again invested with its characteristic featurelessness. Whether the patient walks straight past me into the consulting room as if scarcely aware of my presence, or whether he displays an effusive, mirthless bonhomie, the restricted relationship is unmistakable. Restriction and expansion alternate throughout the analysis.

THE DIVERGENCE

To sum up; ignoring the effect of the external environment, the schizophrenic personality depends on the existence in the patient of four features; (i) a conflict that is never decided between life and death instincts; (ii) a preponderance of destructive impulses; (iii) hatred of external and internal reality; (iv) a tenuous but tenacious object relationship. This peculiar endowment makes it certain that the schizophrenic patient's progression through the paranoid-schizoid and depressive positions is markedly different from that of the non-psychotic personality. This difference hinges on the fact that this combination of characteristics leads to a massive resort to projective identification. It is therefore to projective identification that I now turn, *but my examination of it is restricted to its deployment by the schizophrenic against all that apparatus of awareness that Freud described as being called into activity by the demands of the reality principle.*

DIVERGENCE OF PSYCHOTIC FROM NON-PSYCHOTIC PERSONALITY

I spoke of Melanie Klein's picture of the paranoid-schizoid position and the important part played in it by the infant's phantasies of sadistic attacks on the breast. Identical attacks are directed against the apparatus of perception from the beginning of life. This part of his personality is cut up, split into minute fragments, and then, using the projective identification, expelled from the personality. Having thus rid himself of the apparatus of conscious awareness of internal and external reality, the patient achieves a state which is felt to be neither alive nor dead.

This apparatus of conscious awareness is intimately connected with verbal thought and all that provides, at the early stage of which I speak, the foundations of its inchoation.

Projective identification of conscious awareness and the associated inchoation of verbal thought is the central factor in the differentiation of the psychotic from the non-psychotic personality. I believe it takes place at the outset of the patient's life. These sadistic attacks on the ego and on the foundations of inchoate verbal thought, and the projective identification of the fragments, makes certain that from this point on there is an ever-widening divergence between the psychotic and non-psychotic parts of the personality until at last the gulf is felt to be unbridgeable.

FATE OF THE EXPELLED FRAGMENTS

In so far as the destruction is successful, the patient experiences a failure in his capacity for perception. All his sense impressions appear to have suffered mutilation of a kind which would be appropriate had they been attacked as the breast is felt to be attacked in the sadistic phantasies of the infant. The patient feels imprisoned in the state of mind he has achieved and unable to escape from it because he feels he lacks the apparatus of awareness of reality, which is both the key to escape and the freedom itself to which he would escape. This sense of imprisonment is intensified by the menacing presence of the expelled fragments within whose planetary movements he is contained. The nature of this imprisonment will become clearer with the discussion of the fate of these expelled fragments, to which I now turn.

In the patient's phantasy the expelled particles of ego lead to an independent and uncontrolled existence outside the personality, but either containing or contained by external objects, where they exercise their functions as if the ordeal to which they have been subjected has served only to. increase their number and to provoke their hostility to the psyche that ejected them. In consequence the patient feels himself to be surrounded by bizarre objects whose nature I shall now describe.

THE PARTICLES

Each particle is felt to consist of a real external object which is incapsulated in a piece of personality that has engulfed it. The character of this complete particle will depend partly on the character of the real object, say a gramophone, and partly on the character of the particle of personality that engulfs it. If the piece of the personality is concerned with sight, the gramophone when played is felt to be watching the patient. If with hearing, then the gramophone when played is felt to be listening to the patient. The object, angered at being engulfed, swells up, so to speak, and suffuses and controls the piece of personality that engulfs it: to that extent the particle is felt to have become a thing. Since these particles are used by the patient as if they were prototypes of ideas—later to become words—this suffusion of the piece of personality by the contained, but controlling, object leads the patient to feel that words are the actual things they name, and so to the confusions, described by Segal, that arise because the patient equates, but does not symbolize.

CONSEQUENCES FOR THE PATIENT

The patient now moves, not in a world of dreams, but in a world of objects which are ordinarily the furniture of dreams. These objects, primitive yet complex, partake of qualities which in the non-psychotic are peculiar to matter, anal objects, senses, ideas, superego, and the remaining qualities of personality. One result is that the patient strives to use real objects as ideas and is baffled when they obey the laws of natural science and not those of mental functioning.

Associated with projective identification is the psychotic personality's inability to introject. If he wishes to take in an interpretation, or bring back these objects I have been describing, he does so by projective identification reversed, and by the same route. This situation was neatly summed up by the patient who said he used his intestine as a brain. When I said he had swallowed something, he replied, "The intestine doesn't swallow." Dr. Segal has described in her paper, which I had the good fortune to see before the Congress, some of the patient's vicissitudes in the depressive position; I would now add that, thanks to this employment of projective identification, he cannot synthesize his objects: he can only agglomerate and compress them. Further, whether he feels he has had something put into him, or whether he feels he has introjected it, he feels the ingress as an assault, and a retaliation by the object for his violent intrusion into it.

REPRESSION

It will be clear that where the non-psychotic personality, or part of the personality, employs repression the psychotic has employed projective identification. Therefore, there is no repression, and

CHAPTER 3:

Arriving and Accepting One's Own Identity

Empathic Exchange: The Key for Creating New Space between Internal and External Wars in the Management of First Episode Psychosis Patients

Sabar Rustomjee

Before I begin, I would like to acknowledge Edward Pinney's work, which has been exceptionally inspirational in demonstrating his personal authenticity and the depth and clarity of his work.

My reason for choosing the above title is to highlight the importance of what I refer to as the "human element" which always exists between "I and Thou" (Martin Buber), meaning all mankind. Naturally, this includes all of us attending this congress, whether or not we are close in relationship, agree or disagree on major or minor points or are of the same race or religion. What brings us together at this moment is an appreciation of how we, as both group and individual psychotherapists, can work together — not with realisations condoning destructiveness both within and outside of us, but my using our own individual human element, our human empathy, which enables us to reach out to one another in a productive manner.

In Edward Pinney's extension of Foulkes' concept of the group matrix, he very wisely notes that "it is the total therapeutic matrix of the therapist and the group that is the therapeutic agent". Clarifying this, he describes how a negative counter-transference from the group leader can lead to verbal as well as physical assaults between group members! This point clearly demonstrates how an internal "war" within the psyche of the group leader can emerge externally and openly in any group in violent forms. I believe this statement does not only apply to group psychotherapy; rather, it refers to a very central issue in life. However, in group and individual psychotherapy, he leader or therapist has the power to either reconstruct where possible a "corrective emotional experience" which is constructive or instead unknowingly and unconsciously become merged in a "destructive emotional experience" which can also be transmitted to the whole group, leading to destructiveness and major or minor anti-group manifestation. The above is also applicable to numerous other settings, especially those involving injustice, leading to both internal and external wars. In this vein, Martin Luther King, in Birmingham jail in 1963, wrote "Injustice anywhere is a threat to justice everywhere".

Let us now look at injustice in external wars that led to internal wars in the minds of famous artists. These internal wars were able to be portrayed by the artists, through art, into meaningful dialogue with us — the viewers.

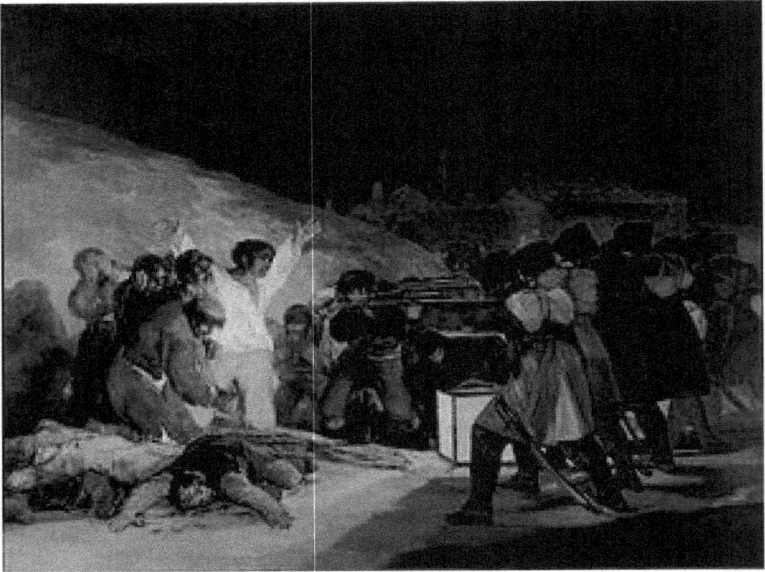

Figure 14.1: The Third of May 1808, by Francisco Goya

External and Internal Wars

EXTERNAL AND INTERNAL WARS ARE PORTRAYED BY ARTISTS

Here, an example of injustice is beautifully portrayed in Francisco Goya's famous painting. *The Third of May 1808*. Napoleon's army, attempting to stop any form of Spanish uprising at the start of Napoleon's quest to conquer Spain and Portugal, brutally executed a small group of unarmed Spanish peasants who were waiting near the Royal Palace in Madrid to get a glimpse of the 13-yer-old son of King Charles IV. It had been rumoured that the boy was being kidnapped and taken to France; the onlookers were curious, but hoping for reassurance. Goya had personally witnessed this scene, it is reported, but that Goya had to wait six years before he felt emotionally capable of paining it!

Prior to this invasion, the Spaniards had lived with a lack of safe space for a number of years under a weak ruler. The Spanish royalty had already been in disarray, like any group with weak leadership. A part of Napoleon's army which had suddenly descended upon them lined up, blending as one in unison, while focusing on their cold lethal rifles, determined to carry out executions without trial, like robots — without any dialogue or question.

This is also the demand put upon soldiers in wars, even when someone obviously blunders as expressed by A.L. Tennyson in his poem, The Charge of the Light Brigade (1870);

Theirs not to make reply,

Theirs not to question why,

Theirs is but to do and die.

The emotions on the faces of these unsuspecting Spanish peasants range from a wish to stare directly and courageously at Napoleon's army, as expressed clearly by the peasant in yellow trousers with the light from a lantern illuminating his face as his emotions challenge and confront the soldiers, even in the face of imminent death. Some peasants express feelings of total horror and despair; others close their eyes, perhaps hoping to be spared any further visual torture; the rest simply resort to prayer.

My aim in presenting this painting is to highlight certain interesting features. The French army represents a very powerful subgroup, but not even on solider is allowed to verbalise in his own concerns: "It is not to question Why? It is but to do or Die". This is at all times the demand of war. The army is commanded to work as one organism, not as separate individuals, no matter what each one's own commonsense conveyed. Although the French take pride in the ideals of liberty, equality and fraternity, during the period of Napoleon's desire for conquest these ideals were not considered important enough to be applied to the life or death of this small group of unarmed Spanish peasants! It should be noted that it is not the issue of desire — whether or not it is based on conquest — but the way in which it is carried out which is the main issue.

Picasso, in his equally famous masterpiece *Guernica* (1937), depicted a similar scene of senseless suffering in war influenced by Goya's painting. We can well imagine the depth of emotional turmoil, the internal wars which both these famous painters who loved Spain dearly, were feeling at the time. *Guernica* has remained synonymous with indiscriminate slaughter and now hangs proudly in the hallway of the United Nations. So, what according to these artists compelled them to produce these works which have been immortalised? In my opinion, among other issues, these paintings bring to life the total lack of the human element of empathy by those unjustly inflicting a death sentence on innocent civilians.

Kofi Annan has said, "Please spreads in one nation as genocidal fury rages in another". We can nevertheless live with the hope that introducing empathy into our own daily lives and work can lead to a greater awareness of human vulnerability, resulting in more humans conduct and less inhuman and senseless suffering. Most importantly, putting ourselves in the position of the other person highlights for us our own and another's irrational anger, our own and another's paranoid anxieties, our own and another's strengths and limitations, and, most of all, the similarities and differences between us.

I agree with Nelson Mandela's belief that "no enemy is invincible and all humans are vulnerable". Hence, he advises. "Keep your friends close and your rivals even closer" (*Time*, 2008). This helps us accept similarities in what we thought were differences and accept differences in what we thought were similarities in our fellow human beings. Such a tolerant and empathic way of seeing life's challenges creates a common ground in which constructive work can be done.

Similarities of Experiences in External and Internal Wars when Compared with First Episode Psychosis Patients

The injustice felt when a strong alien army opens fire without warning and executes a very small group of harmless, unarmed peasants on their own soil resembles the total lack of justice which is often felt by our first-episode psychosis patients towards the invasion of their minds by powerful psychotic thoughts. This is experienced most acutely when they sense a total lack of empathy by their own parents.

"My parents stare at me all the time, even when I ask them not to. So? I stare back. I try to scare the devil out of their bodies now!" one courageous patient said to me. His own terror of being overwhelmed by alien thoughts of the devil entering his mind, and how upset, alone and helpless he felt, was lost on his parents. It is true that his parents had become engrossed in their own fear and helplessness and could not be empathic towards their only son's terrifying experiences at this crucial time. Hence, my patient felt totally cut off from them and preferred to remain defiant by staring angrily, rather than submit to feeling tortured by his parent's lack of empathy and understanding. This is similar to both aspects of Goya's painting, that of the defiant peasant who outwardly stares back at Napoleon's soldiers while inwardly feeling the same fear as the other peasants — those who shut their eyes to prepare themselves for the inevitable loss of everything they had lived for, namely their journey in life so far, their land, their space, that of their ancestors, their own lives and those of their families.

Safe space can be destroyed in a flash when any form of external or internal violence, including a totally unexpected psychotic illness, descends on a person without warning or preparation. These patients already had their safe space destroyed once through psychosis and now lived in constant fear. They realised that it would take time to recovery and wondered if total recovery was ever possible. I was fully aware of this during every minute of every session. Hence, I decided not to make any supportive or non-empathic remarks, which in their existing paranoid state could easily have destroyed our relationship and as a result adversely affect their hopes for regaining normality.

Keeping Boundaries in Place and Being Attuned with Empathic Flexibility

One of the important features for maintaining trust and encouraging creativity and productivity in any group is to keep certain vital boundaries intact at all times, while allowing for empathic flexibility in other areas. It is of crucial importance to "prevent violence, uncontrollable behaviour, shame, hurt and humiliation at all times. To do so, the group leader needs to be able to protect the more helpless members in a group, especially when the group is unable to do so" (Pinney, 1995).

Empathy, combined with strong leadership and the capacity for reflection, is the key. This is the difference between one leader and another. A leader with empathy, whether in a group or organisation, will never humiliate a member just to prove a particular issue, even if it is a boundary issue. When boundaries are enforced in a robotic way without understanding why a person wishes to violate them, incorrect and irreconcilable decisions are often made.

Boundary Issues Regarding the Group Leader's Ability to Use Control and Ensure a Safe Space without Threats of Violence

An example: In one of my other heterogenous groups composed of patients who were not suffering from psychosis, but had narcissistic, grandiose and omnipotent tendencies, two male members got verbally entangled in a conflict. One said to the other, "Let us go to the park outside and settle this matter once and for all". Obviously, both wanted me to take sides, while at the same time wanting me to feel helpless and impotent in the face of their male muscular strength. Instead, I said in a loud, clear and firm voice, "If anyone takes even one step outside the group room at this moment, you cannot return to the group ever again". Both members instantly pretended that nothing had happened and after a few minutes of the group talking about superficialities, the group started to talk more meaningfully and productively about the issue that had precipitated the conflict. I did not humiliate either member, but encouraged the group to look into group-as-a-whole issues of rivalry between themselves, with me as leader, the group attempting to project their own helplessness onto myself.

Similarly, it is important that members are not humiliated simply because they come late. Even if it is a routine occurrence, it clearly signifies than an existing problem has not yet been resolved. Once again, more meaningful work can be done in an empathic work group culture rather than in an accusatory demanding manner. With recently hospitalised members, one of my guidelines is that the leader must acknowledge that the patient made considerable effort simply to get out of bed, get dressed and arrive safety to attend the group. I value equally those who struggle to come on time as well as also those who attend against all odds, e.g. heavy medication, lethargy, persecutory delusions, depression, etc. The time boundary of ending on time is maintained and not extended for latecomers or others, except in certain life-threatening circumstances. First-episode psychosis or chronic patients with psychotic disorders often feel that they have not only lost their friends, parents and entire future, but also that nobody can ever create a safe-enough space to hear or understand them. Their lives at times can feel so burdensome that violence, murder or suicide may seem like acceptable alternatives. However, when strategies to counteract these helpless thoughts are put into place, these patients have every possibility of overcoming their fears and not putting them into action.

An Experiential Group Project with First-Episode Psychosis Patients

My presentation will now describe a 22-month Experiential Group project with patients suffering from first-episode psychosis.

DETAILS OF ORGANISATION

A first-episode psychosis unit associated with a psychiatric out-patient clinic was launched in a region of Victoria where such a service had not existed, as a new venture spanning adult and adolescent mental health services. About a year of preparation went into starting the unit. We had meetings with staff from well-established units elsewhere in Victoria and realised that one of the major difficulties would be the effort of transporting even highly motivated patients to the venue, following discharge from a psychiatric hospital. We would have to rely on the parents, caregivers or existing community-assisted transport avenue for patients who lived miles away from the unit. The rest of the patients would have to rely on their own motivation and mobility or on the unit staff, to help with transport. We had monthly meetings with the general outpatient team whose members also covered our work absences if required. A healthy network for this venture was now put into place.

Patients were selected for the group from referrals of those who had been discharged from hospital within the past two years. The selection was based on an initial face-to-face assessment while patients were in hospital, along the lines of routine selection for most small groups. Socialising between members after group sessions was allowed; however, bringing these outside meetings back to the next group session was highly encouraged.

An unspoken, but very visible feature, was that myself — a consultant psychotherapist employed for the training in individual and group psychotherapy to psychiatry trainees and all other multidisciplinary staff — would be in sole charge of the unit. So, there was acknowledgement that supportive, expressive group psychotherapy was a useful treatment modality for first-episode psychosis patients. Total trust was placed in me and my cotherapist to provide responsible leadership with empathy and containment. My cotherapist was a very pleasant and friendly male in his early 30's who had experience with borderline inpatients. We had great respect for each other's work. We spend time before and after each session reflecting and assessing the event which had occurred.

THE OBJECTIVES OF THE UNIT

1. To treat a group of patients of both genders between the ages of 16 and 25 for whom a serious mental illness, affecting their thought processes and mental state, had been their first encounter as a patient in a psychiatric hospital. Their hospital admission needed to have been within the past two years; by doing so, we eliminated chronic patients. Those patients with dual diagnosis during their hospitalisation, including the intake of marijuana and other addictive drugs which had precipitated their psychoses, were included.

2. To help with the client's rehabilitation into the outside world. To this end, a community hall situated about 15 minutes by public transport outside the regional hospital and outpatient area was selected. They would be attending in familiar territory, but sufficiently far away so as to

discourage them from feeling too involved, by constantly dropping into the hospital where they had been admitted.

3. To attempt to actively involve parents and caregivers so as to give them support in gaining a clearer understanding of what was happening to their son or daughter, through individual or family sessions at the outpatient clinic as appropriate, as well as bi-monthly evening sessions at the local community hall.

4. To provide group psycho-education once a month in the evenings at the community hall, not only to the patient, but to all family members, caregivers, and staff who wished to attend. The importance of maintaining an empathic outlook on their sick patients as well as not having very high expectations of themselves was highlighted.

5. It was hoped that through all of the above, there would be a reduced risk of relapse among these young patients. In essence, our aim was to initially create a group culture with safe space, and, when this was mastered, to attempt to extend it through psycho-education to their homes, so they could feel free to discuss their personal "internal wars" — their constant internal conflict and turmoil — whenever they were able to do so. The group culture needed to reflect empathy, sensitivity, authenticity, trust and non-aggressiveness as well as encourage our patients to be as free from destructive criticism and shame as was possible for them. It was hoped that such a benign yet reality-based culture would help the patients regain their lost self-esteem through verbal as well as non-verbal dialogue, expressions with the group through art, music, indoor and outdoor sports, as well as informal communications with each other and with the external world.

The Work of the Group and its Guidelines

Our group could be described as a partially structured, flexible, undemanding group without any visible tension. By allowing the patients to have as much autonomy as was appropriate to their current mental state, and by discussing whatever they brought up with no pressure to continue their chain of thought, they felt a sense of freedom, with mutual trust between us. We hence attempted to convey a corrective emotional experience. No demands were ever placed on them, and as therapists we were constantly aware of their limitations in both thought and action. We were aware how drained of energy they often felt. Simply making an effort to attend as often as was possible was sufficient indication of their motivation. The rest would take time. They needed constant ego building and our full attention along with tolerance at all times.

The main boundary issue was that there was to be absolutely no physical violence. Their medications would be attended to by their own personal psychiatrists.

Details of Sessions

The sessions were held once a week from 9.15am to 2.30pm. The first session (9.15-10.30am) lasted 1¼ hours, followed by a ¾ hour tea break from 10.30 to 11.15am. This was followed by a second session of 1¼ hours until 12.30pm. We recognised the clients' poor attention spans and were accordingly very flexible. The hall had a piano and an attached basketball court. As expected, group members stayed with us and chatted informally during their tea break. Either they or my cotherapist often played music during break. Nevertheless, there was total flexibility, if they wanted instead to leave the community hall during this time, to do shopping etc. In fact, most enjoyed being together. A number of the patients had a good sense of humour and tried to joke around. The jokes were usually repetitive, but they would all laugh at them anyway. The sicker patients were never put under any stress to contribute, but they did attend regularly and engaged in activities that suited them for as long as their concentration span allowed them to do so.

This is how the usual sessions started. Both my colleague and/or I arrived early to arrange the seating. Some clients would also often come early. They were invited to come with either one of us who went to the local bakery and together we bought freshly made cakes and pastries, soft drinks and fruit. The clients enjoyed the delicious food and often gave us orders in advance for the following week regarding their first, second or third choices. This "ice-breaker" set the stage for them feeling this was not a formal therapy group, but that we were extremely flexible and boundaries were flexible although they were clearly always in place. They respected us as we did them.

We would spread a variety of work materials on the large table, namely paper and coloured pencils; origami materials; occupational therapy materials such as fabric colours with stamps for printing on handkerchiefs if they chose to do so; as well as travel magazines or National Geographic magazine so that, if they wished they would simply turn the pages and that would help group or individual discussion. Alternatively, patients were allowed to simply wander around for a while and then sit down, whenever and wherever they wanted.

Our main documented therapeutic material was through my cotherapist, who happened to be a very talented impromptu artist. He would quickly draw whatever the patients were saying as a group, making the group theme crystal clear. If the patients disagreed, they would correct him and draw something different themselves. We filed everything done each week and brought the same folder weekly so they could add anything new if they wished. These pictorial representations helped them to remember what they had done each week and how far they had improved. They all became proud of the work done, which gave them a sense of achievement. The start was a drawing of Atlas carrying the burdens of the globe on his shoulders. Then there was a very funny caricature of me with huge spectacles, sitting behind an igloo and sucking a chocolate icy-pole, with the caption compiled by the patients from the guidelines I had given. It read: "We talk of everything, from icy-poles to igloos, that is everything that begins with I". This was read every week, followed by peels of infectious laughter. This brought out the feeling that this was a safe space where anything could be said or discussed without reprimand.

GROUP MEMBERS

I will describe a few group members.

Client A: Talked in a very transparent way about his difficult relationship with both his parents since his breakdown. With our encouragement, he started writing *Guidelines for Parents* and guidelines for us. He wrote: "Whom can we turn to when we felt nobody had even the slightest clue of what we were going through? It does not help when our own parents say 'We are there for you', but then they cannot believe whatever we say, and also don't want to give us the time to listen to our version of what is best for us. So, here is our gift to you now". His advice to hospitals was, "Every hospital should have a dog". As my cotherapist drew the do, another group member joined in the fun and said, "Look Grandma, the dog has no balls!" [This statement, obviously addressed to me, was also a source of massive entertainment for them! They had now entered an empathic safe space. Anything could really be said and no one would humiliate or shame them. The practical possibility or impossibility of whatever the group said did not matter. The fact they could speak openly and everyone would hear them was productive.]

Client B: Joined in telling us how he avoided conversation with his parents who hounded him daily as to why he would or would not do something. He had found an excellent escape route by saying repeatedly to every question they asked by replying, "Just because". This stopped their repetitive questions. He said he had been totally psychotic while in hospital, thinking he was Jesus Christ! His remark was joined by most other who said, "So did we!" I asked, "Then how did any of you know which one was the real Christ?" They all burst into further peels of laughter at what they felt was a totally stupid question. Each one said, "I of course knew for sure I was the real Christ, the others were only faking it. What else?"

Client C: With the help of the cotherapist, wrote a poem describing how he ran out of the ward at the height of his illness, hoping to buy more marijuana and was picked up in a couple of hours by the Police. It was only four weeks later he said that he realised why he had run away: "The penny finally dropped, that I was still sick!" he said with new insight.

Client D: Said he had always wanted to be better than Einstein and also to become a professor. He said his symptoms started at age 20, soon after his parents broke up. He then spent $300 on books, one of which was on chaos theory. "Because I could not understand it. I thought it must be very good", he continued. "I then started to read Einstein's relativity theory. I know E=MC² now." No-one in the group ever challenged him about anything he would say. They nicknamed him "Our Professor".

Client E: Although he said and did the most atrocious and outwardly aggressive things in the group, never really worried either me, my cotherapist or other group members. We were confident we could contain his aggression. He was probably the most intelligent and the least predictable. However, he never hurt anyone. He was the only one who asked us and brought his girlfriend along every session. She drove him to the sessions and fit into the group very well. She brought and discussed books she had read with others. No-one could fathom, if anything that E said was what he meant to be discussed further in any way. He seemed to say, "I like to be in control at all times. Please do not ask me anything". H was neatly dressed at most times.

He knew that after we left the hall, a group of very elderly women came — some in wheelchairs. He would write little notes to them and paste them all over with sticky tape, probably testing us. The content revolved around wanting to be left alone by scaring them off. He would write in bold letters: "Beware, You Christians are Sinners. Satan is here. Drugs are God. We are all crazy. Don't fuck with us. Take our football again and we will curse you!" Another time he wrote on top of the sugar container in chalk. "This jar is full of Arsenic. Use it and see!" Everyone would have a giggle, while either my cotherapist or I would remove them carefully in front of him and paste them in the group journal, just like everything else. He appeared content with that, knowing he had been heard and acknowledged. His other favourite saying was "Go, Kill the Pigs!" said provocatively, in a testing way, but without anger or malice.

He was in fact very popular with the group and often invited all of them to his rich mansions. The feedback was that all who went had a good time, with no dramas. I sometimes wondered if maybe some part of him wanted to be involved with us as our entertainer while at the same time he did not want to get close to us either! He kept a certain distance from everyone — even his girlfriend! My cotherapist and I decided not to interpret any of his aggressive actions, but simply to contain them. By our response we normalised it. His similar provocative outbursts gradually diminished. About six months later, he started a course of study and left the group, but still entertained the group members he knew!

Client F: Was in a state of continuous dissociation with a fantasy figure, not knowing when he was a fantasy figure, whom he knew previously as a friend — Adam — and when he was back to his usual self. His psychosis had been precipitated, he said, by experimenting just once with MDMA and Cocaine. He had started using marijuana at age 14! Most times, he would laugh uncontrollably and start dancing, saying his legs could not stop dancing and that he liked to be a clown! His symptoms too gradually settled.

There were three females with psychotic symptoms, delusions and hallucinations. One joined in with the male members, but the other two drew and painted and talked mainly with me, but remained somewhat distant from the others.

In retrospect, I made one significant error. I should have added a further guideline — that here would be no discussion about any member's religious beliefs. One female questioned a male group member very forcefully about his religious beliefs, which in all probability was a major factor in him leaving the group prematurely. He gave the reason that transport was difficult, which was also a factor, but maybe not the most important one!

As longstanding group members began to improve, and got employed in low stress, suitable work, it was time for the group to end. They summarised their current values in life as follows:

There will always be

Someone to love

Someone to live for, and

Something to look forward to.

Final Outcome

This experiential group for First Episode Psychosis patients lasted 22 months. It was initially expected that members would attend approx. 9-10 months. This was a pilot group, from which others have since started in this clinic. A total of 38 patients joined. Five dropped out after a couple of session and 33 had what we felt was a productive experience, depending on their length of attendance. Of these, 10 patients attended regularly for 40 working weeks (holiday period excluded); 8 attended for 12 weeks; 10 attended for 8 weeks and 5 for between 3 to 8 weeks.

Only one patient who was one of those who dropped out early

after a couple of sessions had a relapse of symptoms and needed further hospitalisation. It was recognised that empathic and supportive group psychotherapy had been very productive for this young age group of patients.

In conclusion, Edward Pinney's own authentic values and their clinical applications have been invaluable.

In the words of Henry Wadsworth Longfellow (A Psalm of Life, 1838), Edward Pinney has left behind him:

Footprints on the sands of time;

Footprints, that perhaps another,

Sailing on life's solemn main;

A forlorn and shipwrecked brother,

Seeing, shall take heart again.

References

Pinney, E. (1995). *A first group psychotherapy book*. Lanham, MD: Jason Aronson   Publishers.

Stengel, R. (2008, July 9). Mandela: his Eight lessons on leadership. *Time Magazine*, 17-22.

Tennyson, A.L. (1870). Charge of the light brigade. *In Little Oxford Dictionary of Quotations*.   Oxford;   Oxford University Press, p.20.

Web Resources

Rabey v. The Queen, [1980] 54 C.C.C. (2d) 1 S.C.C. http://wps. prenhall.com/ca_ph_blair_law_1/6/1550/396810.cw/ index.html [last accessed 6th December 2015]

Jean-Christophe: Novel by Rolland
http://www.britannica.com/topic/Jean-Christophe   [last accessed 7th November 2015]

https://www.pinterest.com/pin/307722587019533395/

Meeting Elizabeth Rohr

I was studying Group Analysis, an international journal, Volume 42, No 2. June 2009. I had met Elizabeth Rohr, Professor for Intercultural Education.

The title of her paper is *Farewell To A Dead Horse: Group Analytic Supervision Training In Post-war Guatemala.*

Key words : Psychosocial work in post-war society supervision training in case work.

This is accompanied by unconscious fears and extremely long death lists. The author described that such a meeting was like riding a dead horse, and also getting down from the dead horse.

Do you look for a stronger whip?

Do you book a training course to learn how to ride a dead horse?

The above reminded me of Raskolnikov in Crime And Punishment. I was told that everybody would stay on the dead horse, trying to keep on riding, ignoring the fact that the horse was dead. They would pretend as if nothing had happened. Nobody looked at reality.

Supervision in training could lead to getting down from the dead horse to create a new future. Fortunately for Little Hans, his father consulted Sigmund Freud and discussed how he should deal with every occasion. Little Hans recovered and was able to become an orchestra leader, without any fear of introducing himself as Little Hans. Raskolnikov also had a happy ending after confessing his sins of murdering a pawn broker and her step daughter and the unborn child. He finally overcame his guilt by confessing his guilt to both his closest partner Sonia, and then to the police. In prison other prisoners looked up to Sonia too. It has been found to be very important to remove self guilt from the child's thoughts. Raskalnikov was able to do so, with help of his companion Sonia, as adults.

Coming up to recent times fathers are taught how to be a most important person in the child's life, which will help the child to be able to understand their father.

Similarly in the experiences of Tom Maine at Northfield, he came to realise that he should not have expected pure recovery from previously very sick Patients, who were transferred to the care of less accommodating environment.

These patients would expect from their superior nurses more care than was possible leading to great turmoil with a result of a change in the Head of the Hospital to Dr.S.H.Foulkes. This change was accompanied by better understanding among treating doctors, superior and recently employed nurses. The rate Of recovery of patients now became more acceptable.

Patients who had primary as well as secondary episodes of psychosis was now better treated. Dr Sabar Rustomjee, psychiatrist and analytic therapist of long standing, was able to start an additional programme where patients were able to converse with each other jokingly; Dr. Sabar would also join in the fun. The rate of improvement was markedly increased.

Neville Symington has also greatly improved the standard of recovery of very longstanding difficult patients. The therapist's ability to identify with the patients problem without frustration has been a major factor to strengthen difficult cases.

REFERENCES

Aiston, G., & Horne, G. (1924). *Savage Life in Central Australia*: Australian Aboriginal Culture Series No. 7. Virginia, NT, Australia: David M. Welch.

Elon, A., (2002). *The Pity of it All: A History of Jews in Germany*. New York: Metropolitan Books.

Altmann, C. (2006). *After Port Arthur: Personal Stories of Courage and Resilience Ten Years on from the Tragedy That Shocked the Nation*. Crows Nest, NSW: Allen and Unwin.

Babyak, J. (1994). *Birdman: The Many Faces of Robert Stroud*. Berkeley CA: Ariel Vamp.

Bateman A. W. (2002) Psychological treatment of borderline personality disorder. Psychiatry 1:1: 17-20.

Benedict, Ruth — *The Chrysanthemum and the Sword* — Mariner Books

Bernard, H. S. & Spitz, H. I. (2006) Training in Group Psychotherapy Supervision. New York: American Group Psychotherapy Association, Inc.

Bettelheim, B. (1976). *The Uses of Enchantment: The Meaning and Importance of Fairy Tales*. New York: Vintage Books.

Bick, E. (1968). The experience of the skin in early object relations. *International Journal of Psycho- Analysis, 49*: 484-486.

Bion, W. R. (1961). *Experiences in groups and other papers*. London: Tavistock.

Bion, W. R. (1967). *Second Thoughts: Selected Papers on Psychoanalysis*. London: Karnac.

Bion, W. R. (1991). *Transformations*. London: Karnac.

Bion, W.R. (1957). Second Thoughts. *Int Journal of Psychoanalysis, Vol 38; Part 3-4: 43-64*, London: Karnac.

Bion, W.R. (1962). The Psycho-Analytic Study of Thinking. *International Journal of Psycho- Analysis*, 43: 306-310.

Blundell, J. W. (Ed.) (1997). *The Plums of P. G. Wodehouse.* London: The Folio Society.

Bollas, C. (1987). *The Shadow of the Object.* New York: Colombia University.

Bollas, C. (2009). *The Evocative Object World.* East Sussex: Routledge.

Borchgrevink, A., (2013). *A Norwegian Tragedy. Anders Behring Breivik and the Massacre on Utoya.* G. Puzey (Trans.). Cambridge: Polity Press.

Bowlby, J. (1973). Separation: Anxiety & Anger. Attachment and Loss (vol. 2); (International psycho-analytical library no.95). London: Hogarth Press.

Catherina M., *Comments on the relation of OCD with Paranoid Psychosis.*

Christie, G. L. (1994). Some psychoanalytic aspects of humour. *International Journal of Psycho- Analysis*, 75: 479.

Christie, G., & Morgan, A. (2000). Individual and group psycho-therapy with infertile couples. *International Journal of Group Psychotherapy, 50(2):* 237-250.

Clarke, D. (2003). Faith and Hope. *Australasian Psychiatry, 11: 2.*

Clarke, D. (2012). *Depression, Demoralisation and Psychotherapy in People who are Medically Ill. The Psychotherapy of Hope.* R. D. Alarcon, & J. B. Frank (Eds.), Baltimore MD: Johns Hopkins University.

Clarke, D. M., Kissane, D. W., Trauer, T. & Smith, G. C., (2005). Demoralization, anhedonia and grief in patients with severe physical illness. *Department of Psychological Medicine, Monash Medical Centre, Clayton, Australia,* p. 96-105

Coetzee, J. M. (2000). *Disgrace.* London: Vintage Books.

Cox, M. (Ed.) (1999). *Remorse and Reparation.* London: Jessica Kingsley.

Dalal, F. (2002). *Race Colour and the Processes of Racialisation.* East Sussex: Brunner Routledge.

de Maré, P., Piper, R. and Thompson, S. (1991). *Koinonia: From Hate through Dialogue, to Culture in the Large Group.* London: Karnac.

Doi, T. (2001). *The Anatomy of Dependence.* New York: Kodansha International.

Edwards, R., & Reader, K. (2001). *The Papin Sisters.* New York: Oxford University.

Eggum, A., Woll, G., & Lande, M. (Eds.) (1998). *Munch: at the Munch Museum, Oslo.* London: Scala.

Ellingson, P. (2013). *The writing is not on the wall. A History of Psychoanalysis in Australia: from Freud to Lacan, 9:* 193. PsychOz.

Erikson, E. (1963). *Childhood and Society.* New York: Norton.

Erikson, E. H. (1969). *Gandhi's Truth: On the Origins of Militant Nonviolence.* New York: Norton.

Ezriel, H. (1957). Experimentation within the psycho-analytic session. *The British Journal for the Philosophy of Science, 7:* 342-347.

Feder, L. (1980). Preconceptive ambivalence and external reality. *International Journal of Psycho- Analysis, 61:* 161-178.

Fonagy, P. (1996). "Attachment, the development of the self, and its pathology in personality disorders". Psychomedia: 26–32.

Freud, S. (1912a). Formulations on the two principles of mental functioning. *S.E.* 12.

Freud, S. (1912b). The Dynamics of Transference. S.E., 12. London: Hogarth.

Freud, S. (1913). Totem and Taboo. S.E., 13. London: Hogarth.

Freud, S. (1916a). Those Wrecked by Success. S. E., 14. London: Hogarth.

Freud, S. (1916b). Criminals from a Sense of Guilt. S. E., 14. London: Hogarth.

Freud, S. (1920a). The Psychogenesis of a Case of Homosexuality in a Woman. S. E., 18: 147-172. London: Hogarth.

Freud, Sigmund — *His life in Pictures and Words* — Univ. of Qld Press, St Lucia, Qld. Australia

Freud, S. (1920b). Beyond the Pleasure Principle

Freud, S. (1923). *The Ego and the Id. S.E. 19.*

Freud. S. — Story of Little Hans and his father — Page 266.

Gandhi, M. K. (1945). *A Thought for the Day. Gandhi Series.* New Delhi, India: Anand T. Hingordni.

Gandhi, M. K. (1983). *Gandhi. Navajivan Trust.* Mumbai, India: Vakil and Sons.

Gandhi, M. K. *Great Works of Mahatma Gandhi.* Delhi, India: Jainco.

Gandhi, M. K. My Experiment with Truth, Part I, Birth and Parentage & The Bhagavad Gita, Introduction. In: *Great works of Mahatma Gandhi.* Delhi, India: Jainco Publishers

Gilligan, J. (1999). *Violence: Reflections on Our Deadliest Epidemic.* London: Jessica Kingsley.

Glowinski, H., Marks, Z., & Murphy, S. (Eds.) (2001). *A Compendium of Lacanian Terms. Anamorphosis.* (p. 14-15). London: Free Association Books.

Gordon, R., & Haynes, J. (1998). *Dialogue in the Analytic Setting. Selected papers of Louis Zinkin on Jung and on Group Analysis.* London: Jessica Kingsley.

Grant, S. (2016). Talking to my Country. Sydney, Australia: HarperCollins Publishers.

Grigg, R. (2001). *Psychosis. A Compendium of Lacanian Terms.* (p. 148). London: Free Association Books.

Grotstein, J. S. (Ed.) (1983). *Do I Dare Disturb the Universe? A Memorial to Wilfred R. Bion*. London: Maresfield Reprints.

Gudmundsson, E. (2013). Sibling transference and family transference in groups and organisations. *Forum: Journal of the International Association for Group Psychotherapy and Group Processes, n.6*; 143-152. July 2014.

Guntrip, H. (1975). My experience of analysis with Fairbairn and Winnicott. *International Review of Psycho-Analysis* 2:145-156;

Guntrip, H. (1975). My experience of analysis with Fairbairn and Winnicott. *Int. Rev. Psycho-Anal., 2:145-156; reprinted Int. J. Psycho-Anal.*, 77, 4 (1996): 737-754.

Hesse, H. (1993). "A Child's Heart" in Miller, A. The Drama of Being a Child. (p. 85). London: Virago.

Hildebrand, D., & Pithers, W. D. (1989). Enhancing offender empathy in sexual abuse victims. In: D. R. Laws (Ed.) *Relapse Prevention with Sex Offenders*. New York: Guildford.

Hopper, E. (1992). The problem of context in group-analytic psychotherapy: a clinical illustration and a brief theoretical discussion. In: M. Pines (Ed.), *Bion and Group Psychotherapy*. (pp. 330-353). London: Routledge.

Hopper, E. (2003a). *The Social Unconscious: Selected Papers*. London: Jessica Kingsley.

Hopper, E. (2003b). *Traumatic Experience in the Unconscious Life of Groups: The Fourth Basic Assumption: Incohesion: Aggregation/Massification or (ba) I:A/M*. London: Jessica Kingsley.

Hopper, E., & Weinberg, H. (2011). *The social unconscious in persons, groups and societies Volume 1: Mainly Theory*. London: Karnac.

Hopper. E. (2005). Countertransference in the context of the fourth basic assumption in the unconscious life of groups. *International Journal of Group Psychotherapy, 55: 1*, 87-114.

Hopper. E (1995) A Psychoanalytical Theory of 'Drug Addiction' : Int. J. Psycho-Anal; Vol 76, p1121. London.

Hunt ,Leigh..........

Isaacs, S. (1952). The Nature and Function of Phantasy (Fifth Discussion of Scientific Controversies). In: King, P. & Steiner, R. (Ed.) (1991). *The Freud-Klein Controversies 1941-45 (New library of psychoanalysis; 11)* (pp. 440-475). London: Routledge [reprinted London: Routledge 1992].

Joseph, B. (1989). *Transference: the total situation, International Journal of Psychoanalysis, 66: 4,* 447-454.

Keats, J. (1988) *Ed Barnard. The Complete Poems. Third Edition.* Penguin Books.

Keogh, T. (2012). *Through a glass darkly then face to face: Malignant narcissism, psychopathy and perversion. The Internal World of the Juvenile Sex Offender, 5,* (pp. 53-72). London: Karnac.

Kernberg, O. F. (1970). Factors in the psychoanalytic treatment of narcissistic personalities. *Journal of the American Psychoanalytic Association, 18:* 51-85.

Kernberg, O. F. (1974). Further contributions to the narcissistic personalities. *International Journal of Psychoanalysis. 55:* 215, 240.

Klein, M. (1948). *Contributions to Psychoanalysis. 1921-45.* London: Hogarth

Klein, M. (1952). *The Emotional Life of the Infant.* London: Hogarth.

Klein, M. (1975a). *Love, Guilt and Reparation: and Other Works 1921-1945.* London: Hogarth.

Klein, M. (1975b). *Envy and Gratitude: and Other Works 1946-1963.* London: Hogarth.

Kotani, Hidefumi / Bonds, White Frances, *Creating Safe Space through Individual and Group Psychotherapy.*

Lacan, J. (1973). *The Four Fundamental Concepts of Psychoanalysis.* Middlesex: Penguin.

Lacan, J. (1977). *Ecrits.* Paris: Seuil.

Lacan, J. (1981) [1973] *Of the gaze as object petit a in The Four Fundamental Concepts of Psychoanalysis* (pp. 67-104). New York: W.W. Norton.

Lande, M. (1980) Edited by Munch, at the Munch museum Oslo (1998), Oslo, Norway: Scala Books/The Munch Museum.

Langs, R. (1994) *Doing Supervision and Being Supervised.* London: H Karnac Books Ltd.

Lannoy, R. (1974). *The Speaking Tree.* Oxford: Oxford University Press

Lansky, M. R., & Morrison, A. P. (Eds.) (1997). *The Widening Scope of Shame.* London: The Analytic Press.

Laplanche, J., Pontalis, J. B. (1983). *The Language of Psychoanalysis.* London: Hogarth Press and the Institute of Psychoanalysis.

Laungani, P. (2003). Sexual Abuse in an Asian Family. *Counselling Psychology Quarterly, 16 (4):* 385-401.

Laungani, P. (2005). Caste, Class and Culture. *Counselling Psychology Quarterly, 18 (1):* 61-71.

Laungani, P. (2007). *Understanding Cross-Cultural Psychology.* London: Sage.

Little, M. I. (1990). *Psychotic Anxieties and Containment: a Personal Record of an Analysis with Winnicott,* (pp. 31-38). London: Jason Aronson.

Livingston, M. S., & Livingston, L. R. (2006). Sustained empathic focus and the clinical application of self-psychological theory in group psychotherapy. *International Journal of Group Psychotherapy, 56 (1):* 67-84.

Mahler, M. (1991). *The Psychological Birth of the Human Infant (Maresfield Library).* London: Karnac.

Main, T. F. (1957). The Ailment. *British Journal of Medical*

Psychology, *30:129-145. doi: 10.1111/j.2044-8341.1957. tb01193.x*

Mandela, N. (2000). *Long Walk to Freedom: The Autobiography of Nelson Mandela* (pp. 11-12). London: Abacus.

Maugham, S. (1915). *Of Human Bondage*. London: Vintage Books.

McWilliams, N. (2004). *Psychoanalytic Psychotherapy: a Practitioner's Guide* (pp. 37, 60-72). New York: Guilford.

Menninger, K. (1973). *Whatever Became of Sin?* New York: Bantam.

Miller, A. (1987). *For Your Own Good: Hidden Cruelty in Child-Rearing and the Roots of Violence*. London: Virago.

Miller, A. (1993). *The Drama of Being a Child: The Search for the True Self,* (pp. 81-145). London: Virago.

Mollon, P. (2003). *Shame and Jealousy: The Hidden Turmoils*. London: Karnac.

Moodley, R., Rai, A., & Alladin, W. (Eds.) (2010). *Bridging East-West Psychology and Counselling: Exploring the Work of Pittu Laungani*. New Delhi: Sage.

Munch, E., Munch (1897-1899) Edited 1993.

Murphy, S. Glowinski, H., & Marks, Z. (Ed.) (2001). *A Compendium of Lacanian Terms*. London: Free Association Books.

Museo Nacional Del Prado, The Prado Guide (2016)

Muthesius, A. (Ed.) (1993). *The Frieze of Life. Munch*. Cologne: Benedict Taschen.

Nitsun, M. (1996). *The Anti-Group: Destructive Forces in the Group and Their Creative Potential*. London: Routledge.

Padel, J. (1996). The case of Harry Guntrip. *Int. J. Psycho-Anal.* (1996), 77, 4: 755-61.

Pines, Malcolm

Pisani, R. A. (2014). Large, Small and Median Group in Group Analysis, In: *Autobiografia Scienza e Arte*. (pp. 289-300). Rome: Edizioni Universitarie Romane.

Rahv, P. (1962), "Dostoevsky in Crime and Punishment," in *Dostoevsky: a collection of essays, ed. René Wellek.* (p. 34). Englewood Cliffs: Prentice-Hall, Inc.

Reed A. W. (1994). *Aboriginal Stories,* (pp. 11-14). Sydney: New Holland Publishers.

Reed, A. W. (1999). *Aboriginal Myths, Legends & Fables.* Sydney: New Holland Publishers.

Elizabeth Rohr, *Group Analysis Journal,* Volume 42 No 2. June 2009.

Rolland, R. (1943). *Jean-Christophe.* Whitefish, Montana: Kessinger Publishing.

Roth, B. E. (1990). *The Difficult Patient in Group: Group Psychotherapy with Borderline and Narcissistic Disorders.* W. N. Stone & H. D. Kibel (Eds.) Monograph 6. AGPA. International Universities Press, Inc.

Rustomjee, S. (1996). Noncompliance in renal medicine. *ANZJP, 30: No. 2.*

Rustomjee, S. (2001). Exploring social disintegration. *Group Analysis, 34:* 115-127. London: Sage.

Rustomjee, S. (2009). The solitude and agony of unbearable shame. *Group Analysis, 42 (2):* 143-155. London: Sage

Rustomjee, S. (2013). Empathic exchange: *The key for creating new space between internal and external wars in the management of first episode psychosis patients. Creating Safe Space through Individual and Group Psychotherapy.* (pp. 187-198). Tokyo: Institute of Psychoanalytic Systems Psychotherapy Press.

Rustomjee, S., & Smith, G. (1996). Consultation Liaison Psychiatry to Renal Medicine: Work with an Inpatient Unit. *ANZIP, 30: No. 2;* 229-237

Rutan, J. S., & Stone, W. N. (1993). *Psychodynamic Group Psychotherapy, 2nd Edition.* New York: Guilford Press.

Sachs, A. (1990). *The Soft Vengeance of a Freedom Fighter, Second Edition*. California: University of California.

Saint-Exupery, A. D. (2012). *The Little Prince*. London: Egmont.

Saul, J. R. (1995). *The Doubter's Companion: a Dictionary of Aggressive Common Sense*. New York: Penguin.

Scheff, T. J. (1987). The shame rage spiral: the case study of an interminable quarrel. In: Lewis, H. B. (Ed.), *The Role of Shame in Symptom Formation* (pp. 109-150). New Jersey: Erlbaum.

Schmideberg, M. (1935). Reassurance as a means of analytic technique. *International Journal of Psycho- Analysis, 16:* 307-333.

Schützenberger, A. A., & Devroede, G. (2003). *Ces enfants malades de leurs parents*. Paris: Payot.

Segal, H. (1975). *Introduction to the Work of Melanie Klein*. London: Hogarth.

Segal, H. (1987). Silence is the real crime. *International Review of Psychoanalysis, 14:* (1) 3-13.

Simmons, R. *Pathological Reactions to Giving a Kidney.* (p. 227-244)

Spiegel, D. (1993). *Living beyond limits: new hope and help for facing life-threatening illness*. New York: Times Books.

Steinberg, J. Levy, N. & Radvila A. (1981). Psychological Factors Affecting or Rejecting of Kidney Transplants. In: *Psychonephrology 1, Psychological Factors in Haemodialysis and Transplantation, Part III*. New York: Springer US.

Steiner, J. (1985). Turning a blind eye: the cover up for Oedipus. *International Journal of Psycho- Analysis, 12:* 161-172.

Stephen, K (1941). Aggression in Early Childhood, *British Journal of Medical Psychology, 18:* 178-190

Stone, W. N. (1996). *Group Psychotherapy for People with Chronic Mental Illness*. New York: Guildford.

Stone, W. N. (2009). *Contributions of Self Psychology to Group Psychotherapy: Selected Papers.* London: Karnac.

Strengal. R — Mandela, His Eight Lessons Of Leadership — *Time Magazine* 17-22

Symington, J. (1984). The survival function of primitive omnipotence. *International Journal of Psycho- Analysis, 66*: 481-488.

Symington, N. (1986). *The Analytic Experience: Lectures from the Tavistock.* London: Free Association.

Symington, N. (1993). *Narcissism: A New Theory.* London: Karnac.

Symington, N. (1996). *The Making of a Psychotherapist.* London: Karnac.

Syson, L., Leonardo, Keith, L. and Stephenson, J. (2011). *Leonardo da Vinci.* London: National Gallery Company.

Ta-Jen Chang — *Creating Inner Safe Space for Schizophrenia* — Chap 15 in book by Kotani and Bonds-White

Tolstoy, L. (2012). *Anna Karenina.* New York: Vintage.

Turquet, P. (1975). *Threats to Identity in the Large Group. The Large Group.* L. Kreeger (Ed.). London: Karnac.

Varvin, S. and Volkan, V. D. (Eds.) (2003). *Violence Or Dialogue?: Psychoanalytic Insights on Terror and Terrorism.* London: International Psychoanalytical Association.

Weldon, E. V. (2011). Perverse transference and the malignant bonding. In: *Playing with Dynamite: A Personal Approach to the Psychoanalytic Understanding of Perversions, Violence and Criminality.* (pp. 50-59). London: Karnac.

Welldon, E. V. (1988). *Mother, Madonna, Whore: The Idealization and Denigration of Motherhood.* London: Karnac.

Welldon, E. V. (2011). Children who witness domestic violence: what future? In: *Playing with Dynamite: A Personal Approach to the Psychoanalytic Understanding of Perversions, Violence and Criminality.* (pp. 84-97). London: Karnac.

Welldon, E. V. (2011). Introduction to forensic psychotherapy. In: *Playing with Dynamite: A Personal Approach to the Psychoanalytic Understanding of Perversions, Violence and Criminality.* (pp. 164-175). London: Karnac.

Whitaker, D. S. (2001). *Using Groups to Help People.* East Sussex: Brunner-Routledge.

Whitaker, D. S., and Lieberman (1964). 51. A. *Psychotherapy through the Group Process.* New York: Atherton Press.

Williams, P. (Ed.) (2002). *Key Papers on Borderline Disorders: With IJP Internet Discussion Reviews.* London: Karnac.

Winnicott, D. W. (1960). Ego Distortion in Terms of True and False Self, In: *The Maturational Process and the Facilitating Environment: Studies in the Theory of Emotional Development.* (pp. 140-152). New York: International UP Inc.

Winnicott, D. W. (1963a). D.W.W.'s Dream Related to Reviewing Jung. In: C. Winnicott, R. Shepherd, & M. Davis (Eds.). *D. W. Winnicott: Psycho-Analytic Explorations.* Cambridge MA: Harvard University Press.

Winnicott, D. W. (1963b). The development of the capacity for concern. In: Maturational Processes and the Facilitating Environment. London: Hogarth Press, 1965, pp. 73-82

Winnicott, D. W. (1982a). Primary maternal preoccupation. In: *Through Paediatrics to Psychoanalysis.* (pp. 300-306). London: Hogarth.

Winnicott, D. W. (1982b). Hate in the counter-transference. In: *Through Paediatrics to Psychoanalysis.* (pp. 194-204). London: Hogarth.

Winnicott, D. W. (1989). *Psychoanalytic Explorations, 4. The Use of an Object.* C. Winnicott, R. Sheppard, & M. Davis (Ed.). (p. 218-240). Massachusetts MA: Harvard University Press.

Winnicott, D.W. (1967). Mirror role of mother and family in child development. In: *Playing and Reality*. Harmondsworth: Penguin.

Winnicott, D.W. (1985). The Theory of the Parent Infant Relationship (1960) and On the Contribution of Direct Child Observation to Psychoanalysis (1957). In: *The Maturational Processes and the Facilitating Environment*. Hogarth Press, Inst. of Psychoanalysis.

Wordsworth, W. (1770-1850). Roe, N. (Ed.) (2002). *William Wordsworth*: Selected Poems. London: Folio Society.

Wurmser, L. (1997). The shame about existing: A comment about the analysis of 'Moral' masochism'. In: Lansky M.R, Morrison. A.P, Hillsdale, NJ, Eds. *The Widening Scope of Shame*. The Analytic Press. (pp. 367-381)

Yalom Irvine — *The Schopenhauer Cure* — Scribe, Melbourne.

Yalom, I. (1975). *The theory and practice of group psychotherapy*. New York: Basic Books.

Yalom, I., & Leszcz, M. (2005). *The Theory and Practice of Group Psychotherapy (5th edition)*. New York: Basic Books.

Pierre-Auguste Renoir

Luncheon of the Boating Party reveals a bustling Parisian modernity and leisure

Only when taken together Luncheon of the Boating Party captivates the viewer. Time destroys human beauty in a few years, but well-preserved paintings last for a lifetime.

CORRESPONDENCE

Dr Sabar Rustomjee

Dear Sabar,

Thank you for your gift of a copy of your excellent book 'From Contempt to Dignity'.

It is a rich compendium of the wisdom you have gained over your years of clinical experience and also the wisdom you have gathered from the teachings of the great clinicians and theoreticians of the past.

I was very interested in the biographical section — how you rose to the challenges to establish your professional career and your reputation as a first-class clinician.

You can also be very proud of what you have done and of the fine and accomplished family you and Piloo have raised.

Thank you once again for the book and very best wishes for the future.

Sincerely,

Alan Large

Diego Velazquez

Noncompliance — demonstrated by pushing away the curtains with Dignity and Self-Safety. The picture presents itself as a slice of life, but which hides readings on many levels behind its apparent clarity.

From Dependence...

to Independence.

I Wandered Lonely as a Cloud
By William Wordsworth

I wandered lonely as a cloud
That floats on high o'er vales and hills,
When all at once I saw a crowd,
A host, of golden daffodils;
Beside the lake, beneath the trees,
Fluttering and dancing in the breeze.

Continuous as the stars that shine
And twinkle on the milky way,
They stretched in never-ending line
Along the margin of a bay:
Ten thousand saw I at a glance,
Tossing their heads in sprightly dance.

The waves beside them danced; but they
Out-did the sparkling waves in glee:
A poet could not but be gay,
In such a jocund company:
I gazed—and gazed—but little thought
What wealth the show to me had brought:

For oft, when on my couch I lie
In vacant or in pensive mood,
They flash upon that inward eye
Which is the bliss of solitude;
And then my heart with pleasure fills,
And dances with the daffodils.

www.ingramcontent.com/pod-product-compliance
Lightning Source LLC
Chambersburg PA
CBHW031115020426
42333CB00012B/94